Critical acclaim for John Taylor
and
Storming the Magic Kingdom

"A Hieronymus Bosch painting in words and sentences about the lowest of modern manipulators and the games they play to loot whatever they can find that offers profit in the American business system."

The Wall Street Journal

"Compelling. . . . Taylor's book is well worth reading. It is sure to change forever our childhood image of a company that is one of America's great institutions."

Business Week

"John Taylor takes the reader through the ins and outs, the complex wheelings and dealings so skillfully that it's understandable even to those of us whose idea of high finance is buying a Megabucks ticket."

The Boston Globe

"[This] clear and detailed narrative propels us rapidly through a convoluted maze of internecine conflict, corporate brinkmanship, Wall Street arcana and arbitrage duplicity. . . . Infused with suspense and intrigue."

USA Today

STORMING THE MAGIC KINGDOM

*Wall Street, the Raiders,
and the Battle for Disney*

by John Taylor

BALLANTINE BOOKS • NEW YORK

For My Mother and Father and
for Maureen and Jessica

♦

AUTHOR'S NOTE

THIS BOOK IS BASED primarily on interviews with participants in the drama that surrounded what is now the Walt Disney Company in 1984. Minutes of board meetings, personal diaries, correspondence, and appointment calendars were also made available by some participants. Documents filed as exhibits in lawsuits and depositions taken during those proceedings provided additional information. The dialogue quoted in conversations reflects the recollection of participants as to what was said. It is taken from interviews and on occasion from depositions, and in most instances was confirmed by other participants.

Many of the individuals who cooperated in this book wish to remain anonymous. To all of them I am grateful. I would like to offer special thanks to Stanley Gold and Raymond Watson, who generously agreed to interviews extending over several days. I would also like to thank Nancy Sweid for her research assistance. I am indebted to Corona Machemer for her exceptional editing. Finally, I would like to thank Jane Amsterdam, the editor of *Manhattan,inc.* magazine, for enabling me to undertake this project, and for many other things as well.

PREFACE

SATURDAY, JUNE 9, 1984, was Donald Duck's fiftieth birthday. Donald, whom Walt Disney Productions liked to describe as "the incarnation of everyman," first appeared in a minor role in the 1934 cartoon *The Little Wise Hen;* in less than five years, he had overtaken Mickey Mouse as Disney's most popular character. He was inducted into the army in the 1942 cartoon *Donald Gets Drafted,* and during World War II he served as a symbol on more than four hundred official military insignias. His career reached its peak in 1943 when *Der Fuehrer's Face* won the Academy Award for best short subject of the year. By the time he officially retired, in 1961, he had appeared in 127 cartoons, 4 animated feature films, and thousands of comic strips.

Disney's formidable public relations machine turned the occasion of the fiftieth birthday of "one of Hollywood's most famous stars" into an extended celebration, a series of events inaugurated in December 1983, when Donald returned to the screen in a new cartoon called *Mickey's Christmas Carol.* The following spring, at a formal ceremony in Torrance, California, "the feisty quacker" was honorably discharged from the United States Army: a lieutenant general presented a retirement certificate signed by the secretary of the army to one of the anonymous individuals who dressed up as Donald at Disneyland, and who was wearing a World War II uniform over his duck costume. Two days later Donald planted his webbed duckprints in the forecourt of Mann's Chinese Theatre in Hollywood, and early in June, together with Clarence "Ducky" Nash, Donald's voice ever since *The Little Wise Hen,* "the famous fowl" began a cross-country tour, attending birthday fetes and galas in fifteen cities. On Friday, June 8, the day before his birthday, he and Nash were hosts at the opening of a Donald Duck film festival in New York.

On that same day, financier Saul Steinberg, who had a reputation
as the most feared corporate raider in the country, announced that he
was going to attempt a hostile takeover of Walt Disney Productions.
He planned to gain control of the company, and then, in order to
maximize his profits, split it apart, or, as they say on Wall Street, strip
off the assets, by selling the Disney studio in Burbank and a portion
of its real estate to other investors. He intended to keep and operate
Disneyland and Walt Disney World himself.

As "the irascible duck" was greeting crowds at Rockefeller Center
in Manhattan—three blocks from Steinberg's office—the top executives of Walt Disney Productions were debating their response to
Steinberg's offer. To accept it was unthinkable. Walt Disney Productions was not just another corporate entity, not just some holding
company in a cyclical industry like natural gas or forestry that suffered
from overcapacity and therefore needed to be rationalized by liquidation of its assets to achieve maximum value for the shareholders. Nor
was Disney just another brand name—though it was, certainly, one
of the most successful marketing stories of the twentieth century. The
company's executives saw Disney as a force shaping the imaginative
life of children around the world. It was woven into the very fabric
of American culture. Indeed, its mission—and it did, they believed,
have a mission as important as making money for its stockholders—
was to celebrate and nurture American values.

Thus, to Disney's executives, Steinberg's move was not merely an
outrageous and ruthless profiteering tactic, it was somehow unpatri-
otic, almost anti-American—and they were not alone in this view.
Expressing the popular reaction to the takeover attempt, Robert
Knight, a staff member of the *Los Angeles Times,* wrote in an op-ed
article in his paper that "while Steinberg and his ilk are making
millions by threatening to tear down what took years to build, Disney
and other creative institutions still are developing ideas, tangible products—and jobs. Steinberg apparently thought nothing of dissolving
an American original, a monument to ingenuity and quality. His
attitude is beyond cavalier. Breaking up Disney to cash in on its assets
would be on the order of smashing a Tiffany vase to get at the penny
that fell inside." Disney executives had actually heard from Jews
voicing support for the company who expressed fears that Steinberg's
actions would provoke an outburst of anti-Semitism, that the takeover

battle might be regarded as an attempt by Jews to topple one of the temples of Protestant America.

Indeed, so pervasive were these feelings both inside and outside the organization that Disney's executives had always believed theirs was the one company a raider would never dare molest. And even after Steinberg made his offer, some of the elder members of the board argued that the company's unique position in American culture, the fact that millions of children loved its films and parks and characters, was protection enough. They thought that stockholders would support Disney because it *was* Disney—that, as children saved the life of Tinkerbell in *Peter Pan* by clapping, so Disney's shareholders would proclaim their faith in Disney and save it by refusing to sell Steinberg their stock.

Unfortunately, however, by 1984 small investors, the ones who might have been moved by such sentimental considerations, were not much of a force on Wall Street. A lot of Disney's stock was in the hands of institutional investors, who handled the portfolios of pension funds and insurance companies and banks, and who were obliged to seek the best short-term returns on their clients' money. Steinberg was prepared to buy the stock of Walt Disney Productions at a price more than $10 per share higher than the figure at which it had been trading before takeover speculation drove it up; the institutional investors were willing and even eager to sell.

To avoid being acquired, Disney's executives had to make the pilgrimage to Wall Street. There they discovered the tiny, incestuous world of takeover mercenaries: men, by and large, at a handful of investment banks, law firms, and public relations agencies, who were sometimes professional adversaries and at other times professional allies, depending on who retained them in any given battle. These men —together with the speculators, investors, and raiders who bought up the stock of a target company like Disney—knew each other and in a number of instances were even friends; they attended the same social functions, ate at the same expensive restaurants, belonged to the same exclusive clubs. In takeover battles they communicated with one another through an informal network of mutual acquaintances and back channels. Theirs was the consummate insiders' world, and their work constituted the ultimate insiders' game.

It was a world about which the Disney executives were largely

ignorant. Indeed, Wall Street itself was an alien arena for most of the
company's officers, who were in the business of running theme parks
and making movies for children. Few of them had a master's degree
in business administration, that purported indicator of expertise in
high finance. They were, for the most part, unfamiliar with the intri-
cate strategies of corporate combat or, equally important, with the
names—and the motives and the values—of the men who had suddenly assumed control of their collective destiny.

Upon learning that it could not count on the goodwill of the
stockholders to avoid a takeover and the subsequent liquidation of the
company, Walt Disney Productions was forced to seek some other
solution. It did, and by the time the sequence of events was over, the
company had changed irrevocably. The side of the Disney family that
had controlled the studio for most of its sixty-year history had been
driven from power, and a new team of executives had taken over and
was making films that bore little if any resemblance to the brand of
entertainment the public had come to expect from Walt Disney Productions. Some people complained that the hostile takeover attempt
and subsequent developments had wreaked havoc with an irreplaceable American institution and with the family of its founder; others
claimed that the replacement of lackluster executives with a flashier
and more contemporary group had revitalized the company, and that
the ensuing rise in the price of Disney's stock vindicated the role of
the raider in corporate America. Parties on both sides argued that,
were he alive, Walt Disney would have agreed with them.

PART · ONE

The Greenmail

1

ROY E. DISNEY, Walt Disney's nephew, had relinquished his office at Walt Disney Productions when he resigned from the studio in 1977. In the years that followed he had become accustomed to working out of his home, and though he acquired another office—eventually he was to own an entire building, the Shamrock Center, on Lakeside Drive in Burbank—he still made the big decisions at the wall-enclosed mansion in Toluca Lake, an affluent neighborhood of North Hollywood. So, on the mild January day in 1984 when he was preparing to take what he believed to be one of the most important steps of his life, Roy Disney was at home, in the den overlooking the backyard, with his wife, Patty, and his attorney, Stanley Gold.

Gold was reviewing the facts: Roy Disney—or, more precisely, his private holding company, Shamrock Holdings—owned about 1,100,000 shares of Walt Disney Productions. In the past year the value of that stock had dropped from around $80 million to around $50 million, a loss that looked even worse because Wall Street was enjoying a rally; in 1983 the Dow Jones industrial average had climbed more than two hundred points. Walt Disney Productions had "terrific stuff," Gold told his client, but it was not producing. Epcot, the new theme park at Walt Disney World in Florida, had cost more than $1 billion to create, and Gold believed that at that price it could not show a decent return on investment. More important, the Disney studio was a disaster. Roy Disney had been complaining for years that the company's expenditure of so much time, energy, and money on pharaonic real estate ventures like Epcot and Walt Disney World had led to the neglect of the film division, which he considered the heart of the company, its creative center. And in fact the studio had not produced a live-action hit since *The Love Bug* in 1969. Except for an animated feature or two, it had been dry for sixteen—*sixteen*—years.

Roy had two choices, Gold told his client. He could sell his Disney stock, swallow the loss, and buy something profitable. Or he could work to replace Disney's current management with a team that would improve earnings.

"Either we get out of this investment," said Gold, "or we get management to our liking. But *this* is crazy."

"So it's all the way in or all the way out," Patty Disney said.

Roy Disney agreed, and repeated his wife's words: "All the way in or all the way out." In the months that followed, the phrase was to assume the character of a refrain for the group around Roy Disney.

With his long nose, his black mustache, his midwestern drawl, with his cigarettes and his persistent cough, Roy Disney vaguely resembled his Uncle Walt. But while Walt Disney had been domineering and manipulative, his nephew rarely asserted himself. Though not without daring—every other year he skippered his yacht *Shamrock,* after which he had named his holding company, on the Trans-Pacific Yacht Race from California to Hawaii—he was a quiet, modest, even shy man, who had spent most of his career at Walt Disney Productions directing and producing nature films such as "The Life of the Beaver" and "The Life of the Peregrine Falcon," which ran on the company's television series, *The Wonderful World of Disney.* He had neither the temperament nor the inclination to manage his own business affairs, and in 1974 he had turned them over to Stanley Gold, a partner at Gang, Tyre & Brown, a small but prestigious Hollywood law firm that specialized in the entertainment industry. Since 1978 Gold had also been chief executive officer of Shamrock Holdings.

In his personal style, Stanley P. Gold was almost the exact opposite of his client. He combined the qualities of a conservative investment banker and a raffish Hollywood deal-maker. His suits were dark, but the pants had pleats. He kept his hair close-cropped, but wore glasses with cherry-red frames. He was a short man who needed to watch his weight; the pounds accumulated quickly if he was neglectful. Volatile and opinionated, he talked in torrents of words, and he liked to have a good time, to fool around—food fights were a tradition at Shamrock management meetings. People found him either colorful and amusing or obnoxious and egotistical. But even his enemies conceded his intelligence and his unusual energy.

Starting with the Disney stock Roy Disney had inherited from his father, Roy O. Disney, Gold had expanded his client's holdings into a diversified portfolio of investments. Since retaining him, Roy Disney had seen his net worth double to around $200 million. He owned everything from cattle ranches to radio stations, as well as the now depressed shares in Walt Disney Productions.

Typically, Gold would present business propositions to his client, who, if Gold recommended them, would almost always give his approval, then leave his attorney to execute the deal. Gold invested aggressively. For example, in 1978 Shamrock had purchased Starr Broadcasting Group, a collection of radio and television stations, in a leveraged buyout, putting up only a fraction of the price in cash and borrowing the rest by using Starr's assets as collateral. The deal resulted in a loud and rancorous quarrel between Gold and William F. Buckley, Jr., Starr's largest shareholder. Gold, echoing charges made by others in a lawsuit, claimed that some of Starr's owners, including Buckley, had looted the company by selling it their personal assets at inflated prices.* The Securities and Exchange Commission had launched an investigation into Starr prior to Shamrock's purchase of the company, and when the dispute and the investigation reached the press, Buckley, with uncharacteristic inelegance, told a reporter for the *Wall Street Journal* that Gold was "full of crap." Gold clipped the article and hung it on his study wall. "Anybody who's called full of crap in the *Wall Street Journal,* by no less a person than William Buckley, has arrived," his wife, Ilene, told him.

Five years later, in 1983, Gold plunged into another corporate battle. Shamrock began acquiring shares in Fabergé, and toward the end of the year it was rumored that Gold might start a proxy fight to oust the perfume company's management and its board of directors

---

*Buckley denied the charges, but agreed to an SEC resolution of the matter in which he stated he would never behave as charged in the future, and he subsequently declared that he would never sit on the board of a public company again.

by persuading other stockholders to join Shamrock in voting for their dismissal at a special shareholders' meeting. When Fabergé's officers elected to sell their company to another corporation—a "white knight"—as a means of avoiding the proxy fight and their probable ouster, Shamrock sold its shares at a handsome profit. More important than that, however, was the confidence the successful maneuver gave Stanley Gold—confidence in his ability to pressure the management of a company to produce the sort of return on investment that he, as the representative of a large shareholder, wanted to see. If Roy Disney chose to hold onto his stock in Walt Disney Productions and go "all the way in," Stanley Gold believed he would be able to act effectively to implement his client's decision.

Through the month of January 1984, Roy Disney mulled over the prospects and examined his own conflicting feelings. He discussed the matter incessantly with his wife, with Gold, and with other close friends, especially his brother-in-law Peter Dailey, a former advertising executive and ambassador to Ireland, Mark Siegel, a partner at Gang, Tyre & Brown, and Clifford Miller, an executive in the public relations agency Braun & Company. This group took to referring to itself—privately, casually, jestingly—as the Brain Trust.

What Roy Disney faced was not just another business decision, not just the loss of some $30 million that he would have to endure if he sold his Disney stock at current prices. The paramount considerations were emotional. Roy Disney's father had been second only to his uncle in the creation and operation of the company: Walt Disney Productions belonged to him as rightfully as it did to his cousins, Sharon Disney Lund and Diane Disney Miller, whose husband, Ronald Miller, had been for the past year the company's president and chief executive officer. Selling his stock, Roy Disney believed, would represent a betrayal of his heritage.

But the alternative—to go "all the way in" and see to it that the company was run the way he wanted—presented potentially devastating complications, complications that had nothing to do with return on assets or depreciating values. Instead, they had to do with the longstanding feud between Roy O. Disney and his brother Walt, a feud that the two men had passed on to their children. They had to do with the fact that Roy E. Disney was barely tolerated, indeed was held in outright contempt, by the executives who had run the company for the last ten years.

In 1923, at the age of twenty-one, Walt Disney, youngest son of an unsuccessful midwestern businessman and farmer, had arrived in Los Angeles from Kansas City, Missouri, where he had created crude animated shorts for local movie houses. His brother Roy, who had served in the navy during World War I, was already in California, recuperating from tuberculosis. The two went into business together, with Walt producing, and Roy arranging the financing for, a series of shorts called *Alice in Cartoonland,* which featured the interaction of a live child actress with animated characters, usually animals. The series enjoyed a modest success, but soon exhausted its formula. Looking for a new gimmick, Walt toyed with a few forgettable characters; then, on a train trip from New York to Los Angeles that was subsequently enshrined in Disney legend, he roughed out his concept of The Mouse.

Mickey and Minnie Mouse made their debut on October 6, 1927, in *Plane Crazy,* a silent short that, while not widely released, did accompany the premiere of the first talking movie, Warner Brothers' *The Jazz Singer.* The following year brought *Steamboat Willie,* the first animated film to employ sound. *Steamboat Willie*'s high point was a musical sequence in which Mickey and Minnie used various animals as instruments, playing, for example, on a cow's teeth as if on a xylophone. (Then and for the next several years, Walt Disney played the voice of Mickey.) *Steamboat Willie* was wildly successful, and before long so were the Disney brothers.

At the time, the two men seemed to move in lockstep, so complete was their immersion in each other's lives. Roy had married his high school sweetheart, Edna Francis, in 1925; the same year Walt had married Lillian Bounds, an uncomplicated young woman from Idaho. Both Disney wives worked at the studio—Edna was inking the frames of Mickey Mouse films while pregnant with Roy Edward Disney, who was born in 1930—and for a while the two families lived next door to each other in a pair of old houses on Lyric Avenue in Hollywood. The success of The Mouse, however, enabled the Walts to move to Woking Way, and the Roys to settle in the San Fernando Valley.

From the outset, Walt assumed all responsibility for the creation of the cartoons, at which Roy showed absolutely no aptitude, while Roy administered the small company's financial affairs. And though each performed essential tasks, it was beyond question Walt who dominated the studio. A few years after its founding he even insisted that its name be changed from Disney Brothers to Walt Disney Productions. According to Roy's son, "Dad kind of buckled under to that." It was an intimation of the divisions and bitterness that would later develop between the two families and within the company.

Despite such tensions, the Disneys remained close during the thirties and forties. Two other brothers, Herbert and Raymond, also lived in Los Angeles, and all four families would get together almost every Sunday during the summer at the Roys' house in the valley, which had a huge backyard. One family would bring barbecue, another chicken, another corn on the cob. After the meal there was usually a vigorous game of croquet. As the match progressed and the brothers surrendered to their competitive instincts, tempers frequently flared—Walt in particular always enjoyed a good argument. While the fights made croquet seem a vicious game to young Roy Edward, they did not prevent any of the brothers from returning the following Sunday for another big meal and another round at the wickets.

Most of Roy E. Disney's childhood memories of his Uncle Walt were of a different quality, however, one more in keeping with Walt Disney's public persona. For example, during a Sunday gathering in 1937, some months before *Snow White,* Disney's first full-length animated movie, was released to ecstatic reviews, seven-year-old Roy was sick in bed, unable to join the rest of the family. His uncle announced that he was "going to try *Pinocchio* out on the kid." Sitting on the edge of Roy's bed, he so mesmerized the child with his account of the puppet's adventures that when Roy saw the film *Pinocchio* two years later, shortly before its release, he was disappointed. The movie's spell was not as powerful as the one Walt Disney had cast when telling the story himself.

For all his exposure to his uncle's magnetism, Roy Edward Disney was not at first inclined to enter the family business. Like his father, he had no talent for drawing. And he had another ambition. Too young for World War II but not too young to catch the aviation fever it engendered, he was fascinated with airplanes. He obtained his pilot's license when he was sixteen and two years later enrolled at Pomona College intending to earn a degree in aeronautical engineering. But he turned out to be no better at mathematics than at drawing; after almost failing calculus he switched to English, and upon graduation, having few other prospects, he drifted into the entertainment business. He started out as a "black suit," or page, at NBC; later, with his father's help, he secured a job as an apprentice film editor on *Dragnet.*

By this time—the early 1950s—the Disney studio, which had won an Oscar in 1949 for its first nature film, *Seal Island,* had established a full-fledged nature department. After almost a year of splicing film on *Dragnet,* Roy Disney was made an assistant film editor there, working on sixteen-millimeter documentaries like *The Living Desert* and *The Vanishing Prairie.*

Walt Disney Productions had changed remarkably since the days of *Alice in Cartoonland.* The great animated works, *Snow White, Pinocchio, Fantasia,* and *Bambi* had been completed, and the studio had begun to produce less memorable animation, such as *Peter Pan* and *Sleeping Beauty.* Walt Disney, meanwhile, had turned his attention to other projects. In addition to the nature documentaries, he was making live-action features, like *Treasure Island* and *Rob Roy, the Highland Rogue.* And, unlike many studio heads, who feared the new medium, he had plunged enthusiastically into television. His first hit, the three-part series *Davy Crockett,* starring Fess Parker, started a national craze among American children for coonskin caps.

But the most important and the most radical of Walt Disney's new ventures during this period was Disneyland. He had nurtured the idea of an amusement park since the thirties; by 1952 he had sketched out the project, but his ever-cautious brother, who considered it just one more of "Walt's screwy ideas," refused to invest more than $10,000 of the studio's money. In another moment enshrined in Disney lore, Walt borrowed the rest of the capital he needed on his life insurance policy. Disneyland opened in 1955 and the following year its gross revenues came to $10 million, one-third of the total gross of Walt Disney Productions.

Laboring furiously to keep abreast of his projects, by now Walt Disney no longer had time for Sunday croquet matches or long bedtime stories. Not only was he the driving force at WED Enterprises, the design studio that created Disneyland, he also picked the producer, the director, and the cast for most films. And in 1955 he started the *Mickey Mouse Club,* which demanded a new one-hour television program every day, five days a week. As Roy Disney put it, "Loving hands at home and all that stuff just went whoosh. Walt didn't have time to sit down and say, 'Hey, gang, what if you do this and this?' Instead he said, 'Do it this way because I've got to leave, I've got twenty-five other meetings.'"

The pressures were reflected in the relationship between the Disney brothers. There had been several serious disagreements over the years, almost always involving Roy's resistance to a risky and expensive new proposal (he had had strong reservations about such seminal Disney projects as *Snow White* and *Seal Island,* as well as Disneyland). But then came a dispute so bitter that the ill feelings it engendered would extend down through the next generation. In 1953, Walt Disney, over his brother's vehement opposition, formed Retlaw Enterprises ("Retlaw" is "Walter" spelled backwards), a private company completely controlling the merchandising rights to the name Walt Disney. In return for licensing the name to Walt Disney Productions, Retlaw received 5 percent of the income from every merchandising deal and was allowed to make an investment of up to 15 percent in every Disney project. Since the Disney name by then appeared on everything from books and stuffed toys to Walt Disney Productions itself, Retlaw began virtually overnight to generate enormous wealth for Walt Disney and his two daughters.

Roy O. Disney believed himself betrayed. Retlaw was more than an insult. It gave the appearance that Walt Disney was siphoning money from the company he and his brother had built together in order to enrich his own family—not all the Disneys, just the Walt Disneys.

The feuding lasted almost a decade, during which time the relationship between the brothers became so poisoned that they refused to speak to each other; eventually their enmity assumed a legendary quality that they themselves perpetuated. Roy Disney, who shared some of his brother's talent for story-telling, liked to describe how, when he and Walt were growing up in Kansas City, they shared a bed which his younger brother frequently wet. "He'd pee all over me," Roy would say, "and he's still doing it." Walt told the same story. "I pissed on him then," he'd say, "and I'm pissing on him now."

The dispute divided the company. The staffs of the financial, legal, accounting, and administrative departments were all "Roy men." Marketing and sales, and the creative divisions such as the studio and the parks, were filled with "Walt men." Rare was the individual who crossed over; those who tried risked their careers.

Finally, in the early sixties, the brothers were reconciled. Walt sent Roy a long letter that was signed "I love you, Walt" and gave his brother a feathered peace pipe, which Roy kept in his office beneath a photograph of Walt. When Roy died, his son took the peace pipe home and placed it on his mantelpiece.

Despite the personal reconciliation, however, the division within the company remained; it was to intensify after the deaths of the two brothers.

By the early 1960s, Walt Disney had turned most of his attention from film to real estate. He had been enraged when dozens of cheap motels, souvenir shops, restaurants, and fast food stands had sprung up around Disneyland in the years after it opened. Not only were they an eyesore, they were making profits that would have gone to Walt Disney Productions had the company had the foresight to acquire the land around the park and build its own facilities. Now, as the planning began for Walt Disney World in Florida, Disney bought 27,500 acres of land in the center of the state and later added 500 more. He foresaw not only a new theme park for children but an entire community supported by futuristic technology and open to the public: a theme park for adults. He called it Epcot, for Experimental Prototype Community of Tomorrow.

Epcot was quite literally Walt Disney's dying dream. On December 14, 1966, he suddenly succumbed to cancer, which had been diagnosed only a few weeks before. Like most people, he was unprepared for his own death; the executive producer of Walt Disney Productions had never grappled with the issue of a successor at the company. The job fell to his older brother, who at age seventy-one wanted instead to retire. Reluctantly Roy O. Disney, who was then president, assumed the title of chairman. Donn B. Tatum, the company's executive vice-president of administration, was named president. Together with E. Cardon (Card) Walker, the former head of marketing, who subsequently became executive vice-president in charge of operations, they formed what came to be called the Disney Troika, instituting rule-by-committee in place of Walt's autocratic managerial style.

Walt Disney Productions grew fabulously during the reign of the Troika. The year Walt Disney died, the company's gross revenues were about $116 million. In 1972, the year after Walt Disney World opened, revenues reached $250 million. But the pressure to complete Walt Disney World had taken its toll on Roy O. Disney, who died less than three months after the project was finished.

Through the remainder of the 1970s, the company was ostensibly run by Donn Tatum and Card Walker. Tatum, named chairman after Roy O. Disney's death, was quiet and intelligent. A graduate of Oxford who had risen through the financial side of the company, he was a "Roy man." Walker, named president of the company, was, by contrast, impulsive and outgoing. He had been hired as a messenger boy in Disney's traffic department after graduating from UCLA in 1938, and except for a stint in the navy during World War II, he had never worked anywhere else. A "Walt man," with the support of Walt's widow, his daughter Diane, and Diane's husband, Ron Miller—who had joined the board of directors shortly after Walt Disney's death and who, at the time of Roy's death, was a producer in the film studio—Card Walker soon made it clear that it was he who was really in charge at Walt Disney Productions. In 1976, in part to consolidate his power, he named Ron Miller head of production at the studio and took for himself the title of chief executive officer as well as president. Overpowered by Walker's energy and ambition, Tatum was relegated to serving as liaison to the investment community and chairing various meetings— "Mr. Outside" to Walker's "Mr. Inside."

While Roy O. Disney was running the company, his son had continued to produce nature films for *The Wonderful World of Disney*, traveling to such places as Kenya, Bahrain, and Alaska to film birds and beasts in their native habitat.* For all the exotic locations, however, a certain routine informed production of these films, and the younger Roy, who in 1955 had married Patricia Dailey, the sister of one of his childhood companions, began at her urging to press in a mild way for advancement. In 1967 he had been elected to the board of directors. The year before his father died, he was named vice-president of sixteen millimeter and placed in charge of the small department producing the nature films. Two years later, as a principal shareholder, he joined Walker, Tatum, and Ron Miller on the executive committee that dominated the board.

Though he had inherited his father's inability to draw, Roy E. Disney was much more interested in the creative side of the business than Roy O. Disney had been. He possessed firm ideas about the ingredients necessary to make good films, and he was troubled by the direction the studio took under Ron Miller and Card Walker. Walker in particular, he felt, had neglected the studio; although he was a Walt man, someone from the creative side, Walker was less interested in films than in real estate, as Walt Disney himself had been in the last years of his life.

The studio had reached its commercial peak in 1964 with the release of *Mary Poppins,* an ambitious musical that combined live action with animated sequences. The most successful film Disney had ever produced, it had grossed more than $45 million, which made it for a time the sixth most popular film on record. Since then, the studio's biggest commercial hit had been the 1969 comedy *The Love Bug,* about an intelligent Volkswagen named Herbie. Such zany comedies—others included *The Boatniks* (1970), *The Shaggy D.A.* (1976), and sequels to *The Love Bug* like *Herbie Goes Bananas* (1979) —tended to ape the style and tone of earlier Disney comedies like *The Absent-Minded Professor* (1961), and its sequel, *Son of Flubber* (1963). In the seventies they became the mainstay of the studio.

*These were eventful journeys; one even allowed Roy Disney an opportunity for political intrigue. In 1972 he was on a two-masted dhow in the Arabian Gulf with the Sheik of Bahrain, who told him that the Shah of Iran would be overthrown. Disney wrote a letter containing this information to Bob Haldeman, a former high-school classmate who had become Richard Nixon's chief of staff. Haldeman had other matters on his mind in 1972 and never replied personally, but several months later Disney did receive a letter from Henry Kissinger, who assured him that the situation was under control.

Roy Disney felt that the film division ought to be encouraging innovation rather than repeating the formulas which had worked years before, and which, to judge from the studio's balance sheet during this period, worked no more. The success of *Star Wars* in 1977 was an indication of the new directions possible in family entertainment, but Card Walker resisted change. Lacking sharp creative instincts, and seeing himself as the man entrusted with Walt Disney's legacy, he favored projects of the sort the master had approved during his lifetime. His approach to creative decisions was epitomized by the question: "What would Walt have done?"

Other executives, taking their cue from Walker, asked the same question year after year at meeting after meeting until it became a sort of incantation for the committees that had been established to make decisions. In fact, Walt Disney's presence hovered constantly over the entire company. In an interview given around the time he became head of the studio, Ron Miller said, "It's uncanny. I start reading a script and suddenly I feel Walt's going to tap me on the shoulder with a suggestion." On the Disney lot, Walt's lingering, ghostly influence became a standing joke. "This is necrophilia," studio hands told each other. "We're working for a dead man."

On more than one occasion, Roy Disney tried to convince the company's management that "the thing about Walt was that he did it different each time." To go around asking "What would Walt have done?" was contrary to the essence of Walt Disney's genius and creativity. "It's the creativity you have to imitate," Roy said. "And no drugstore in the world sells that."

Neither Card Walker nor, after he took over the studio, Ron Miller took Roy Disney seriously, however. For one thing, as a Walt man, Walker had had a strained relationship with Roy O. Disney (at one point years earlier, Roy O. was said to have tried to fire him). For another, Walt Disney had reportedly once told Walker that "My nephew will never amount to anything." The prevailing view was that Roy E. Disney was ineffectual and weak. Around the lot he was known as "The Idiot Nephew."

Given this attitude, it was not surprising that most of Roy Disney's suggestions and requests—to produce a feature film, for example, or to participate in the planning of Epcot—were rejected. Finally, in early 1977, after an intolerable year during which, as vice-president of sixteen millimeter, he had to report directly to Ron Miller as head of the studio, he decided to pursue the possibility of becoming an independent producer with a contract to make films for Walt Disney Productions. Though independent production contracts had always been regarded as unacceptable at Disney, which preferred to maintain absolute control over the films bearing its name, he thought that perhaps an exception could be made for the son of one of the founders. He and Stanley Gold met with Card Walker and Donn Tatum to explore the idea.

Walker refused to hear of it. "What do you want to do, Roy, make *Deep Throat*?" he asked.

Roy Disney, a conservative family man, was flabbergasted.

"No, I don't want to make *Deep Throat*," he said. "That's the last thing in the world I want to make."

"We're just trying not to do Herbie the Love Bug for the fifteenth time," Gold added. "It was cute the first time."

Walker did not seriously believe Walt Disney's nephew wanted to make *Deep Throat*. But he did believe that to depart from the established Disney formulas was tantamount to heresy and would be disastrous. Walt Disney Productions was the only Hollywood studio with name recognition. It signified a wholesome and—equally important—predictable brand of family entertainment. People went to see Disney movies for no other reason than that they *were* Disney movies. Any film that was not identifiably Disney in tone or content might as well be *Deep Throat;* it would destroy the audience's preconception of a Disney movie. There would be no independent production contract.

On March 4, 1977, Roy Disney resigned from his position at Walt Disney Productions. "Dear Card," he wrote.

It is with deep regret that I hereby tender my resignation as Vice President and employee of Walt Disney Productions, due to what seem to me to be deep and irreconcilable philosophical differences with present management. . . .

As I have previously told you . . . the creative atmosphere for which the Company has so long been famous and on which it prides itself has, in my opinion, become stagnant. I do not believe it is any longer a place where I, and perhaps others, can realize our creative capacities. Motion pictures and the fund of new ideas they are capable of generating have always been the fountainhead of the Company; but present management continues to make and remake the same kind of motion pictures, with less and less critical and box-office success. It disturbs me that lately the Company has double-billed current releases with its classics, apparently in order to shore up grosses.* This to me represents a serious erosion of the Company's assets and evidences to me that the Company is no longer sensitive to its creative heritage. Rather, it has substituted short-range benefits, obtainable from exploitation of the Company's past productions, for long-range creative planning.

Under the present circumstances, I believe it is best that I attempt to express myself elsewhere in the industry, while continuing to serve as a member of the Board of Directors and, as always, remaining vitally interested in the affairs of the Company. As the largest individual shareholder† and a Director, I naturally expect to be consulted in advance of any proposed changes in management or corporate financial policy which may affect the future of the Company and the interest of the shareholders.

Regretfully yours,
Roy E. Disney

Now, seven years after his resignation, Roy Disney was more concerned than ever about the erosion of the studio's creative spirit; the fall in the price of Disney's stock indicated that the concern was spreading. But any move he made against management was certain to rekindle the old feud between the Walt men and the Roy men, and

*Disney re-released each of the classics every seven years—the time the company believed it took for a new child audience to reach viewing age.
†Roy Disney at that time owned about 3 percent of the stock of Walt Disney Productions. Collectively the members of the Walt side of the family, who had sold off much of their Disney stock in an earlier diversification program, were said to own around 11 percent; none of them individually was believed to own more than 2 percent.

between the two sides of the Disney family. Even worse, his own abilities would be called into question again. The "idiot nephew" business would resurface. The publicity would be horrible. If he failed, the whole endeavor would be little more than an exercise in humiliation.

"You know how it will be," Stanley Gold said. "You and I are going to be described as a know-nothing producer and a shyster lawyer. And you might as well hear it from me first because you are going to hear it four ways from Sunday."

Roy Disney, however—after numerous meetings with his advisers and consultations with his children, whose fortunes were also at stake —decided to take the risk. Some thirty days after their first conference, he and Patty Disney and Stanley Gold were again sitting in the Disneys' den.

"What do you think, Roy?" Gold asked.

"Let's try for the brass ring," said his client. "So what are we going to do?"

"I haven't figured that out yet," replied Stanley Gold.

2

IN 1953, Ronald Miller, six-foot-five and two hundred pounds, a student at the University of Southern California and a starting right end on the school's football team, met Diane Disney on a blind date. After going out with him for three months, Diane told him one night that her father had said, "When in the hell is that guy going to ask you to marry him?" A couple of weeks later, Miller proposed. Walt Disney quickly blessed the engagement, and the two were married on May 9, 1954.

"For some reason, [Dad] and Mother liked Ron the minute they met him," Diane Miller said in an unpublished interview in 1968. "And I never could figure out why. Because Ron was very shy. He was not very articulate. . . . He was kind of a fizzle at education. We had, I think, in common our total failure at being students." (They both dropped out of USC before graduating.)

At the time of the marriage, construction on Disneyland had just begun, and a crew was in the process of ripping out the orange groves on the land in Anaheim. Shortly after his wedding, Ron Miller became the third person hired to work on the project: He served as liaison between Disneyland and the park's designers, driving back and forth with blueprints.

"I think at first he didn't like it," Diane Miller said. "He worked under C. B. Wood [who had been hired to oversee construction] . . . and definitely felt he was there as the son-in-law of Walt Disney. He was nothing but an errand boy. He had nothing to do, didn't know what was happening. Woody at the time had Ron thinking Dad's some kind of crackpot, that he can't do all these wild things he wanted to do at Disneyland. Ron would come home and tell me, 'Your father's some kind of crackpot, and he can't do all these things he wants to do at Disneyland.' It was a bad beginning."

Fortunately, the military intervened. Miller was drafted and served in the army for two years, then joined the Los Angeles Rams as a tight end. "Walt saw me play in two games," Miller said in an interview (given at the same time as his wife's, and also unpublished), "one in which I got rapped in the nose and was knocked unconscious. And in the other I was laying a block for Tank Younger [a teammate]. Instead of laying a block for Tank, I tackled my own man. And I got my ribs caved in and [Walt] saw that. . . . I knew he was up there. And he was just a jinx. I believed it, and I think he believed it. He wouldn't go to the games after that. . . . If he goes, I get racked up. If he doesn't, I don't get racked up. It's that simple."

After that second game, Walt Disney called his son-in-law. "That looks like a rough life," he said. "The opportunities are here [at the studio]. Why don't you become a member of the Screen Directors' Guild?" The Rams' coaches tried to retain him; he could sprint fifty yards in six seconds and had what one reporter called "uncanny leaping ability." But after one year of pro ball, Ron Miller went into the movie business.

He started his career at Walt Disney Productions as a second assistant director on *Old Yeller.* Before long he was a first assistant director for the television program *Zorro* and for *Swamp Fox,* which ran on *Walt Disney Presents,* the program that subsequently became *The Wonderful World of Disney.* Inexperienced and reserved by nature, however, Miller rarely spoke up around the lot, and this at times irked his father-in-law. "I remember Dad expressing frustration," Diane said in her interview. "Like if I was at the house there in the morning or I would be there eating when Dad came home, he'd say, 'You know, Ron frustrates me. He never opens his mouth in a story conference.' I'd tell Dad at the time, 'Ron is shy. He doesn't want to open his mouth.' Then I'd go home and tell Ron, 'Dad thinks you ought to open your mouth in a story conference.' That can be good and bad. I know it took Ron a while to get to the point where he could assert himself. And when he would, Dad would tell Mother, Mother would tell me, and I would tell Ron that Dad was delighted because Ron opened his mouth in the last story conference."

After working on the Pageantry Committee for the 1960 Winter Olympics in Squaw Valley, Miller was made an associate producer on such Disney shows as *Daniel Boone, Slaughter,* and *Moonpilot.* Once, a second unit director was needed to shoot some scenes for *Moonpilot* in San Francisco. Miller agreed to do the work himself, and was preparing to travel north when his father-in-law called him.

"Goddammit," Walt Disney said. "What do you want to be, a second unit director or a producer?"

"A producer," Miller replied.

"Then let's forget the second unit director."

Throughout his early years at the studio, Ron Miller felt that Walt Disney was shaping his future. "He knew," Miller said. "He knew how to guide my life."

"I think he was thrilled with the way Ron came along and grasped it," Diane Miller said. "And actually, Ron had no training for anything else. He was like a blank notebook. Dad could take him and mold him in his pattern. . . . I think the nicest thing I ever did for Dad was that through some quirk of fate I was able to marry a man who was able to fit into Dad's dream, Dad's organization. In turn Dad was able to give this man I married something that he loved to do, something that he was uniquely qualified for."

Miller's position as Walt Disney's heir seemed to be cemented in the final days of Walt's life. Not long after the two men returned from a boat trip they had taken together in Canada, Disney's cancer was diagnosed, and doctors removed his left lung at St. Joseph's Hospital in Burbank, across the street from the Disney studio. Recovering from the operation, Walt Disney introduced Miller to his nurse.

"I want you to meet my son," he said.

"You mean son-in-law," said the nurse, who knew who Ron Miller was.

"No," said Walt Disney. "My son."

Less than twenty years later, on February 24, 1983, Ron Miller was made president and chief executive officer of Walt Disney Productions. He was still a handsome man: tanned, strong-featured, physically vigorous; arriving at the studio as early as five-thirty in the morning, he would often be gone by three to play golf or tennis. Before becoming chief executive he had frequently appeared at work dressed in such combinations as tomato-red pants, white shoes, and a white shirt; now he was inclined toward more subdued attire. He owned a Porsche, a green handmade English Jensen, a vintage Rolls Royce Corniche, and Walt Disney's old black Mercedes, and he and Diane and their seven children moved between their house in Encino, their vineyard in the Napa Valley, and a ski chalet in the Rockies. Fast cars, a glamorous job, a rich wife, time in the sun: Ron Miller seemed to embody the good life as it was defined in Southern California.

Despite the privileges his marriage had brought him, however, Ron Miller apparently harbored a certain ambivalence about his relationship with the Disney family. He was defined, if not by himself then by others, in terms of his father-in-law. He knew, he told his friends, what people said behind his back: that he was "just a good-looking jock" who had only made it as far as he had because he was married to Walt Disney's daughter. And the marriage had been at times a difficult one. In fact, not long after Miller became chief executive he and his wife separated, and gossip about the Millers' rocky relationship had fueled speculation concerning instability at the company that had in turn contributed to the decline in Disney's stock so troubling to investors like Stanley Gold. Now, after less than a year as Disney's chief executive, as Roy Disney was exploring his options with the Brain Trust, Miller was preparing for the company's 1984 annual meeting, at which he hoped to allay the investors' concerns. The numbers did not yet show it, but, he believed, he had begun at last to reverse the fortunes of Walt Disney Productions—to achieve the success that would enable him to emerge once and for all from the shadow of his father-in-law.

Like Roy Disney, Ron Miller realized that the problems of Walt Disney Productions were to some extent rooted in the studio. There was certainly no arguing with the fact that throughout the 1970s, the film division's contribution to the company's overall revenues had become smaller and smaller: Before the opening of Walt Disney World in 1971, it had accounted for more than half the total annual revenues of Walt Disney Productions; by 1979 it produced a mere 20 percent of total revenues, and half of that came from the periodic reissue of the animated classics.* The formulas that had worked for Disney in 1969, when the original Herbie movie was released, had become obsolete; indeed, the audience itself had changed. Theater attendance was dominated by young adults whose tastes ran toward violent movies like *Jaws* or raunchy comedies like *Animal House,* while, continuing a trend that had begun twenty years earlier, the families with small children who once flocked to the movies were turning increasingly to television for entertainment. With each passing year, Disney's share of the overall movie market had shrunk. At the same time production costs had risen enormously. "Disney never made a movie for more than $5 million," entertainment analyst Lee Isgur said in 1973; the average Disney movie actually cost considerably less. But the films that Disney could make for $3 million in 1970 cost $9 million in 1980, with inflation representing only half that increase. And Disney's typical efforts, such as *The Unidentified Flying Oddball* (1979), could not show a profit at $9 million.

Nineteen-seventy-nine was a particularly dreadful year. The studio's animation department was still dominated by the surviving members of a group Walt Disney had called the Nine Old Men, master animators who had been with the company since the thirties and who had participated in the creation of the Disney classics. But the master animators could not go on forever, and during the past several years the studio had worked to nurture a new generation of talent; one of the most promising of the younger animators was Don Bluth, a soft-spoken former Mormon missionary. In September 1979 Bluth walked out of Walt Disney Productions, complaining that the studio was skimping on the production values that had made the classics so remarkable. Lakes no longer reflected their surroundings, raindrops no longer splashed when they hit the ground, curls of smoke no longer floated from fires. (So meticulous was the attention to detail in *Snow White* that, for example, the water trickling from a bar of wet soap was slightly filmed with suds and glistened in candlelight.) Bluth also declared that Disney's stories had degenerated into saccharine mush,

---

*This decline in the studio's percentage of total revenues reflected in large part the growth of the theme parks. Still, with inflation taken into account, the studio's revenues had remained virtually flat from 1970 ($68.8 million) to 1979 ($144.1 million), a period in which the consumer price index roughly doubled.

devoid of the dark undercurrents of fear, loss, and death that linked the classics to traditional fairy tales. Eventually sixteen of Bluth's colleagues joined him, and together they set up a competing studio financed by Richard Irvine and James Stewart, two former Disney executives. So enraged was Ron Miller at this "betrayal" that in a magazine interview he called Bluth a "son of a bitch."

The following year Card Walker told Donn Tatum that he wanted to become chairman of the board before he retired, and Tatum graciously stepped aside. Walker in turn named Ron Miller president and chief operating officer; in February 1980, the appointment was approved unanimously by the directors, who traditionally acquiesced in management's proposals.

Though Ron Miller had been made head of the film studio in 1976, during the late seventies it had been Card Walker who controlled the types of movies Walt Disney Productions made, and he had selected projects by asking "What would Walt have done?" Even if he had been inclined to discuss fresh material, he had not had the time: Epcot had absorbed almost all his attention. Now, although Walker was still chief executive officer, Miller's new position as second in command gave him some opportunity to carry out the changes he hoped would revitalize the studio. As a first step, he asked Thomas Wilhite, the company's twenty-seven-year-old publicity director, to take charge of "creative development for motion pictures and television." Wilhite, who was immediately labeled a baby mogul, had never produced a picture in his life. But he was young and energetic, and he had superb organizational skills (while a college student at Iowa State he had persuaded Groucho Marx to come to the campus for his first major public appearance in ten years). Wilhite realized that the Disney concept of family entertainment needed to be redefined. "I don't think there have been any films that have been really successful at reaching a wide audience by aiming exclusively at children," he said in an interview some months after becoming vice-president for creative development. "You have to reach children, young adults, and adults to have a really big hit." Not that Disney would ever abandon the family. Ron Miller told the same reporter: "The day we make an R picture is the day I'm gone from this company."

Tom Wilhite rapidly embarked upon several ambitious projects designed to reach the wider audience required for success. He signed up Elliott Gould to appear in *The Last Flight of Noah's Ark* and *The Devil and Max Devlin*. He arranged for the studio to finance *Never Cry Wolf*, an independent production—Disney's first—about a naturalist's experiences observing wolves in the Canadian Arctic. His most daring venture was *Tron*, a $21-million science-fiction adventure with computer-generated animation about a software programmer trapped in his own video game.

But *Tron*, released in 1982, fizzled, in the process drawing attention to the role of the stock analyst as movie critic: After screening the movie, Ted James, a San Francisco analyst for Montgomery Securities, advised his clients to sell Disney. Other analysts followed suit, and Disney's stock fell 2.5 points in one day. Most of the other Disney movies released in 1981 and 1982 fared poorly as well. The two Elliott Gould movies bombed; so did *Condorman*—about the comic adventures of a cartoonist; *Night Crossing*—about a family fleeing Eastern Europe in a homemade balloon; *Popeye*—a musical directed by Robert Altman; and *The Watcher in the Woods*—a 1980 Bette Davis film withdrawn from the theaters after dismal reviews.* Disney's one success during this period was *The Fox and the Hound*. A 1981 animated feature that was largely the work of those young animators who had not walked out with Don Bluth, it won favorable notices and took in around $50 million at the box office.† As the fortunes of the film division declined—it had income of $34.6 million in 1981, $19.6 million in 1982, and a loss of $33.3 million in 1983—Disney began to make fewer pictures. In 1983 it released only three: *Never Cry Wolf, Trenchcoat*, and *Something Wicked This Way Comes*; since the costs of maintaining the studio remained fairly constant, the result was that overhead came to account for 30–35 percent of the total costs of the few films Disney did make, as opposed to roughly 20 percent at other studios.

During those same years, Disney's top executives were embroiled in a debate over the company's identity. Miller and Wilhite's push to

---

*The film was reshot and released again, with a different ending, in 1981, but still performed abysmally.

† Although this figure exceeded the revenues generated by *Mary Poppins*, in constant dollars it was less than half that for the earlier film.

produce more contemporary movies encountered stiff resistance not only from Card Walker but also from such second-level executives as James Jimirro, the head of the Disney Channel, a cable television service started in 1983, and Richard Nunis, who oversaw the theme parks. Both Nunis and Jimirro believed that more "modern" movies might damage the company's reputation as a purveyor of children's entertainment and thus harm the performance of their own operations, which depended heavily for their drawing power on the Disney name and the happy, wholesome American values it represented.

The Disney values were not universally applauded. Walt Disney had been ridiculed for decades by critics like Pauline Kael, who called the firm a purveyor of "corrupt popular culture," and Richard Schickel, who, in his biography *The Disney Version,* called Disney's work often "vulgar," "tasteless," "crassly commercial," "sickeningly sentimental," and "crudely comic." Walt Disney Productions had been attacked for its politics: The Chilean novelist Ariel Dorfman had, in one of his books, criticized the Donald Duck cartoons set in foreign lands for their disrespectful attitude toward the Third World. And Disney had been accused of promulgating loose morals: according to the *Wall Street Journal,* a youth committee in Helsinki once persuaded the city council to cancel library subscriptions to Donald Duck comics because Donald and Daisy were unmarried; because the parentage of Hewey, Dewey, and Louie—the three mischievous nephews —was unknown; and because Donald's short sailor suit left his rear exposed. Even on the occasion of his birthday, Donald Duck did not escape criticism: That spring the National Coalition on Television Violence issued a report ranking his cartoons among the most violent on television and singling out for special condemnation the frequent spankings he administered to his nephews.

Such charges, which the company dismissed as ridiculous, were part of a long-standing and more general complaint about hypocrisy at Walt Disney Productions—a complaint given a particular edge in light of the fact that Walt Disney Productions arguably took its image more seriously than any other company in the United States. It was an old company joke that Walt Disney could not have been hired to work at Disneyland. Walt cursed vigorously, chain-smoked, liked a stiff drink at the end of the day, and wore a mustache; the employees at Disney's theme parks tended to be clean-living and conservative, and were forbidden facial hair.* Company policy also required them to remove their Mickey Mouse or Donald Duck name tags if they went into a bar for a drink. Disney even tried to impose grooming standards on visitors, at one point forbidding women in halter tops to enter the parks. Behavior suggestive of homosexuality was also taboo.

The accusations of hypocrisy were at once accurate and irrelevant. While the criticism of Disney's "aesthetics" is of the sort levied against almost all enterprises that traffic in the commerce of entertainment, it was true that a gap existed between the social standards Disney upheld and the personal behavior of many of the men who set them. But Disney's executives fussed and fretted over the company's image precisely because Disney was in the *family* entertainment business. More than that, Disney did market a value system. Disneyland and Walt Disney World were not called amusement parks but "themed entertainment experiences": In addition to providing the "guests" with good clean fun, their object was the inculcation and celebration of virtues ranging from rugged individualism to the primacy of the nuclear family. The experience offered by the parks and by Disney films could be intermittently frightening or sad, but it was not designed to challenge the assumptions of customers or assault middle-class values. Any film that departed from this tradition could erode Disney's following not only among movie audiences but also in the vacation industry.

On the other hand, it was impossible to deny that while attendance at the theme parks steadily climbed, fewer and fewer people were showing up at Disney movies. Instead, even in the more conservative climate of the 1980s, audiences evidently preferred films like *Porky's*, a tasteless comedy in which sexually preoccupied high school boys talked in an unending stream of obscenities and expended considerable energy trying to spy on naked girls.

Disney executives became obsessed with *Porky's*. They hated the movie for its offensiveness, its lewdness, its leering sexual exploitation. For them, *Porky's* came to epitomize just the sort of movie Disney

---

*They also tended to be white and gentile. Walt Disney, like other conservative businessmen of his time, was not inclined to hire blacks or Jews.

would never make. But it was so maddeningly successful. Released in 1982, *Porky's* grossed more than $70 million at the box office, making it one of the top-ten grossing films of the year. Disney's most successful 1982 film was *Tex,* a contemporary tale of an alienated Texas teenager played by Matt Dillon; it had box office receipts of only $9 million. *Tex* was a promising movie: Well received by critics, it was faithful to Disney's worldview, but starred a hot new adolescent idol. Nonetheless, teenagers shunned it in droves. The situation was so frustrating it impelled Card Walker to the view that if Disney could not produce movies which were both successful and wholesome, it should close down the film division altogether—except for the occasional project Walt would have wanted to do.

The Card Walker faction was concerned for more than the company's image. They also worried that if Disney made the sort of movies put out by other studios it would become *like* the other studios —a place ruled by greed, status-mania, and self-indulgence, with constant executive turnover, stretch limousines, liberal expense accounts, gigantic bonuses, and—who knew?—even drug abuse and promiscuous sex. Disney prided itself on the distance it maintained from the rest of the movie industry and on the absence of Babylonian behavior around the lot. (The board of directors even rejected as improper the suggestion that Disney raise money for movies through tax shelters, a practice common at other studios.) And despite its conservative ways, or because of them, the studio enjoyed tremendous loyalty from its staff; Disney executives always seemed to be awarding someone a twenty-five- or forty-year pin. Employees tended to refer to the rest of the entertainment industry as "Hollywood" (though Columbia, Warner Brothers, and NBC also had studios in Burbank) and to Hollywood as "over there" or "over the hill." Card Walker and his supporters believed that this isolation was to be cherished and protected—it helped make Disney unique.

Ron Miller did not want Disney to make movies like *Porky's,* but he did think it should be producing films like *E.T.* and *On Golden Pond.* Card Walker did not disagree, but said that if Disney had produced those movies, he would have cut the scene in *E.T.* where one boy called another "penis breath" and the scene in *On Golden Pond* where Katharine Hepburn gave the finger to some rambunctious teenagers. Tom Wilhite, with Ron Miller's support, urged the studio to create a second label under which it could release movies with more mature themes (he suggested calling the new label Hyperion, after the original Disney studio on Hyperion Avenue). Card Walker and his supporters resisted the concept.

Such was the situation in the fall of 1982, when Miller, dissatisfied with the performance of Wilhite's films and his management of the studio, began to search for a more experienced executive to run the film division. He considered approaching Dennis Stanfill, the former head of Twentieth Century-Fox Film Corporation. And he actually did approach Michael Eisner, the president of Paramount Pictures Corporation, but Eisner was interested only if he could run the theme parks too, which essentially meant that he wanted to run the entire company. Miller looked elsewhere. One day during a golf game, he mentioned his search to William Self, who headed Disney's television department at the time, and Self recommended Richard Berger, whom Miller hired in March 1983. An immaculately tailored man with silver hair and dark eyebrows, Berger was senior vice-president of world-wide productions at Twentieth Century-Fox. He had a reputation as a troubleshooter who could assert control over pictures that had gone over budget or fallen behind schedule or both, as was most often the case. He also had sharp commercial instincts and an intuitive feel for the youth market. At Fox he had been involved in the production of, among other films, *The Rose, Brubaker, The Final Conflict,* and *Six Pack,* and the distribution of, ironically, *Porky's.*

Four months after his arrival at Disney, Richard Berger wrote a position paper endorsing the proposal for a second label. "Time and television have permanently changed the look of the industry and the look of movies," Berger wrote.

> Mores and lifestyles changed rapidly and successful filmmak-
> ers adapted by mirroring those reflections in their productions.
> Disney remained insular, set in its own way of doing things and
> remote from accelerated change in the marketplace. . . . If our
> organization is to be strong and competitive as a live-action
> movie studio, we have no choice but to be guided by prevailing
> taste. . . . The alternative for Disney in the present day is to

cease competition as a feature filmmaker or continue to bear the burden of embarrassing and self-defeating write-offs and legitimate stockholder reaction. . . .

Looking at the major box office successes of recent years, there were very few that couldn't have been produced by Walt Disney Productions, but our organization was probably never considered for those properties. The industry's perception of Disney was—and to a certain extent remains—that we didn't have the welcome mat out for them. We weren't interested in serious adult fare, we are terribly hard-nosed negotiators, our standards were outdated, we wouldn't pay for big stars, properties might not be properly positioned by association with Disney, they would lose control to studio executives who would make their work conform to the Disney "mold."

Believing that many Disney executives had only the vaguest notion of what current audiences liked, Berger concluded with an admonishment: "From my conversations, in the short time I have been at the studio, I believe we all have to go to the movies more often."

The fact that Berger's memo circulated was an indication that he and Ron Miller had won the debate over the studio's future. In May, Card Walker, following plans announced at the 1983 annual meeting at which Miller was named chief executive, had stepped down as chairman. Raymond Watson, who replaced him, was an advocate of change, and the obstacles to reform at the studio were more easily overcome.

To help settle the issue of the film division's identity, Disney commissioned the polling firm of Yankelovich, Skelly & White to do a market research study of the Disney name. The resulting report established that Walt Disney Productions was the only motion picture studio with name identification: It meant a movie for children. One nineteen-year-old queried in the study said he "wouldn't be caught dead" going to a Disney movie because he would be laughed at by his peers. However, he said, he looked forward to the day when, older and married, he could take his own children to Disney movies.

Such results indicated that from a long-term point of view, Card Walker had perhaps not been wrong in insisting that Disney protect the purity of its image. Disney movies had never been very popular with adolescents, and the members of the postwar generation, who had enjoyed Disney movies as children in the fifties and who by their huge numbers had made these movies enormously successful, had naturally outgrown them by the sixties and seventies. But as that generation began settling down and raising children, Disney's brand of family entertainment might well enjoy a resurgence in popularity. Yankelovich, therefore, endorsed the concept of a second label for more "adult" fare and tested several names, including Silvermine, Tapestry, and Touchstone. The last seemed best to Richard Berger because it embodied the notion of a test of quality, of a standard Disney would maintain in all its films regardless of their intended audience.

The Touchstone label was to make its debut with the PG film *Splash,* a "high-concept" comedy about a mermaid.* Interestingly, Richard Berger had passed on *Splash* when it was offered to him at Fox because he thought the extensive underwater sequences made it prohibitively expensive. Tom Wilhite, however, had grasped its potential. With his guidance, the script was revised and much of the underwater action deleted. But by the time *Splash* was ready for release, Wilhite, unable to accept Berger as his superior, had left the studio.

Scheduled to open in March 1984, shortly after Disney's annual meeting, the movie was to be the centerpiece of Ron Miller's demonstration to the shareholders that the necessary steps were being taken to reestablish his company's creative credentials—and, not incidentally, to give a boost to its stock. Almost everyone who had seen the film in previews had been enchanted, although some Disney executives, including Jim Jimirro of the Disney Channel and Jack Lindquist, marketing vice-president for the theme parks, worried about the damage to the corporate image that might result from its sporadically foul language and the few fleeting and partial glimpses of the actress Daryl Hannah's bare breasts (her hair was glued strategically into place to prevent an *entire* breast from floating into view). Despite the

---

*A high-concept movie is one in which the appeal or situation can be expressed in one snappy sentence, as in: A young man falls in love with a mermaid who can only come out of the water for short periods.

movie's PG rating and the disguise offered by the new label, they insisted that the company publicize its own explanation of Touchstone before Walt Disney Productions was charged with producing pornography. Miller reluctantly agreed. And so, shortly before the annual meeting, at which *Splash* was to be screened for shareholders, Disney ran a full-page newspaper advertisement describing its new Touchstone label and appearing to dissociate the parent company from the movie's more risqué moments.* Nevertheless, as he made his final preparations to face the shareholders at Walt Disney World outside Orlando, Ron Miller believed that such official expressions of uncertainty as the newspaper advertisement would be obviated when the assembly saw the film itself; *Splash* was at once a clear signal that the turnaround had begun at Disney and a vivid indication of the studio's new direction.

---

*In fact, Disney had already broken the nudity barrier in its own name with *Never Cry Wolf,* which had been released three months before *Splash,* in December 1983, and in which actor Charles Martin Smith ran naked through the Canadian tundra. But that was a nature movie.

3

IN AN ARTICLE from the *Los Angeles Times* that the Disney
public relations department never tired of quoting, Raymond L.
Watson was said to have the "kind of reputation the late Walt
Disney loved. His favorite hobby is his family and his passion is
proving that large, imaginative projects can be profitable." Lean and
friendly, with quiet tastes, Ray Watson lived with his wife, Elsa, and
his well-behaved son (his two daughters were grown) in a handsome
but unremarkable ranch-style house in the hills overlooking the Pa-
cific above Newport Beach. His private life was moderate and orga-
nized. As he jogged in the morning, he listened to taped books on a
Sony Walkman. He liked light jazz, to which the stereos in both his
house and his car were tuned.

Improbable though it may seem for the chairman of Walt Disney
Productions, Ray Watson knew little of the film business, and reading
screenplays bored him. But then, it had never been Ray Watson's goal
to run Disney. His previous career had not even been in the entertainment industry.

An architect by trade, Watson had spent most of his professional
life with the Irvine Company, the large agricultural concern that,
during the postwar housing boom, had converted much of its hundred
thousand acres of farm and grazing land in Southern California to
commercial and residential real estate. Entire towns were built on land
Irvine once used for grazing sheep and growing asparagus, and
Watson had overseen much of the development and construction,
including that of Irvine, California, one of the first, largest, and most
successful planned communities on the West Coast.* He was presi-

*Watson was one of the first architects to use market research to determine consumers' tastes
and needs in housing. He did studies to discover the façades and lot sizes preferred by various

dent of the Irvine Company from 1973 until 1977, but left when it changed owners, and, as an independent developer, had gone on to help turn former pastures near the village of Newport Beach, south of Los Angeles, into a sprawling bedroom community of affluent homes and condominiums centered around a vast upscale mall.

Watson's involvement with Walt Disney Productions had begun in 1964, when Walt Disney, in search of someone with experience in planned communities to inspect a mock-up of Epcot, had called him at the recommendation of a mutual friend. Disney had envisioned a city of twenty thousand residents with a fifty-acre central hub enclosed in a glass dome that would keep out rain, heat, cold, and humidity. Skyscrapers and a thirty-story hotel would rise through the dome. A series of transportation spokes were to carry inhabitants and visitors to outlying residential or industrial complexes. Epcot was to have schools, churches, apartments, offices, stores, restaurants, clubs, theaters, parks, tennis courts, golf courses, and marinas. It was simultaneously to display and to utilize the most futuristic technology available: a monorail, a vacuum-tube trash disposal system, an underground utility tunnel, a central computer system to control everything from streetlights to hotel reservations. "Epcot . . . will always be in a state of becoming," Walt Disney wrote. "It will never cease to be a *living blueprint of the future,* where people actually live a life they can't find anywhere else in the world today."

Because Epcot, like Disneyland, was to be open to paying visitors, however, Disney intended to regulate the lives of the city's residents almost as thoroughly as the climate in the dome. Representative local government was ruled out. No residents were to be permanent. Pets would be forbidden, dress codes would be enforced, and residents would be expelled for unbecoming conduct ranging from drunkenness to unmarried cohabitation.

The concept, Ray Watson told Walt Disney during their first meeting, was terrific. But, he said, Disney was going to have to subsidize the people who lived there. No one would volunteer to live for long in a place where he would be watched when he went out in his

---

income groups, the floor plans best suited to families with younger or older children, the size of kitchen needed by a retired couple; and Irvine's architects designed houses based on these studies. Some architectural critics maintained that the approach lacked creativity, but Watson felt he was providing people with the types of homes they desired.

pajamas to pick up the milk, where he couldn't have a dog or a cat, where he could be expelled if he didn't conduct himself "properly," as visitors who misbehaved were expelled from Disneyland. It was not a natural way to live.

Walt Disney appreciated the advice and asked Watson back again, and after Disney's death, Card Walker and Donn Tatum occasionally invited him to Florida to critique various aspects of the construction of Walt Disney World—the first stage in Walt Disney's plans for the Florida property. As the company's involvement in real estate increased, Watson's advice proved so useful that in 1973 he was asked to join the board.

By that time Epcot had assumed a shape radically different from the one envisaged by Walt Disney. The glass dome, the twenty thousand residents, the churches and schools had all been sacrificed as impractical, and Epcot recast as a theme park for adults. There were to be pavilions sponsored by various nations and by corporations on subjects like space and the oceans; "audio-animatronic" figures—talking robots—of Ben Franklin, Mark Twain, and Will Rogers; and a geodesic dome 164 feet high with 954 panels called Spaceship Earth. Although the initial response to Epcot from potential sponsors had been disappointing—each had to pay $25 million, according to *Business Week,* merely to acquire a ten-year license to operate a pavilion —and as a result, the number of foreign pavilions was scaled back from seventeen to eight, Epcot was nonetheless one of the largest and most expensive private real estate projects ever undertaken anywhere. Its ultimate cost of $1.2 billion was more than triple the original estimate.

Epcot Center opened on October 1, 1982. Hundreds of costumed Disney employees stood in ranks along the walkways and on the pavilion roofs, moving and turning to instructions shouted through a loudspeaker. Columns of costumed men and women carrying American flags and standards with the Epcot insignia streamed into the plaza. Musicians in silver space suits climbed onto the stage and struck up a brassy rock tune. Teams of sequined dancers jumped and twirled. Twenty thousand balloons and a thousand pigeons were released. A family was chosen from among the crowd at the turnstiles to be the first to enter the park, and Card Walker introduced them—Richard

Cason, his wife, Paula, and their children Ricky, Chris, Jennifer, and Jody—to a cheering crowd. The Casons, who had been waiting at the gates since six in the morning, were given complimentary lifetime passes to Epcot and Walt Disney World. Then, amid a scuffle of photographers, Richard Cason held a "press conference."

"You wouldn't believe this, but I dreamed about it," he told reporters. "Eleven years ago, we came to the opening of the Magic Kingdom and I watched the First Family and I said to myself, 'I'd like that.' And here we are."

As the pageant proceeded, thousands of eager visitors were clambering off the monorail from Walt Disney World and the trams that had carried them from the parking lots. They were forbidden to enter the park, however, until the ceremony ended, and as the music and dancing continued, some of the more impatient among them began to boo, marring the ceremony somewhat. But eventually the turnstiles were unlocked and the waiting crowds flowed through the Spaceship Earth Plaza heading for the Land pavilion, sponsored by Kraft, or Exxon's Universe of Energy, for the miniature Eiffel Tower or the Chinese temple or the United Kingdom pavilion, with its cute tea shop, for the Mexican pavilion, which boasted a marimba band, or the reproduction of the Butchart Gardens in the Canadian pavilion. Disney had expected attendance on opening day to be light, but the park reached near-capacity. The company's executives were ecstatic. So was Wall Street. Shortly after Epcot opened, Disney stock reached $84 a share.

All of the directors of Walt Disney Productions except Roy Disney (who refused to attend because he was appalled at Epcot's cost) had flown to Orlando to participate in the park's debut, and following the opening ceremony, they gathered in a conference room at the Contemporary Resort Hotel. It was here that Card Walker, after enthusing about Epcot's promise, abruptly announced that he intended to retire, and that Ron Miller would succeed him as chief executive officer.

This, at least, was no surprise. Miller's appointment had been considered a foregone conclusion in Hollywood for years. Indeed, Walker had openly expressed his intentions in an interview with *Fortune* prior to Epcot's opening. "Nobody doubts that the Disney board will approve Miller," the magazine reported. Ron Miller had been the company's president and chief operating officer since 1980, Walt Disney had seen him as his "son" and heir, and he enjoyed the strong backing of the Walt side of the family. In a statement he issued later, Walker said, "Miller's succession was part of long-established strategy to ensure an orderly transfer . . . and assures a continuity of the entertainment philosophy of Walt Disney."

After the meeting, Walker asked Ray Watson to join him, Donn Tatum, and Ron Miller for breakfast the next morning in Walker's suite. There, as Ron Miller sat beside him in silence, Walker told Watson that in his opinion the younger man lacked the necessary business experience to run Disney on his own, that he would need a helping hand in his new position. What was required, Walker said, was an arrangement similar to the one that had existed between himself and Donn Tatum. Tatum had played Mr. Outside, representing the company to the business community and meeting with analysts. Walker had played Mr. Inside, actually directing the affairs of Disney. As president and chief operating officer, Ron Miller had shown that he could run the company. Now the question was who should be Mr. Outside to Ron's Mr. Inside. The meeting broke up with the three men agreeing to explore the matter further back in Los Angeles.

Watson was puzzled by the inconclusiveness of the conversation and its implications concerning Miller's role. Although the younger man had been the company's second-ranking executive for three years, like his cousin-by-marriage Roy Disney, he rarely spoke up at board meetings, and consequently to the outside directors he was something of a cipher. As soon as Watson returned to California he set up an appointment with Ron Miller.

"I've thought about this thing and I'm still confused," Watson said when the two met in Miller's office.

"Ray, let's cut through it," Miller replied. "We're talking about you."

Watson was stunned. "For me to do what? You're talking about me, but I don't know what you want to talk about."

Miller told Watson that he, Card Walker, and Donn Tatum had been discussing this matter for a year. They had considered bringing in an outsider, but they had been leery of recruiting someone who might not understand or respect the Disney culture. The values that made Disney unique, that elevated it from a mere corporation into an American institution, could easily be destroyed by someone insensitive to its idiosyncrasies. The Disney executives knew Ray Watson and were confident that he shared their feelings about Disney. They wanted him to become chairman of the board and help Miller run the company.

"It's because Card doesn't have confidence in me," Miller said. "He thinks I need help." Miller seemed not to resent Walker's lack of faith.

"Well, what do you think, Ron?" Watson asked. "Let's forget about what Card thinks. What do you think?"

"I think I need help, too," Miller said.

While Watson considered Miller's proposition, the other outside directors began to debate the issue of Walker's successor. Though Miller's appointment had not been a surprise to them, they knew little of his capabilities, and some of them, including Philip Hawley, the chairman and chief executive of Carter Hawley Hale Stores, and Caroline Ahmanson, a philanthropist and businesswoman, had misgivings. They consulted the investment bankers at Morgan Stanley & Company, who had worked with Miller in his capacity as chief operating officer and who were, they discovered, unimpressed; more than anything, Miller seemed to them inexperienced. It was suggested that Walker remain with the company for another year to train a successor, be it Miller or someone else. But Walker was sixty-six years old and in uncertain health. Also, he was an assertive man, and he apparently realized that if he remained he would inevitably dominate any chief-executive-in-training and thus frustrate the process. He refused to change his mind.

Sensing the opposition that was beginning to form, and the trouble it might generate later, Watson had a frank conversation with Ron Miller, asking him directly if he did want the job and felt himself prepared for it. To back out at the beginning would be embarrassing, but to be forced out a couple of years down the road would be worse.

Miller was aware that a number of the directors were less than enthusiastic about appointing him to run Walt Disney Productions, but if anything, their reluctance strengthened his determination to take the job. "No, I *want* it," he told Watson. "I can do it."

Watson decided that he, too, wanted the position that had been offered him. Even though he still had only the vaguest notion of what his duties would entail, the fact that Disney was in transition convinced him that it would be an exciting place to work. He would agree to be chairman, he told Card Walker, if he could take the job part-time.

So it was that at the annual meeting in February 1983, when Ron Miller was elected president and chief executive officer of Walt Disney Productions, Ray Watson was named vice-chairman. Card Walker wanted to remain chairman until after he flew to Japan in April to open the Tokyo Disneyland. He would relinquish the title to Watson on May 1.

Since Ron Miller had spent virtually his entire career at Disney's film studio, he knew very little about the theme parks or the consumer products division, which licensed the Disney characters. Moreover, a number of projects, such as the plan to build hotels on the raw land around Walt Disney World, demanded expertise in real estate. So, increasingly, Ron Miller turned for advice to Ray Watson, who soon was immersed in the staggering array of decisions that need to be made daily at a company as large and diversified as Disney. He attended meetings on everything from new Epcot pavilions to personnel budgets. Occasionally, Miller would even ask his opinion on a script. Before long, Watson was spending two days a week at the studio, then three, then four. His own company, Newport Beach Development, suffered from neglect. By the time he was officially designated chairman, Walt Disney Productions was consuming almost all of Ray Watson's energy. Shortly thereafter, Miller approached him with a proposal: Would he consider coming on full-time?

"I've been thinking about it," Watson replied. He had found the work at Disney challenging and rewarding; after all, the company was involved in some of the largest and most complex private real estate projects in the country. Also, Watson's worries about his role had proved unfounded; Miller welcomed him. He was needed. He was productive. So Watson severed all ties with Newport Beach Development and became an active Disney executive.

He immediately had his hands full. In recent years the staff of WED Enterprises, the division that engineered and designed the parks, had swollen to more than two thousand employees as it labored to produce the rides and exhibits for both Epcot and Tokyo Disneyland. As happened at all architectural firms, massive layoffs became necessary once the projects were completed, unless, of course, additional projects had been planned.

They had not. And one of the reasons why, Watson discovered, was that Walt Disney Productions, a Fortune 500 company, a company with revenues of more than $1 billion a year, had no business plan. It had *never* had a business plan.

Watson believed that a business plan was a great discipline for a company. It concentrated everyone's mind on overall objectives. It helped ensure the harmonious interaction of different divisions. It guaranteed that you would not wake up one morning and find that all your projects were completed and you had two thousand people on the payroll with nothing to do.

After persuading Ron Miller that a business plan was essential, Watson arranged a meeting with all the divisional managers, where he learned to his amazement that no one had ever set goals for the divisions, either. The managers came to work, made what money they believed they could for the company, then went home. Almost twenty years after Walt Disney died, the firm was still run as it had been run under his reign, when gross revenues were $119 million and earnings were less than $10 million. Watson set out to establish growth targets for every division—but he was quickly diverted by a more pressing matter.

It had become evident that for the company's fiscal year 1983, which ended on September 30, net income would be down—in fact, it fell 7 percent to $93 million—and that the decline, following an 18 percent drop in 1982, would have a discouraging effect on Wall Street. Analysts were predicting that earnings would fall much more drastically in the year ahead, and in no time, both Wall Street and Hollywood began to talk of the company's potential as a takeover target.

One problem was that attendance at Epcot, despite all the initial fanfare and optimism, was dropping. With its national and industrial pavilions, it seemed to potential visitors to be just another world's fair at a time when the country was glutted with such expositions, notably the disastrous 1981 fair in Knoxville and the New Orleans fair, which was scheduled to open in 1984. Another problem was the Disney Channel: Only half the number of households the company had predicted would subscribe to its channel on cable television had actually signed up. And as far as the public was concerned, the film division was still in wretched shape; the movies that were expected to turn it around had not yet been released.

"We need to know what others think they know," Watson told Ron Miller when the company's vulnerability to a takeover was first noticed in the fall of 1983. One way to find out was to assume Disney's management was going to do a leveraged buyout; on that assumption, they could look carefully at every asset the company had and see how much it would bring if sold.

Miller agreed, and soon thereafter Watson hired Stan Ross of Kenneth Leventhal & Company, one of the premier real estate accounting firms in the country, to analyze Walt Disney Productions for a potential leveraged buyout. How much money could be borrowed against the company's assets? How much would they bring if sold? The investigation had to be done very quietly, very privately, because all sorts of investors would start stockpiling Disney shares if word got out that management itself was thinking of buying the company.

Since Disney carried little debt, the analysis was relatively simple. The value of the theme parks was obvious: Together they grossed approximately $1 billion a year; they could sell for up to $2 billion. It was more difficult to produce a figure for the value of the film library. The 25 animated features, the 119 live-action films, and the more than 500 cartoons, television programs, and other shorts were worth anywhere from $250 million to $1 billion, depending on the buyer's plans to exploit them and the endurance of their popularity in years to come. And Disney's real estate, primarily the seventeen thousand undeveloped acres in Florida, also had an undetermined value, since it depended on the size of the blocks to be sold and their prospects for development. Many people were doing what Ray Watson called cocktail party analyses of Disney's real estate: standing around, drink in hand, calculating that since a broker had just sold a five-acre plot near the property for $100,000, it must be worth $20,000 an acre, and since there were seventeen thousand acres, the land altogether was worth $340 million. Watson knew this was foolishness—one seventeen-thousand-acre parcel could not fetch the same price as seventeen thousand one-acre plots. Nonetheless, it was the sort of argument a raider could use to persuade investors to join in a hostile takeover.

Leventhal presented its analysis in November, by which time the stock was trading at $58 a share. It showed that a buyer—whether a raider or management itself—could leverage the company's assets to borrow much more than the $2 billion its 34.5 million outstanding shares were currently worth. The theme parks alone were worth that. Walt Disney Productions was decidedly vulnerable.

Having assumed they were going to do a leveraged buyout for the purposes of analysis, Watson, Miller, and Disney's other senior executives now discussed attempting one in earnest. But a leveraged buyout would require selling off parts of the company to pay down the debt accumulated during the buyout; the result would be to destroy the synergy that bound the divisions together and created a whole greater than the sum of its assets. Also, it was the opinion of their advisers at Morgan Stanley that if management offered to buy the company for a certain price, say $65 a share, it would be hard for them to maintain a principled objection if a raider stepped in and offered to pay $66 a share. Management's offer would inaugurate a bidding war, and Morgan Stanley believed that in the end the management group would be outbid; by proposing a leveraged buyout, the advisers said, Disney's executives would only be "shooting themselves in the foot." They also made the obvious point that the one way to improve the atmosphere in the investment community was to get the company's stock price back up.

The company had scheduled its 1984 annual meeting to begin on February 28, a Tuesday, in order to encourage the participants to spend the preceding weekend at Walt Disney World, and many of the shareholders did just that, whirling through rides like the Mad Hatter Teacup at the Magic Kingdom, shopping for Mickey Mouse T-shirts on Main Street, exploring the science and technology pavilions at Epcot, playing a few holes at one of the three golf courses, eating at the Polynesian Village, boating on the artificial lakes, and camping at the Fort Wilderness Campground, where the electric outlets were "themed" (Disney's term) with fiberglass bark to look like real trees.

The annual meeting itself was less fun. "I hope they're nice," Ron Miller told a bystander as he looked out over the more than three hundred stockholders gathered in the Ballroom of the Americas at the Contemporary Resort Hotel. Always shy and self-conscious, Miller hated to speak in public and had an outright fear of talking off-the-cuff to large audiences; whenever possible he read from a prepared text. Nonetheless, as Disney's chief executive, he was answerable to the shareholders, and so, standing at a podium at the front of the ballroom, Miller gave his speech about the Touchstone label and his hopes for *Splash*, and noted that in fiscal 1983 attendance at Disney's theme parks in Anaheim and Orlando had climbed 42 percent, that revenues had jumped 23 percent to a record $1.3 billion—the sixteenth consecutive year of record-breaking revenues. Then he began taking questions from the floor.

The shareholders were not nice. Unimpressed with Miller's attempt to appear upbeat, most of them concerned themselves with the distressing details of Disney's financial statement. Despite the record-breaking revenues, net income had declined from $100 million in 1982 to $93 million as a result of operating losses in the film division and start-up costs associated with the Disney Channel. Earnings per share —the company's income divided by the number of shares on the market—had dropped 10 percent. As earnings had fallen, so had the market price of Disney stock.

One shareholder stood up and said, "My mother asked me what stocks to invest in and I advised her to buy Disney when it was at eighty-five. It started going down, and she keeps calling me and asking me why, and I say, 'Don't worry, Mother. It will come back up, it's a great company.' I'm tired of answering her question now, so if I give you her number, will you call her and explain what's going on so she will get off my back?"

As the floor of the ballroom erupted in laughter, Ron Miller said, "I'll give her a call."

Another shareholder asked Miller about a rumor that Coca-Cola was going to take over Disney.

"The rumor did persist on Wall Street, here in Florida, in California," Miller said. "I took the occasion to call Don Keough, who's the president and chief operating officer of Coca-Cola. He flatly denied it. As far as I'm concerned, the case is closed."

If Ron Miller's hopes for the annual meeting were not realized, his hopes for *Splash* were. Critics greeted the film warmly, as did the adolescents who had proved so resistant to the Disney logo. *Splash,* in fact, provoked more enthusiasm than any Disney movie in more than a decade and grossed over $25 million at the box office in its first twenty days. Only one sour note marred its release. *Splash* opened on March 9, the day Roy Disney submitted his resignation from the board of Walt Disney Productions.

4

WELL BEFORE the annual meeting, Stanley Gold had begun to act on Roy Disney's decision to "reach for the brass ring." Within a short period he acquired 550,000 shares of Disney, bringing Shamrock's total stake in the company to 4.7 percent of its outstanding shares. At a price of between $49 and $55 a share, he figured the stock had about a $5 downside and a $25 upside; that is, it would fall only so low before someone stepped in to try to take over the company, but if earnings should improve, it could climb by more than 25 points. At the very least, Gold reasoned, his client would benefit from any speculative leap the stock might take if it did draw a raider. Whatever way you looked at it, Walt Disney Productions was a good investment.

Gold also contacted an old friend and mentor, Frank Wells, who had been a partner at Gang, Tyre & Brown when Gold joined the firm in 1968. Wells had resigned the following year to become a vice-president at Warner Brothers, and Gold had inherited a number of his clients, including Roy Disney's brother-in-law Peter Dailey. Thus it was indirectly through Wells that Gold had become Roy Disney's adviser, and though their careers had diverged, the two men both lived in Beverly Hills and occasionally they would bump into each other in the neighborhood or at the nearby UCLA track, where they both ran.

The two met for lunch at Wells's sprawling stucco house off Sunset Boulevard. Over the meal Gold explained Roy Disney's decision to go "all the way in" at Walt Disney Productions, and he asked Wells, who had quit Warner Brothers in 1982 after serving for five years as president and co-chief executive, if he wanted to join their ranks with the idea of perhaps going to work at Disney should something come of the enterprise.

Wells was intrigued. He liked challenges; when he left Warner Brothers he had decided that the time had come to fulfill one of his life's ambitions and climb the tallest mountain on every continent. After scaling six of his targeted peaks and coming within two thousand feet of the summit of Mount Everest, he had returned to Los Angeles and was currently serving as a consultant to Warner Brothers. It was not terribly exciting work, a fact that made Gold's proposition that much more enticing. But there were certain potential conflicts of interest.

First, Wells said, he would have to clear the matter with Warner. Second, in recent years he and his wife, Luanne, had become fairly good friends with Ron and Diane Miller. Before he could surface and take an active role he would have to go to Ron Miller and explain the situation. "I want him to know I'm prepared to help in any way I can to bring the two sides together, whether there's a job for me or not," Wells said.

"Everything's aboveboard," Gold replied. "I don't mind your doing that."

Through the rest of the meal, the two men reviewed the strengths and weaknesses of Disney's management, including Gold's doubts about Ron Miller's ability to run the company. They discussed the role Wells himself might play if he were to join Disney, and tossed around other potential additions to or replacements for Disney's senior officers.

"I'm going to give you the best advice you've ever had on the subject," Wells said. "Whatever else you do, get Michael Eisner."

Gold, of course, knew of Paramount's president, but it had not occurred to him to interest Eisner in Disney.

"Michael Eisner ought to be running that company," Wells went on. "He's hot. He's got a track record. You do everything you can to get him and I'll help."

In a very short while, Frank Wells became an indispensable member of the Brain Trust. He and Stanley Gold began meeting almost every day, and they quickly fell into a routine. At six-thirty most mornings, Wells would drive his blue Mercedes the four blocks from his house to Gold's and the two men would make the car trip together to the UCLA track, all the while discussing developments and opportunities. They would jog together for a mile, and then, as Gold continued to circle the track, Wells would run up and down the bleachers to strengthen his legs for mountain-climbing. After that, they would return to Gold's house for juice, coffee, and more conversation, which often continued until midmorning.

In the last week of February, Gold and Wells flew to New York and retained the investment banking firm of Lazard Frères & Company to work up a thorough corporate profile of Walt Disney Productions, one that would, like the analysis produced by Kenneth Leventhal for Disney's executives, rigorously evaluate the company's assets to determine their worth. At Lazard's offices in Rockefeller Center, Gold and Wells also sat down with Peter Jacquith and Donald Petrie, the two Lazard partners assigned to the account, to review possible courses of action.

One option was to launch a proxy fight. If the Brain Trust could persuade enough stockholders to vote with Roy Disney at a special shareholders' meeting, they could install new directors who could then depose Miller and bring in someone like Frank Wells or Michael Eisner. In a full-blown proxy fight both the board and the dissident shareholders would hire professional proxy solicitors, who would send out mailings, give presentations, and hire hundreds of people (usually part-time actors and models) to work around the clock making tens of thousands of telephone calls to everyone from the professional money managers who controlled big blocks of stock to widows who might own a mere hundred shares, with the object of persuading them to vote for their client. A proxy fight could be exciting—even fun. It was certainly something for the Brain Trust to consider.

Another possibility would be for Roy Disney himself to attempt a hostile takeover of Walt Disney Productions. He could simply make a tender offer for all or part of the outstanding shares at a certain price above their current market value. But Walt Disney Productions might sell for as much as $3.5 billion—$100 a share—which was, of course, a lot more money than Roy Disney had. And even if he could get the company for as little as $60 to $70 a share, he would have to resort to some sort of leveraging to raise the funds, borrowing the needed money with a pledge to repay the loan by selling off some of Disney's assets once it had been acquired. That, however, would mean breaking up the company, which Roy Disney and the Brain Trust did not want to do any more than Disney's management did.

Yet a third possibility was to encourage another big company to buy Walt Disney Productions. Over the years a number of corporations, from Westinghouse to American Express, had showed an interest in acquiring Walt Disney Productions, usually to obtain control of either its invaluable film library or its huge tracts of real estate. And though almost everyone who worked at Disney believed the company was a special place, and feared that in a merger it might lose the attributes that made it so distinctive, Gold and Roy Disney would have preferred to see it the subsidiary of a large corporate parent if that would improve its management. After all, such had been the fate of most other Hollywood studios. Charles Bluhdorn of Gulf & Western had acquired Paramount; the oil billionaire Marvin Davis and the commodities trader Marc Rich had taken over Twentieth Century-Fox; the financier Kirk Kerkorian owned MGM/United Artists; Coca-Cola owned Columbia; and Steven Ross had merged his company, which had been founded on a chain of funeral parlors, with Warner Brothers to form Warner Communications. To the Brain Trust, a merger was a viable option, assuming that the appropriate corporate partner could be found.

After meeting with the Lazard partners, Stanley Gold still was not sure what he was going to do, but before leaving New York he also retained Herbert Galant, a senior partner of the law firm Fried, Frank, Harris, Shriver & Jacobson. A man with considerable experience in corporate mergers and acquisitions, Galant had worked for such takeover barons as Sir James Goldsmith and had advised Getty Oil when it tried to have Gordon Getty removed as a trustee of the Getty Trusts.

Gold and Wells were still in New York when Disney's annual meeting ended. Roy Disney, as a director of the company, had attended, and afterward he and Patty flew up from Orlando in the Shamrock jet to have dinner with the two men, then give them a lift back to the Coast. The Disneys took a suite at the Ritz-Carlton, where Gold and Wells were staying, and the four gathered there for a room-service dinner. Gold was on a severe diet at the time; he could eat only fruit. The others, under no such restrictions, ordered a bottle of vodka.

Wells and Gold reviewed for the Disneys their session at Lazard Frères. They also discussed the potential conflict of interest caused by Roy Disney's position on the board of Walt Disney Productions: He was privy to the board's most secret deliberations, but at the same time was withholding from the other directors information of vital interest to the company, namely, his own embryonic plans to try to oust management. If he was going to continue to explore that avenue, he would have to sever all ties with the company.

Wells wanted Roy to tell him what kind of pictures the studio *should* be making. They talked about *Splash,* about the debut, in a Disney film, of bare breasts, albeit wreathed in the actress's waist-length yellow hair, and about their dissatisfactions with Disney's management.

As the evening wore on, everyone grew increasingly animated. The dinner turned into an impromptu party which lasted until 2:00 A.M. Stanley Gold miraculously managed to cling to his diet, but by the end of the evening he figured he had devoured $50 worth of hotel pears.

On the morning of March 9, 1984, Ray Watson was attending a meeting in the conference room adjacent to his office when his secretary received a hand-delivered letter dated March 8:

PERSONAL AND CONFIDENTIAL

Dear Ray,

Effective this date I hereby resign as a director of Walt Disney Productions.

I would like to thank the shareholders of Walt Disney Productions for giving me the opportunity of serving as a director for the last seventeen years.

Very truly yours,
Roy E. Disney

Watson was shocked. The letter seemed so sudden, so precipitate, so out-of-the-blue. Even more disturbing, Roy Disney did not offer the slightest explanation for taking such a drastic step.

Ray Watson had sat on a good many boards, and usually he could recognize the signs of dissidence as they began to emerge in a director. Most board members made no attempt to hide them. After all, as the saying went, a director really had just one job: to support the chief executive or to replace the chief executive. Roy Disney had never given any public indication that he was unhappy, and he had rarely opposed measures proposed by the management. In fact, in Ray Watson's eleven years as a Disney director, he could recall only one time when Roy Disney had voted against management on an issue before the board. That was the decision in 1982 to purchase Retlaw Enterprises from the Walt side of the Disney family so that Walt Disney Productions would once again control the merchandising rights to Walt Disney's name. And as Watson remembered it, Roy Disney had said he opposed that proposal because he thought the price was too high.*

Watson was aware, of course, of the old feud between the Walts and the Roys. He was also aware of the animosity between Roy Disney and Ron Miller, and between Roy and Card Walker, who, though he had retired as chief executive, remained a director of the company. These quarrels, however, were generally considered ancient history; they predated Watson's involvement in the company's management, and he knew of no recent flare-ups.

In any case, whatever complaint Roy Disney had, Watson wanted to straighten the matter out. The company needed Roy's support. He was the one member of the Disney family—not counting Ron Miller, who was related only by marriage—to sit on the company's board. Also, he was the company's largest shareholder, and stock analysts would view his resignation as yet another indication of trouble at Disney.

Immediately upon receiving the letter, Watson called Shamrock Holdings. A receptionist with an extraordinarily cheery voice explained that Mr. Disney was out of town and wasn't expected back soon. Over the next few days, Watson tried several more times to reach Roy Disney; each time he was told that Mr. Disney was traveling, or that Mr. Disney wasn't in today, or that Mr. Disney couldn't be reached. Finally, he sat down and wrote a letter suggesting that the

---

*Actually, the issue was a pivotal one for Roy Disney, rekindling many of the Roy family's concerns about the Walt side's taking advantage of the company for its own benefit. He believed that the rights in question should always have belonged to the company.

two of them get together and discuss whatever the problems were that had caused a person of such importance to the company to leave the board. Roy Disney, however, did not respond, and Watson, a busy man with a tight schedule and responsibilities that seemed to grow every day, dropped the matter.

In the second week of March a rumor began to travel through the skein of alliances and friendships that bound Hollywood and Wall Street. Investment bankers in Century City passed it along to their clients. Agents and producers discussed it over lunch at Mortons and Spago. But the rumor was given the most attention within the international entertainment empire that was Walt Disney Productions. It spread rapidly through the sound stages and the animation department at the Burbank studio; it was pondered by Japanese executives in the Tokyo Disneyland and by crew supervisors on the circuit of roads that ran beneath the Magic Kingdom in central Florida. The rumor was that Roy Disney had resigned from the board and shrouded himself in silence because he planned to try to take over the company from outside.

5

O N FEBRUARY 24, 1984, a week before Disney's annual meeting and two weeks before Roy Disney resigned from the board, Saul Steinberg, the chairman of Reliance Group Holdings, had lunch with an investment banker at an exorbitantly expensive restaurant in midtown Manhattan. The object of the lunch was to explore investment opportunities for Reliance, and to that end the investment banker recounted for Steinberg some of the current Wall Street gossip, including the rumor that Coca-Cola, which already owned Columbia Pictures, was in pursuit of Walt Disney Productions.

Reliance should look at Disney, the banker said. Something was going to be happening there.

Steinberg was not galvanized by the suggestion. Shrewd investors avoided the movie business; it was so unpredictable, so dependent on the vagaries of public taste and the fitful inspirations of filmmakers. However, he would, he said, consider looking at the values.

After lunch Steinberg returned to Reliance headquarters at Park Avenue and Fifty-second Street, to his office on the twenty-ninth floor with its gracefully curving walls of blond wood covered with plaques attesting to the variety and magnitude of his philanthropic interests. On the wall behind his desk were two gray marble tablets inscribed in English and Hebrew:

The Eleventh Commandment Do Not Talk On The Telephone To The Press	On the Eighth Day Saul Rested

Steinberg punched in Disney's trading code on the Quotron video terminal beside his desk. In seconds a quick summary of Disney—last sale price, trading patterns, earnings per share, dividends paid—appeared on the screen. The company was trading at $49 a share, down from a fifty-two-week high of $84. Steinberg picked up the telephone, dialed his research department, and asked for an investment analysis on Walt Disney Productions.

Steinberg was a short, chunky man with large jowls, a shock of thick black hair, and a pleasant manner. When he grinned and rolled his eyes, which he sometimes did to amuse his wife, Gayfryd, he looked almost jolly. But in business circles Steinberg was known as a pirate who acquired companies in hostile takeover battles, then ruthlessly disposed of management. He was widely viewed as the very incarnation of the corporate raider; executives of vulnerable companies had literally panicked upon learning that he was buying their stock. An article on him in *Fortune* magazine was entitled "Fear and Loathing in the Boardroom."

In truth, Saul Steinberg had not actually acquired a company in a hostile takeover since 1968. But on more than a dozen occasions, he had sold stock he had bought back to a company at a huge premium because the company's management feared he *would* take it over. The victims of this "greenmail" ranged from Chemical Bank to Quaker State Oil Refining. "I have greenmailed more companies than [anyone else]," he declared in a 1985 article in *Manhattan,inc.* magazine.

For many years, a certain notoriety had surrounded Steinberg's personal life: At the time of his divorce from his second wife, Laura, who decorated his thirty-four-room Park Avenue triplex with leopard skins and elephant tusks, she had filed a stockholder's suit accusing him of misappropriating Reliance funds for his personal benefit, including the support of a cocaine habit.* But by 1984 he had been welcomed into the New York establishment. After all, his labors had made him one of the richest men in the United States, with a personal fortune estimated at $400 million, and he was one of the city's most generous philanthropists. By his own estimate he had given away almost $50 million before he was forty-five, much of it to the Metropolitan Museum of Art, whose Frank Lloyd Wright Room he under-

*After the settlement she said all of the accusations and charges were "totally untrue."

wrote. Now, having been transformed into a figure of social consequence, he and Gayfryd, his third wife, could count among the guests
at their black-tie dinner parties such notables as writer Jerzy Kosinski
and Arthur ("Punch") Sulzberger, publisher of the *New York Times*.

Nevertheless, Steinberg had never repudiated his renegade corporate tactics. He was still capable of raiding a company, and to assure
success he maintained at Reliance Holdings one of the most thorough
research staffs on Wall Street; its analysts counted themselves among
the most experienced, and the most highly paid, in the business.*

Within days of Steinberg's request for a Disney profile, an exhaustive portrait of the company's assets, operations, financial performance, and prospects had been produced. It was presented on schedule
to Steinberg; his brother Robert, the president of Reliance; Lowell
Freiberg, the senior vice-president and treasurer; general counsel
Howard Steinberg (who was no relation to Saul, though sometimes it
didn't hurt to let people think so); and George Bello, another executive vice-president and Saul Steinberg's longtime friend.

The Reliance analysis confirmed the vulnerability of Walt Disney
Productions. The liquidation value of the company—its price if all its
assets were sold off—approached and perhaps exceeded $100 per
share. Many of the assets, such as the film library, were underused;
others, such as the seventeen thousand acres of raw land surrounding
Walt Disney World, were altogether *unused*. And, industry sources
had told the Reliance analysts, Disney chief executive Ron Miller was
indecisive, inarticulate, and uncomfortable with numbers.

"Perfect," Saul Steinberg said. "Precisely the kind of company we
should be involved with. There are enormous opportunities here."

Walt Disney Productions had for years been one of the more interesting stocks on the market. It was a very volatile security, which had,
over time and under the impetus of various events such as strikes,

---

*Steinberg's insistence on flawless research dated back to his days as an undergraduate at the
Wharton School of Management at the University of Pennsylvania in the late fifties. A professor
had suggested he write his senior thesis on the decline and fall of IBM. Steinberg's research
indicated that, received opinion to the contrary, IBM was not in decline. Instead, Steinberg
concluded, by the end of the century it would dominate the computer industry, and after
graduating, he began to buy IBM computers and lease them to corporate customers. Before he
was twenty-eight, he had made his first million—and had developed a profound distrust of the
research of others.

stock splits, dividends, and gasoline shortages, fallen as low as $3 a share and climbed higher than $100. In 1973, for example, after Walt Disney World had been operating for its first full year, and attendance had exceeded even the company's own ambitious projections, Disney's stock hit $123. The following year, during the oil crisis, when attendance at the theme parks dropped because of the gasoline shortage and the market collapsed, it fell below $17. And the stock behaved in peculiar ways. The value of most companies' shares declined when the chief executive died, particularly if the executive was a vigorous leader. The stock of Walt Disney Productions rose nine points after Walt Disney's death: He was considered so irreplaceable that investors believed the leaderless company would make an irresistible takeover target. But while they did exist at that time, corporate raiders and the takeover battles they provoked were much less common in the mid-sixties than they were to become in the early eighties, and a threat to the company never materialized.

Much had changed in the nearly two decades since Walt Disney died. Now raiders, who could be prompted into action by relatively minor indications of vulnerability, were an increasingly significant force in the marketplace. And indeed, within days of Roy Disney's resignation from Disney's board, the staff of Michael Bagnall, the company's chief financial officer, noticed a pattern of unusually heavy trading in Disney stock. Normally, around two hundred thousand Disney shares were traded every day; by mid-March, that figure had climbed to more than nine hundred thousand. The most logical explanation was that someone was accumulating a lot of the company's stock. Someone was "taking a position." The identity of the purchaser would remain unknown, however, unless and until 5 percent of the total shares outstanding had been acquired. At that point the purchaser was required to file a Schedule 13D with the Securities and Exchange Commission declaring the amount of stock purchased, the dates of purchase, and the reasons for the purchase. Until then the Disney people had to subsist on the rumors. The experience was like sitting in a small boat and watching the waters roil and churn as some unknown creature circled just beneath the surface.

Disney's staff was not alone in its observation of the unusual trading pattern; anyone who tracked the market, anyone with a Quotron, could see it as well. The first to take note, because it was their business, were arbitrageurs, people who made their money speculating in the stocks of takeover targets. But institutional traders quickly learned of it too, as did retail brokers; by the time the press picked up the story, Wall Street was awash in speculation about the mysterious buyer.

On March 22, Phillip Wiggins, a reporter for the *New York Times,* described the trading pattern and the rumors about the purchaser's identity in the *Times*'s "Market Place" column. The leading suspect, according to Wiggins, was not Roy Disney but Rupert Murdoch. The predatory Australian publisher, known mostly for his cheesecake-and-mayhem tabloids such as the London *Sun* and the New York *Post,* had been trying to expand into television and movies. A month earlier, he had bought 7 percent of Warner Communications in an effort to seize control of that conglomerate. Steven Ross, the chairman of Warner, had resisted, and the ensuing battle had helped popularize such colorful Wall Street colloquialisms as "poison pill" and "shark repellents," describing the various defensive maneuvers undertaken by the hapless Warner. In the end Ross had been able to drive Murdoch off only by selling 29.5 percent of his company to Chris-Craft Industries, a white knight friendly to Warner's management. Now, with Disney's stock heating up, it was said that Murdoch, having been denied Warner, had decided to move on another entertainment company.

The rumors created considerable bewilderment and alarm among the Disney executives, and they turned to the company's professional advisers. Robert Greenhill, a managing director of Morgan Stanley who had founded his firm's mergers and acquisitions department, was one of Wall Street's most experienced takeover specialists. And when Disney's executives had hired Kenneth Leventhal & Associates to evaluate the company's assets, they had, at the recommendation of Morgan Stanley, also placed the law firm of Skadden, Arps, Slate, Meagher & Flom on retainer.

Skadden, Arps was not hired to do any standard legal work for Disney; its lawyers found that sort of boilerplate tedious. Instead, the firm, which had made its mark in the art of corporate warfare under the direction of its managing partner Joseph Flom, was one of a handful a company could turn to for strategic advice when it was besieged by raiders. But Skadden, Arps was also a firm that a company could hire if it wanted to conduct a raid. Hence, a large number of corporations kept Skadden, Arps on retainer so that its lawyers could instantly be summoned in the event of a threatened takeover, and as a precautionary measure to prevent Skadden, Arps from going to work for any potential opponent. During times of tranquility, executives who had retained them tended to think the Skadden, Arps attorneys had an enviable arrangement, collecting handsome commissions for doing essentially nothing. But should a threat suddenly loom up, it was no small comfort to know that they were there.

And the Disney executives felt threatened. Shortly after the *Times* article appeared, Ray Watson called Bob Greenhill at Morgan Stanley, who elaborated on some of the current speculation. "What can we do if this is a real threat?" Watson asked. The question was too complicated to answer over the phone. Watson and Ron Miller were preparing to fly to Paris to explore possible sites for a European Disneyland with French officials (the idea had been under consideration at Disney since the early seventies, but the fabulous success of the Tokyo Disneyland had given new impetus to the project); they agreed to stop in New York to discuss the takeover rumors with their advisers.

The consultations began with a dinner for the Disney people hosted by Morgan Stanley in one of the firm's elegantly appointed private dining rooms on the thirtieth floor of the Exxon building on Sixth Avenue. In addition to Watson and Miller, Mike Bagnall attended as Disney's chief financial officer. Bob Greenhill brought along two Morgan Stanley partners, Byron Rose, a member of the corporate finance department, who had handled Disney's account for years, and Peter Kellner, from mergers and acquisitions. Joe Flom of Skadden, Arps came alone.

Because Disney had not previously been involved in any mergers or acquisitions, its executives had not met Bob Greenhill before, and some time was spent on introductions, backgrounds, mutual acquaintances. Before long, however, the talk turned to takeovers as Greenhill, the very incarnation of the distinguished, urbane investment banker, began describing his experiences in the business and outlining the options that were available to a company like Disney. The point he stressed most heavily was that Disney ought to extend its line of credit, and ought to do it as quickly as possible.

Virtually all companies maintained lines of credit with banks that enabled them to borrow a fixed amount of money on demand. Disney already had a $300-million line with the Bank of America, and Ray Watson failed to see the need for more. It cost more money to maintain a larger line of credit, for one thing, and Disney wasn't expecting to make a major purchase anytime soon. Besides, the company had a long and solid relationship with the Bank of America; if Disney ever did need to increase its line of credit, it should have no difficulty doing so.

Greenhill dismissed these objections. In his experience, once somebody started a takeover, or threatened a takeover, lines of credit dried up. "I don't care how good a relationship you have with your bank," he said, "you won't be able to get them. So if you want them you must get them before the threat appears, not afterwards."

Flom, a slender, elfin man who smoked a pipe, disagreed. In his opinion it was unnecessary—and possibly dangerous—for Disney to extend its line of credit. "I think that just signals things," he said. Flom was a legendary negotiator, but he was far less articulate than Greenhill in freewheeling conversation, often pausing, searching for words. Sometimes his sentences seemed to get lost in his pipe smoke. "It signals that you're getting ready for some massive something," he went on. "And that will inflame the problem, draw attention to yourself."

Greenhill did not disagree. Nevertheless, he told the Disney executives, once a takeover battle started they might need capital—for whatever reasons—and they might not be able to get access to it. He recommended that they obtain as much credit as they could.

For whatever reasons. The words had a distinctly ominous ring. Watson pushed Greenhill to specify those reasons, but Greenhill side-stepped the query. Instead, reiterating the possibility that Disney might find itself without access to capital at a crucial moment, he cited some examples of companies that, when suddenly faced with a threat, had discovered that banks believed it unwise to lend money to a firm whose future was in question: "Their friendly banker said, 'Gee, I'm sorry, but we've got a policy against increasing lines under these circumstances.' "

The Disney people were convinced. When they returned from France, they hastened to the Bank of America. On March 27, the operators at the Disney switchboard in Burbank set up a conference call among the company's board of directors. The "special telephonic meeting" was brief and formal. Mike Bagnall had arranged to more than quadruple Disney's line of credit, to $1.3 billion. The board needed to endorse the measure. The eleven directors were polled; they approved unanimously.

It was a timely act. Two days later the company learned that it was not Rupert Murdoch who had taken the position in Disney. On March 29, Reliance Financial Services Company, a division of Reliance Group Holdings, filed a Schedule 13D stating that it had purchased 6.3 percent of the stock of Walt Disney Productions "for investment purposes." Reliance said it had begun acquiring the stock on March 9, the day Disney released the information that Roy Disney had resigned from the board.

Ron Miller and Ray Watson, worried about Roy Disney and Rupert Murdoch, had never even heard of Reliance or its chairman, Saul Steinberg. Watson called Bob Greenhill, who described Steinberg's background and passed along the rumor, already circulating on the Street, that he might attempt a hostile takeover of Disney. Greenhill recommended that the company's executives return to New York posthaste to review the situation.

Steinberg's name was quite well known in other circles, however. Within days, Disney's stock rose $4 a share on the strength of his reputation, as abitrageurs began to stockpile blocks of the company's stock in anticipation of a takeover battle.

6

EXTRAORDINARY SECURITY surrounded Morgan Stanley's mergers and acquisitions department on the twenty-ninth floor of the Exxon building. First, a guard in the skyscraper's cavernous marble lobby cleared all visitors to the firm. A receptionist on the twenty-ninth floor provided another checkpoint. Locked doors leading into the mergers and acquisitions department, which could only be opened with special magnetic cards, offered additional security. Individual office doors were usually locked as well, and the department had paper shredders in place of wastebaskets. To prevent opportunities for trading on inside information, members of the firm's research and trading departments were usually not even permitted to enter the sanctuary where the specialists in mergers and acquisitions like Peter Kellner, a Morgan Stanley director, had their offices.* Slight of build, with pale blue eyes, sandy hair, and a composed, somewhat dry manner, the man assigned to run the team handling the Disney account exuded urbanity—an impression reinforced by the upholstered Empire chairs, the leather settee, and the antique writing table in his office overlooking the Hudson River.

Kellner's first step was to instruct the junior members of his team to work up a valuation of Disney more extensive than the one recently completed by Leventhal & Company. (This was the third valuation of the company underway in New York at the time; both Reliance and, on behalf of Roy Disney, Lazard Frères were in the midst of similar

---

*Morgan Stanley's concern with security had become almost obsessive in the wake of a scandal that had traumatized the firm in 1981, when two of its investment bankers admitted to systematically selling confidential information to outsiders who used it to trade stocks.

projects.) He needed a firm grasp on the value of Disney's assets because Morgan Stanley would be responsible for advising management on any offers made for the company and for writing the "fairness opinion" that would be required by the SEC to explain how and why any major transaction—a sale of assets or an acquisition—undertaken by the company was in the best interests of its stockholders. Morgan Stanley also retained its own legal counsel, Shearman & Sterling, because the firm could—and probably would—be sued by stockholders unhappy with whatever advice it rendered if a takeover battle actually took place.

Three days after Steinberg filed his first 13D, Ray Watson and Ron Miller flew back to New York. It was the Disney executives' first full immersion in the atmosphere of an investment bank, and Morgan Stanley struck them as a singularly frantic place. The investment bankers wore beepers, and it seemed to Miller and Watson that every time they were five minutes into a discussion with Kellner, his beeper would begin to sound. Usually, another client sought his immediate attention on the telephone or his partners required his presence elsewhere, and Kellner would disappear.

This was particularly frustrating to Watson, who liked to talk a subject out. And what made it worse was that he and Miller were left to sit staring at the walls in what the Disney executives thought had to be the most unattractive conference room in New York; it was adorned primarily with framed copies of documents known in the trade as tombstone ads. Usually run in the *Wall Street Journal* or in ponderous financial magazines like *Institutional Investor,* the tombstones listed stock issues Morgan Stanley had underwritten or mergers it had arranged. As decoration, they left a lot to be desired. Watson started kidding Kellner about this. "You guys have spent a great deal of time designing the ugliest rooms I have ever been in," he said.

Despite the interruptions and the waiting, however, the Disney executives did manage to learn from both the investment bankers and from Joe Flom at Skadden, Arps that only a few methods of averting a takeover existed, and that none was foolproof. One option, called the crown jewels strategy, required the company to cripple itself by selling off the assets the raider considered most desirable. Or the company could turn to a white knight, or pay greenmail to the raider, which would enrage the rest of the stockholders, since they would not be offered the same opportunity to sell their stock for a premium.

Everyone abhorred greenmail.

"No way will we do that," Watson told Kellner and Flom. "That is offensive to us."

Bob Greenhill agreed. "We have never in our history recommended that any company pay greenmail," he said.

Another defensive strategy was the poison pill: The company could make itself an undesirable takeover target by arranging to take on a huge debt load or to make extraordinary purchases if a raider bought more than a certain percentage of its stock. Still another technique was for a company to make acquisitions by exchanging new shares of its own stock for the stock of the acquired company. This would dilute the holdings of the raider; if a company made enough acquisitions and issued enough stock it could, theoretically, prevent the raider from ever gaining control. Joe Flom, however, cautioned the Disney executives that it was self-defeating to make acquisitions merely to issue new stock. Undeniable business advantages had to accrue to Disney. Otherwise the other stockholders, whose holdings would be diluted along with the raider's, would protest vehemently, and some would certainly sue.

The Morgan Stanley bankers focused on a strategy of acquisitions. Indeed, for some time Morgan Stanley had been urging Disney, which maintained a strong balance sheet and carried little debt, to diversify by buying up other companies, but management, preoccupied with Epcot and Tokyo Disneyland, had not been seriously interested. With those projects finally behind them, diversification made more sense than ever, and Peter Kellner and the Disney executives discussed several television stations and cable TV companies they might want to consider.

The discussions, however, were preliminary, exploratory. They struck Ray Watson as disorganized, and after three days of them he became impatient. A builder, Watson was used to accomplishing objectives by choosing among concrete options, and no one at Morgan Stanley or Skadden, Arps seemed to have any definite proposals to offer that might actually eliminate the Steinberg threat. Instead, the talk was about being in a "reactive mode," about waiting to see what Steinberg would do next.

Joe Flom in particular seemed maddeningly vague. Watson recognized Flom's tactical genius, but he chafed at his inability, or refusal, to address specifics. When Watson tried to force him to answer a question, Flom would get halfway through a sentence and then switch to another subject. If Watson tried to return to the original topic, Flom would say, in his distracted way, "Well, there are a lot of balls in the air."

It was his favorite expression, and Watson teased him about it. "I know there are a lot of balls in the air, Joe," Watson would say. "Can't we get one of those balls down out of the air and talk about it before going on to the next?"

But Flom would not do so, and Watson was still frustrated when he caught a late afternoon flight back to Los Angeles on Wednesday, April 4; since Joe Flom happened to be taking the same plane on business unrelated to Disney, the two men sat together, and inevitably wound up discussing Steinberg. Watson, who disliked all the mystery surrounding Reliance's acquisition of Disney stock, wondered why, instead of waiting for Steinberg to make his intentions clear, they could not simply contact the man to find out what his plans were. It seemed natural just to have a conversation. Flom said he was going to see Steinberg in Los Angeles; they were scheduled to attend the same gathering. He would ask if a meeting could be arranged.

Steinberg and Flom were both on the guest list for an unusual and exclusive annual event: the High-Yield Bond Conference held by the investment bank Drexel Burnham Lambert. Commonly known as junk bonds, high-yield bonds were corporate securities that the investment rating services Moody's and Standard & Poor's considered risky or below investment grade. Drexel, an extremely aggressive firm, specialized in creating such bonds and then finding buyers for them. The bonds had become popular among corporate raiders, who used them to finance takeovers; as a result Drexel's annual junk bond conference had become a sort of raiders' summit, jokingly referred to as the predators' conference. Raiders like Saul Steinberg and T. Boone Pickens, arbitrageurs like Ivan Boesky, and takeover attorneys like Joe Flom all put in an appearance. In fact, most of the individuals responsible for the surge in corporate turmoil during the early 1980s gathered at the conference to fraternize and catch up on the latest takeover techniques.*

As he had promised, during the conference Flom suggested to Steinberg that he sit down with Ray Watson for a talk about Disney. Steinberg usually did not meet with the executives of a company if he was contemplating hostilities against it. Such meetings were rarely productive and often quite unpleasant, given the propensity of executives to become emotional, even hysterical, about a situation that Steinberg viewed with detachment.

Nonetheless, Flom persuaded Steinberg to make an exception, and he arranged for Watson to see the Reliance chairman the following Monday at 4:30. But Steinberg neither appeared nor called to cancel. After Watson had left several messages at his hotel, Steinberg finally telephoned. He was civil, but unforthcoming. He had decided against meeting with Watson; he didn't know what he was going to do yet, and was returning to New York to consider his options. "I'll get back to you within ten days," he said.

To Watson, this was distinctly menacing. It seemed incredible to him that Steinberg had bought millions of dollars' worth of Disney stock but *didn't know what he was going to do. Yet.* Was he making a veiled threat? Watson came to the conclusion that Steinberg knew exactly what he was doing. Steinberg had a game plan.

Joe Flom disagreed. Steinberg was an opportunist, the attorney said when Watson called. He had seen a possible opportunity at Disney, but had yet to determine what his next move would be. Flom added that Steinberg probably wasn't sure he could arrange the financing to make a tender offer.

Watson, who had never before done business in such a manner, was not reassured.

At Reliance headquarters, the phones rang constantly during the first two weeks in April. Arbitrageurs, brokers, and bankers passed along information and gossip about Disney in the hope of receiving a hint

---

*It was a standing joke that the hostile-takeover trend would end if someone—presumably a distraught corporate executive—set off a bomb at Drexel's bond conference.

from Reliance executives of the nature of Steinberg's interest in the company. Was this a passive investment? Would Saul make a tender offer to buy out the other shareholders and take over the company? Would he take greenmail? Several Disney shareholders called expressing their approval of Steinberg's move, which had already driven up the price of the stock. And everyone, of course, had suggestions. Steinberg was urged to buy Disney in order to expand its licensing and to exploit the old movies and television programs gathering dust in the studio vaults. Callers from France, Spain, and Singapore said they wanted Disney to open theme parks in those countries.

To all inquiries Reliance executives replied that Steinberg had no specific plans regarding Disney, that he simply thought it a good investment. Few believed them. All raiders said that initially.

"Why Disney?" Steinberg was asked by one Reliance director seeking a deeper explanation.

"I have a special fondness for children," Steinberg replied.

Reliance kept buying. By April 9, its holdings had climbed to 8.3 percent of the company's outstanding shares. Two days later they comprised 9.3 percent. Reliance had become by far Disney's largest shareholder, sweeping up more than $150 million worth of stock in little more than a month because Disney was "a good investment." On April 25, Steinberg filed an amended 13D saying he intended to acquire 25 percent of the company.

Disney let Steinberg know through Wall Street channels and statements in the press that it was extremely unhappy with his behavior, which was "not in the best interests of the company." But Disney's opinion meant nothing. The stock was publicly traded. Anybody with the cash or the credit could buy it. And so far, Steinberg was maintaining that his purchases were for investment purposes. Of course, he could file another 13D at any moment stating that he had changed his mind and had decided to acquire the company, but perhaps he *was* buying for investment purposes. He had, after all, held huge blocks of stock in such companies as Gibraltar Savings Association for years without ever trying to take them over. Disney's management would have to live with the uncertainty.

Meanwhile, Watson and Miller had a company to run. In mid-

April there was a series of meetings at WED to discuss additional pavilions planned for Epcot. And Watson was searching for people on the East Coast who could help to exploit Disney's undeveloped land in Florida. He called James Rouse, an old friend who had renovated Faneuil Hall in Boston and the South Street Seaport in New York. He also called Roger Hall, a former neighbor whose son had played on the same baseball team as Watson's son, David. Hall, who had moved to Boca Raton, was president of the resort communities division of the Arvida Corporation, one of the largest and most successful real estate management companies in Florida.

Disney was getting ready to do some development in Florida, Watson said. Would Hall and his company consider participating as a consultant? Though it was premature to talk about a joint venture, by coming in early Arvida would make itself a natural joint venture partner.

Hall was interested. Arvida had never done such a thing before, but Disney was special and so was Disney's Florida property. "Let me think about it," Hall said.

On the Disney lot that spring, supervising the final cut of his picture *Baby . . . Secret of the Lost Legend* and beginning preproduction on his next movie, *My Science Project,* was a free-lance film producer named Jonathan Taplin. A former rock promoter who had served for a time as Bob Dylan's stage manager, Taplin had produced such movies as *Mean Streets* and *The Last Waltz.* He had been one of the first independent producers hired under Richard Berger's new regime at the studio, and while on location in the Ivory Coast for *Baby,* he had occupied himself by reading through a stack of Disney's annual reports. Like everyone else, he concluded that Disney was undervalued, and when he returned from the Ivory Coast in March he called Richard Rainwater, who oversaw non-oil investments at Bass Brothers Enterprises in Fort Worth, Texas. A year earlier, Taplin had tried to interest Rainwater in investing some of Bass Brothers' money in a leveraged buyout he was attempting to put together for a small movie production company called Lion's Gate. "We don't have time for five-million-dollar deals," Rainwater had told him then. "Come back when you've got something bigger."

"I've got something bigger," Taplin said when he got the Bass lieutenant on the phone. "Much bigger." He then flew to Fort Worth and proposed that the Basses invest in Disney.* The company was going to turn around, he told Rainwater as the two men examined its financial statements. When that happened, Disney's stock would soar.

Rainwater did not disagree. But, he pointed out, at that time the Bass brothers had their capital tied up in other big investments, principally 9.9 percent of Texaco. To get what they wanted out of that company, they might have to go as high as 25 percent, and *that* would require another $2 billion in cash. "So we can't think about purchasing a hunk of Walt Disney right now," Rainwater said.

Taplin, however, was irrepressible. Back in Burbank, he rather presumptuously wrote Ray Watson a memo offering the Disney chairman his advice on how the company might improve earnings by exploiting the film library and expanding production at the studio. When he dropped the proposal off at Watson's office, the two men began discussing Steinberg.

"You ought to talk to Richard Rainwater about the threat to the company," Taplin said.

Unbeknownst to Taplin, Ray Watson knew Richard Rainwater. When Watson left the Irvine Company in 1977, Rainwater had called to tell him that Bass Brothers would be willing to finance him if he was looking for a venture capital partner. Watson had turned the offer down because he wanted to remain independent, but he had found it generous, and he and Rainwater had stayed in touch, later collaborating on a proposal—ultimately unsuccessful—to buy the old Fort Worth Airport. So Watson felt comfortable calling the Bass Brothers executive on the sensitive matter of Saul Steinberg.

"You have an incredible company," Rainwater said. "I'm going to put together a task force called Save Disney."

This was Rainwater's way of talking. He asked Watson whether

*Taplin thought that by bringing the Basses into Disney he would at the very least earn a nice finder's fee—it was a Bass tradition to reward their friends handsomely—and he might be able to talk his way into a position at the studio. Eventually he was indeed compensated by Rainwater, and the deal struck him as such an interesting and easy way to make money that when his two Disney movies failed he became an investment banker at Merrill Lynch. "What I'm doing at Merrill Lynch is like rock and roll was in 1968," he later told a reporter for *Vanity Fair.* "It's the highest adrenaline rush anybody could ever have."

Disney was investigating options independently or leaving everything in the hands of its advisers. Watson said he was willing to talk to anyone who had ideas. Rainwater then suddenly changed course. Taplin, it turned out, was not the only person to have brought Disney to his attention. "Ray," he said, "did you know we own Arvida?"

Watson did not. Rainwater explained. The year before, Bass Brothers Enterprises and Arvida's management had acquired Arvida from the bankrupt Penn Central Company in a leveraged buyout that had cost them only $20 million in cash. So the Basses knew all about Watson's telephone call to Roger Hall. They were also aware that Disney might be forced to make acquisitions as a means of deterring Saul Steinberg.

"Did you ever think about buying Arvida?" Rainwater asked Watson.

"No, I've never thought about it."

"Well, would you?"

"It depends on what the terms are," Watson said. "If it makes business sense, we'll talk about it."

After he submitted his resignation from Disney's board, Roy Disney was besieged with calls from arbitrageurs and reporters. The syndicated financial columnist Dan Dorfman, he was told, had announced he was going to find Roy Disney "wherever he is" and get an interview. When Disney complained about the hounding, his friend Cliff Miller recommended that he simply disappear. So he changed his phone number, closed up the home in Toluca Lake, and moved with Patty to their beach house at Capistrano. Once there, he bought an answering machine. The Disneys felt slightly ridiculous about these melodramatic precautions. "It's Dorfman," Patty Disney joked when a light airplane circled the house for half an hour. "He's going to jump from the plane and find you after all."

Throughout March, as Saul Steinberg accumulated his position in Walt Disney Productions, the Disneys and Stanley Gold waited for Lazard Frères to complete its study of the company's operations, financial records, corporate bylaws, loan commitments, and SEC filings. Gold might have been expected to be dismayed by Saul Steinberg's presence on the scene, if for no other reason than that Steinberg presumably could muster the resources to acquire Disney more easily than Roy Disney could. But Gold was not dismayed. In fact, he believed it to be a good omen. Steinberg would create chaos, and Gold wanted chaos. He thought that whoever was better at managing chaos would prevail, and unlike Disney's executives, unlike most people, Gold told himself, he was comfortable in a chaotic situation. Chaos didn't scare him. In fact, he thrived on it.

Nor was Roy Disney particularly disturbed by the possibility that Steinberg, the man known for creating fear and loathing in the boardroom, might seize control of the company Roy's father had helped found. When newspaper accounts of Steinberg's interest first appeared, Gold had asked his client which he preferred, Steinberg or current management. "I'm not especially crazy about either of them," Roy Disney said. "But if that's the choice, I'll take Saul Steinberg."

Unlike Watson and Miller, Gold and his client knew who Saul Steinberg was. The year before, Shamrock had entered into an oral agreement to acquire WICS, a television station in Springfield, Illinois, owned by Reliance. When Steinberg backed out of the deal, Stanley Gold sued. "You're crazy," his friends told him. "You're asking for a lot of trouble." Nonetheless, Gold persisted. It was only a few weeks after the case was settled out of court, late in January 1984, that Steinberg began acquiring Disney stock. One more or less facetious theory held that he had done so to teach Stanley Gold and Roy Disney a lesson.*

At the end of March, Roy and Patty Disney, Frank Wells, Stanley Gold, and Mark Siegel, Gold's partner at Gang, Tyre & Brown, all flew to New York for a presentation by Lazard Frères, whose analysts had concluded that Disney was worth approximately $82 a share in a liquidation. The studio and film library accounted for about 30 percent of the company's value; the real estate, theme parks, and consumer products division represented the remaining 70 percent. If Roy Disney wanted to acquire Walt Disney Productions, he could, by selling off the theme parks and real estate, recover much of his investment and still retain control of the studio and the film library. While

---

*A similar joke, circulating at Reliance, had it that Saul Steinberg had told his staff to "go after Watson," meaning go after IBM, which had been headed by Thomas Watson and which was the company Steinberg had described in his Wharton thesis, but that the staff had taken him to mean Ray Watson and Disney.

not eager to split up the company, the Brain Trust was tantalized by the prospect of taking it over. They wanted to explore the idea further. Lazard Frères, however, was a relatively small firm without the capacity to arrange the more than $2 billion in financing needed. If the Brain Trust intended to proceed, the next step would be to find someone who did have that capacity.

After their return to Los Angeles, Wells and Gold discussed "the situation," as everyone had taken to calling it, with renewed intensity. Since they still ran together almost every morning, these conversations often took place during the drive to the UCLA track. Was a tender offer possible? Who would vote with them in a proxy fight? What assets would they sell if they did buy the company? What would Steinberg do? What would Disney do in response? Sometimes, wanting to finish their conversation after they had arrived at the track, they walked a lap or two before starting to run, and one day they became so engrossed in the matters at hand that they spent the entire hour walking around the track, then climbed back into Wells's car. Didn't run a yard.

"You've got to meet someone," Wells announced in mid-April. "I've checked around town and the guy who can raise money better than anyone else in the whole world is Mike Milken."

It sounded promising to Gold.

"I'll set up an appointment," Wells said.

Michael Milken, the head of the Los Angeles office of Drexel Burnham Lambert, was an almost mythical figure on Wall Street. His admirers believed him to be a genius. At age thirty-nine, he was said to be the highest-paid individual in the business, earning $25 million a year (more than $100,000 a day), which was approximately one-tenth of Drexel's total earnings.* Mike Milken was the man who had, to put it simply, invented junk bonds. While a student at the Wharton School—the same business school Saul Steinberg had attended—he had discovered that many smaller companies in new industries which, lacking "histories," suffered from poor credit ratings, actually made quite good investments, and he had begun devising bonds for them.

---

*By July 1986, according to *Business Week,* the figure had risen to an estimated $40 million a year. Four months later, however, Milken's stature, and even Drexel Burnham's very future, was put into question when Milken was subpoenaed in the insider-trading scandal then wracking Wall Street.

Though the bonds involved considerable risk for the investor, they had much higher yields than better-rated bonds, and corporate raiders soon discovered another use for them. The raiders could form corporations that were empty shells, then issue bonds in the shell corporation's name—bonds backed only by the assets of the company they intended to seize. Carl Icahn, T. Boone Pickens, Sir James Goldsmith, Victor Posner, Carl Lindner, Meshulam Riklis, the Belzberg family of Canada, and, of course, Saul Steinberg had all come to Mike Milken at one time or another to issue junk bonds to finance their takeover ventures. As a consequence, Milken had developed a network of contacts among the raiders that was without parallel on Wall Street. (It was he who had hosted Drexel's High-Yield Bond Conference in Los Angeles that Steinberg and Joe Flom had attended.)

A rather humorless man who wore a toupee, Milken was a fanatical, obsessive worker. He would begin his day at his office on the corner of Wilshire Boulevard and Rodeo Drive in Beverly Hills at five-thirty in the morning and often remain at his desk until midnight, going through three shifts of secretaries. His Saturdays and Sundays were occupied as well, and he sometimes scheduled appointments as early as four-thirty on Sunday morning. As though he had no time to spare for more normal conversation, Milken tended to speak in blunt, telegraphic statements. "My message to you is: Buy," he would tell one investor. "My message to you is: Offer fifty a share," he would say to another. After reviewing matters with Stanley Gold and Frank Wells, he decided it would be possible to put together the financing that would enable Roy Disney to buy Walt Disney Productions. "It's doable," he said. "It's a doable deal. I can see the numbers." Then he and his associates went to work. For investors, they turned in part to savings and loan associations, some of which by the early 1980s had shed their reputations as conservative thrifts and become major investors in the junk bonds used to finance raids. Charlie Knapp, the daring and controversial chairman of the Financial Corporation of America, agreed to invest.* So did the Dade County Savings & Loan Association.

---

*The following month, FCA was forced to restate its earnings after an investigation by the Securities and Exchange Commission into its accounting practices. In August the SEC required the company to restate earnings a second time; the resulting figures showed one of the largest losses for a single quarter by any savings and loan institution. Two weeks later, Knapp resigned as chairman.

Through the last two weeks of April, Frank Wells and Stanley Gold met repeatedly with Mike Milken and his associate Peter Ackerman to review their progress. Wells and Gold would run at five-thirty in the morning, and then, hot and sweaty, jog right into Drexel's Beverly Hills office for their appointments with Milken's people, who invariably wore suits and ties. One morning Gold was supposed to meet Milken at 5 A.M., and Ackerman wanted to see Gold first. It was a bit early to squeeze in a run beforehand. Gold rose at four and was shaved, showered, and dressed by four-thirty for his four-forty-five meeting with Ackerman. It was pitch dark outside. "You must have another woman," Gold's wife, Ilene, said to him as he left. "It's four-thirty in the morning and you're telling me you're going to a business meeting?"

7

B ECAUSE IT WAS now actually "in play," Walt Disney Productions had become more than an object of keen interest among Wall Street's arbitrageurs: Speculation in the stock had begun in earnest. One of the most aggressive arbs, as they were called, was Ivan Boesky, whose firm, Ivan F. Boesky & Company, was worth more than $100 million. Dubbed "Piggy" on Wall Street for the gluttonous size of his investments, Boesky (who was also known as "Ivan the Terrible") took inordinate risks and had himself described his behavior as a compulsion, once saying: "It's a sickness I can't control." Characteristically, he took a huge position in Disney.*

Once arbs bought into a company, they were, as shareholders, owners, and they often proceeded to make proprietary demands, usually by calling up the company's executives to insist on being given information or to offer unsolicited advice. Ray Watson began to receive such calls in April. One of the first was from Ivan Boesky. At that point Watson had never heard of Ivan Boesky—just as he had never heard of Saul Steinberg a month earlier—and so his secretary took a message. Watson called Peter Kellner at Morgan Stanley.

"Who is this Ivan Boe-esky?" he asked.

Kellner sighed, and began to explain.

Boesky wasn't the only caller. With the arbitrageurs, Steinberg, and Roy Disney all circling Walt Disney Productions, a host of financiers attempted to exploit the company's dilemma by offering, as the Basses had, to sell it *their* companies for a hefty profit. In late April,

---

*Boesky's nicknames and his description of his "sickness" assumed new meaning years later, in November 1986, when he admitted to trading on inside information, paid a $100 million fine (the largest in Wall Street history), and was barred for life from the American securities industry.

Raymond Chambers, president of Wesray Corporation, a private investment firm in Morristown, New Jersey, read a newspaper article about Disney's defensive maneuvering. In 1982 Chambers and his partner, former Secretary of the Treasury William Simon, had acquired a small company called Gibson Greetings through a leveraged buyout in which they and their associates had put up $1 million in cash, borrowing the rest against Gibson's assets. Eighteen months later they had taken Gibson public for a profit of $70 million. But Chambers and Simon still controlled 38 percent of Gibson's stock, which, with the company trading at around $18 a share, was worth about $45 million. If Disney could be persuaded to acquire Gibson at the right price, they might be able to double their money. Chambers called an old friend, Eric Gleacher, a managing director of Morgan Stanley, and suggested that Disney look Gibson over. The two companies were an ideal fit, Chambers said. Gleacher said he would pass the idea on to Peter Kellner.

About the same time, Kellner got a call from the Minneapolis financier and raider Irwin Jacobs, who wanted Disney to take a look at a moving and storage company called Minstar that he had seized in a hostile takeover. Jacobs felt that if someone was going to take advantage of Disney, it might as well be he. It also seemed to him that no one at Disney knew how to handle Steinberg. Jacobs felt he could. So, he told Kellner, he did not want to sell Minstar outright to Disney. He was proposing that the two companies merge, which would allow Jacobs and his associates to come in and straighten out Disney's management.

Kellner was not enthusiastic. He thought Jacobs, far from doing his clients a favor, was simply trying to parlay his odd collection of tiny companies into a big minority position in Disney. Moreover, Jacobs's proposal seemed to carry the faint threat that Jacobs would move on Disney if the company did not buy Minstar. But Disney dwarfed Minstar, and Jacobs too, for that matter. Kellner told him that Disney was not at present interested in merging with Minstar.*

While Chambers and Jacobs tried to sell their companies to Dis-

---

*Jacobs subsequently said in a deposition and in an interview for this book that during their conversation Kellner had told him, "We've got Saul Steinberg in check. There's nothing he's going to do. And we've got ten deals ready if he does. We'll give him the bones of this company. He'll get nothing." Kellner denied in a sworn affidavit ever making any such statements.

ney, others thought fear of the raider might make the Disney executives put Walt Disney Productions itself on the market. Thus in mid-April Sidney Sheinberg, the president of MCA, told Ron Miller that it would be "a shame" to have Disney acquired at its current depressed price, since it was "one of the great institutions in our business." Could MCA "be helpful"? Miller and Watson met with Sheinberg and MCA chairman Lew Wasserman to discuss ways MCA might "help" Disney. The MCA executives did not tell their Disney counterparts that they were also in touch with Stanley Gold and Roy Disney to see whether MCA could be of "help" to *them* should they attempt to take over Walt Disney Productions.

While all these balls were, as Joe Flom might have put it, in the air, the press had started to lavish attention on the Disney story. The tone of much the coverage was struck in an article that ran in *Business Week* in mid-March. It examined the reasons behind the rundown in Disney's stock and drew attention to the poor performance of the studio and the disappointing attendance at Epcot. The article was viewed by Disney's public relations department as unfairly harsh, but stories in the *Wall Street Journal,* the *New York Times,* and the *Los Angeles Times* were scarcely more favorable.

Part of the problem was Ron Miller. Some of the Disney people, as well as some of Disney's advisers at Morgan Stanley and Skadden, Arps, felt that when he granted an interview Miller tended to talk too much and often failed to strike the seamlessly unflappable attitude expected of top executives. For example, when questioned about takeover rumors by *Business Week,* he had said: "Of course we're nervous. It's a concern of everyone in the organization. The rumors are too prevalent." It was not the sort of remark that inspired confidence. Afraid that the coverage would get even worse if a takeover attempt ensued, Erwin Okun, Disney's vice-president for corporate communications and head of its public relations office, sent a memo to Watson and Miller about the need to prepare for battle. "In the event that we become a takeover target," he wrote, "our counterattack strategy should immediately involve the services of a topflight financial PR firm knowledgeable in the rules of Wall Street combat."

There were really only two public relations agencies with that expertise, and they could almost always be found on the two opposing sides in a hostile takeover. One was a small independent firm called Kekst and Company, whose founder, Gershon Kekst, had ties to many raiders and had represented Saul Steinberg for years. The other firm was Hill and Knowlton, a subsidiary of the mammoth advertising agency J. Walter Thompson. Hill and Knowlton's vice-chairman, Richard Cheney, had been involved in more takeover battles than any other PR agent in New York. At Erwin Okun's suggestion, Walt Disney Productions hired Dick Cheney.

In late April, Watson, who had returned to New York to confer with Kellner and Flom, met the new member of the team. It was an inauspicious discussion.

Cheney suggested that Disney's management send out a Donald Duck or some other toy or gimmick to all the company's shareholders.

Watson thought the idea ludicrous. "What are you talking about?" he asked. "What are we going to do, send Steinberg a bunch of Donald Ducks?"

Cheney explained that if they enclosed return cards for a Donald Duck toy in the quarterly reports that are sent to brokerage houses, who forward them to their customers, the individuals who owned Disney stock would contact the company directly asking for the gift, and this would then provide Disney with a list of their names, which would be extremely useful in the event of a proxy contest. Cheney had used this trick successfully in the past. "We'll give these return cards for the ducks or whatever to the Street names," he said, referring to the large brokerages.

To Watson, who had never heard the phrase "Street names," Cheney seemed to be suggesting a trite public-relations ploy. Disney had no need to send out gimmicks to get people to love the company, he told Cheney. What Disney needed was to make people understand what was happening and what might happen, and get some sympathy for that. He suggested that Cheney acquaint himself better with the company before offering any more advice; Cheney, on the other hand, left the meeting thinking Watson knew very little about the ways of Wall Street.

Saul Steinberg's position in Disney, and fear about his intentions, created a sense of urgency with regard to another matter of concern:

executive compensation. Frugality was a tradition at Walt Disney Productions. The company had always paid its executives poorly by Hollywood standards, and their expense accounts were meager. Even that virtually universal industry perk, the stretch limousine, was denied them because of Walt Disney's conviction that people should work for his company because they loved it, not because they had been seduced with luxurious extras—a belief at once shamelessly self-serving and conducive to the preservation of Disney's image. By the 1980s, however, the abysmal salaries at Disney had become an industry joke; indeed, they were one reason why the studio had encountered difficulty attracting fresh talent. Ron Miller's annual salary of $375,000 put him among the lowest-paid of senior executives in motion pictures, though his company was the largest studio after the six majors. The salaries of other Disney executives were similarly small. In fact, so low were the company's pay scales that in the past Disney had been excluded from the motion picture industry's annual study of executive compensation at the insistence of executives from other studios, who believed the Disney salaries, by bringing the overall average way down, would have a detrimental effect on their own incomes.

Employment contracts were also a sore point. Walt Disney had felt an aversion to them; he had expected people to trust him. After Richard Berger had become head of the studio and complained that he could not attract decent directors or actors without offering them contracts, new arrivals to the studio had been given them, but longtime Disney employees continued to labor without. Tension was inevitable, and with the advent of Saul Steinberg, it had increased. Middle-level executives assumed—not without reason—that their jobs would be in jeopardy if the raider seized control of the company and liquidated it. Those without contracts were particularly vulnerable. If a takeover became at all likely, valuable employees would probably begin to respond to the blandishments of headhunters, as executive recruiters were called (much to their dismay), and leave Disney for more lucrative and less uncertain jobs elsewhere.

Thus, the time had come for Disney's directors to reconsider the company's compensation policy. And the discussion had to start with Ron Miller. For one thing, the salaries of the other executives were pegged to Miller's. For another, though Miller had a three-year contract (as did Watson), more than a year had passed since his promotion to the top post. It was time for a raise, if only to demonstrate to the public that the board of directors had complete confidence in its chief executive.

"We ought to decide Ron Miller's somebody we want to have here," Watson told members of the board's compensation committee on the morning of April 30, shortly before the full board convened, and five days after Steinberg had announced his intention to increase his holdings in Disney to 25 percent. "We ought to give him a contract that's commensurate with his job or we ought to get a new CEO."

Convinced, the committee voted to recommend raising Miller's salary, and thus Watson's as well, which depended on Miller's; the full board accepted the committee's recommendation. As chief executive, Miller was now to receive $500,000 a year—still low by Hollywood standards—and Watson $425,000. It was also agreed to extend the two executives' contracts for another two years.

At the same meeting the board also passed, unanimously and with little discussion, several amendments to Disney's corporate bylaws suggested by Joe Flom, and designed to make it easier to hold a raider at bay. One change allowed the board to give a mere twenty-four hours' notice before holding an unscheduled "special meeting," thus enabling it to respond more quickly to breaking events. Another changed the record date determining which shareholders could vote in a proxy contest to forty days after the initiating shareholder filed his "consent" with the SEC that announced his intention to hold such a contest. The maneuver would give the company more time to marshal its forces and take other defensive measures. It was the corporate equivalent of clambering into the bunkers.

Whatever the intentions behind the new employment contracts for Ray Watson and Ron Miller, they had a decidedly undesirable side effect. The press widely described them as "golden parachutes," a term used for excessive compensation packages executives sometimes awarded themselves when faced with a takeover threat. Disney argued that the contracts were not real golden parachutes, because they contained no clauses specifying that the executives were to receive huge bonuses if they lost their jobs in the event that an outsider acquired Disney. The distinction was lost on most reporters, however, and a move to demonstrate confidence in Disney's management was taken instead as evidence of anxiety.

Watson and Miller, however, were too preoccupied with other matters for the misunderstanding to prove more than a minor irritant. The defense of Disney had become an all-consuming task. On May 1, the day after the board meeting, Watson, Miller, and Mike Bagnall returned to New York and the ugly conference rooms at Morgan Stanley.

By that time Disney's officers, together with the investment bankers, had decided to pursue a strategy of acquisitions. Because the undertaking was secret, Morgan Stanley had given it the code name Project Fantasy, after the animated classic *Fantasia.* Kellner and the members of his team (younger associates who rotated in and out of various assignments) were logging twelve to twenty hours a day in their quest for suitable acquisition candidates. They scoured annual reports and the more detailed statements corporations filed with the SEC. They looked at everything from a chain of movie theaters to a cruise line, and conducted in-depth investigations of more than two dozen companies in entertainment, broadcasting, and consumer products. They would eventually approach twelve. As Kellner was to say later in a deposition: "We looked virtually at the world as a starting point and over time narrowed it down."

ABC was a promising candidate. So was Binney & Smith, the maker of Crayola Crayons. So was the Wrather Corporation, which was run by John D. Wrather, Jr., an old friend of Walt Disney's, and which consisted of a collection of odds and ends such as the leases on the mothballed ocean liner *Queen Mary* and Howard Hughes's gigantic wooden airplane, the *Spruce Goose,* the rights to *Lassie,* and the Disneyland Hotel—a piece of real estate Walt had always coveted.

Listening to reports from the investment bankers on all these companies was an ordeal for Watson and Miller. After absorbing the reactions of the Disney executives to a particular analysis, the Morgan Stanley people would retire to another room to discuss alternatives, leaving them to sit for what seemed like hours in the conference room with the tombstone ads. Then too, Kellner was still wearing his beeper, and frequently had to excuse himself from meetings to attend to other clients.

As they explored possible acquisitions, Watson and Miller were also inundated with proposals from various firms that wanted to be "of service." They had already sat through a presentation from Bank of America, which was beginning to orchestrate leveraged buyouts and wanted to undertake such a venture for its longtime client. Now, in New York, they listened to a similar pitch from Kohlberg, Kravis, Roberts & Company, the biggest name in the field. Even though Joe Flom had advised against a leveraged buyout by Disney's management because it would unleash a bidding war that management would surely lose, the idea continued to appeal to Ron Miller and Mike Bagnall. If Disney's managers bought the company themselves and took it private, the takeover threat would simply disappear. They could then all get back to the business they knew, the business of entertaining families.

The Disney officers were becoming desperate. They described themselves as "fighting for our lives," by which they meant they were fighting to defend the very existence of the company. Saul Steinberg was preparing to lay siege to and then plunder Walt Disney Productions like some corporate Visigoth. While this seemed criminal to the Disney executives, it was all perfectly legal, and it had begun to dawn on them that it could really happen. If they took the wrong step. Or unless they took the right one. Feelings were naturally aroused in such a situation, but as he sat through the various presentations, Ray Watson, at least, made an effort to suppress all emotion. The company, he told himself, was in the middle of a game much like chess, and the only way to win was through the most searching analysis of every option on every move.

On April 20, 1984, Bass Brothers Enterprises sold its stake in Texaco back to the oil company for a 12 percent premium. The $1.28-billion package of cash and preferred stock yielded Bass Brothers a pretax profit of $400 million—which critics promptly decried as greenmail —and freed them for other deals. On May 9, Richard Rainwater put in a call to Charles Cobb, the chief executive of Arvida.

"Chuck," Rainwater said, "how's that joint venture with Disney shaping up?"

Cobb said the deal was on hold. Arvida executives had made a presentation to Ray Watson in early April, but the Disney people had since become preoccupied by Steinberg.

"Would you like to do business with them?" Rainwater asked.

"Definitely," Cobb replied.

"Now that we've sold the Texaco stock we have the wherewithal," Rainwater said, and went on to recount his previous conversations with Ray Watson and Jonathan Taplin. The Basses, he told Cobb, could make an outright investment in Disney. Or they might want to take another approach and merge one of the Bass Brothers companies with Disney. Arvida, for example. The Basses believed that Disney, with its new $1.3 billion line of credit, and with Steinberg rapidly closing in, would be willing to pay handsomely for the right acquisition.

Cobb immediately grasped the possibilities. Disney had bought its 28,000 acres of land in central Florida to avoid a repetition of what had happened in Anaheim, where cheap motels, restaurants, and souvenir shops had sprung up around the theme park and siphoned off profits Walt Disney felt should have gone to Disneyland. But Disney had never built more than a few hotels and restaurants on the Florida land and had developed only 3,500 of the total acreage. Another 7,500 had been set aside as a nature preserve. The remaining 17,000 acres just sat there, though admittedly a good portion of it was bog. And cheap motels, restaurants, and souvenir shops had sprung up on its perimeter. Disney had again failed to capitalize on its own drawing power. If Arvida merged with Disney, however, Chuck Cobb could turn his team of skilled developers loose on all of that raw land. Cobb thought it was a terrific idea.

"Let's move, then," Rainwater said. "We need to come up with an offer quickly."

The next day Cobb and his associates flew to Fort Worth to meet with Rainwater and Sid Bass. By noon they had agreed to offer Arvida to Disney for $300 million. For a variety of reasons, including tax considerations as well as Disney's presumed desire to diminish Steinberg's holdings, payment would be made not in cash but in Disney stock issued to cover the purchase price. Rainwater called Peter Kellner, who said the proposal sounded interesting but that Disney would require the Basses to sign a "standstill agreement" promising not to buy additional Disney stock for several years and pledging to support the company's management. Sid Bass, however, was opposed to standstills on principle. The capitalist system only worked, he felt, when shareholders had the right to vote with or against management as they saw fit. He would sign no agreement giving up his rights as a shareholder.

When Kellner insisted, it was decided to delay discussion of the issue until the Disney executives had had an opportunity to review Arvida. Rainwater then called Ray Watson, who, having returned to New York, was staying at the Helmsley Palace on Madison Avenue. "We want to make a proposal," he said. The following morning, Cobb and Sid Bass flew to New York to present Arvida to Disney's officers.

Based in Boca Raton, Arvida was one of the biggest real estate and development companies in Florida, specializing in planned communities like Boca West, a 1,400-acre project on the outskirts of Boca Raton with expensive homes and pricey shopping centers designed around four golf courses to create a resort atmosphere. Arvida also owned oil fields, theme parks, and various other Florida properties.

In 1965 the Penn Central Corporation had acquired a controlling interest in Arvida. Then, in 1970, Penn Central had filed for bankruptcy; it had emerged from Chapter Eleven in 1978, but with what to many seemed an excessively bureaucratic management, and within a few years Arvida's executives decided they wanted their company to become independent again. In the fall of 1983, Chuck Cobb persuaded Richard Rainwater, whom he knew slightly, to join him in a leveraged buyout of the company. Rainwater had never seen any of Arvida's properties, but, over dessert at a Fort Worth restaurant, he agreed to invest $14 million on behalf of the Basses. Arvida's managers had kicked in $6 million, then borrowed $183.6 million against Arvida's assets, for a total price tag of $203.7 million. Now, six months later, Sid Bass and Arvida's president were proposing that Disney buy the company for $300 million.

Arvida intrigued Ray Watson, and the next day, a Saturday, the Disney executives, accompanied by some Morgan Stanley real estate experts, flew to Boca Raton. There they met Bass associate Alfred Checchi, who flew in from Texas, and then spent the weekend hopping from one Arvida property to another in a chartered jet. It was an enjoyable outing. All the Disney officers liked Chuck Cobb. Ron Miller even relaxed enough to crack a few jokes about Steinberg.

Watson and Miller returned to New York Sunday night, and additional Disney staff arrived from Los Angeles. Morgan Stanley's analysts rapidly digested the financial information on Arvida, and, by the end of the following day, Watson was almost prepared to begin negotiations. But there was still one significant reason to hesitate, and that was the Basses themselves.

The purchase of Arvida would make Bass Brothers Enterprises one of Disney's largest shareholders, second only to Saul Steinberg's Reliance. Given Steinberg's already huge position in Disney, did the company want a second group of controversial investors, a group that some called raiders and greenmailers, holding a second significant block of its stock? Neither Joe Flom nor the Morgan Stanley people considered this a good idea, especially if a standstill remained unobtainable.*

But Sid Bass arranged for Watson and Miller to have lunch with him and Al Checchi the following day, May 15, in a private dining room at the Carlyle Hotel. During the meal, Bass, who had a sober and gentlemanly manner, and who had been educated at Andover, Yale, and Stanford, never mentioned Saul Steinberg or Arvida or even Disney. Instead, he talked about himself. He was pained, he said, by his reputation—he was not a raider or a greenmailer, and he wished to allay any fears the Disney executives might have about doing business with him and his family.

The roots of the Bass fortune extended back three generations to a wildcatter named Sid Richardson who had traded oil and gas leases from a lunch-counter pay phone. Richardson's only partner was his nephew, Perry Bass, and when Richardson died in 1959, Perry Bass had wrapped all the family's holdings into a new company called Bass

---

*In fact, Sid Bass had come to New York with another proposal in addition to Arvida. Bass Brothers was awash in cash from the Texaco deal, and Bass suggested to Peter Kellner that his company buy a large block of preferred stock in Disney, on top of the stock it would receive if Arvida went through, as a means of forestalling Steinberg. However, Morgan Stanley's wariness of Bass Brothers Enterprises was such that the discussion came to nothing.

Brothers Enterprises. In 1969 Perry Bass had retired to devote himself
to sailing (he became a navigator on Ted Turner's yacht *American
Eagle*), and had turned the company over to his eldest son, Sid Richardson Bass, who was then twenty-seven.

While the bulk of the Bass fortune remained in oil and gas, Bass
Brothers Enterprises had become under Sid Bass a $4-billion conglom-
erate with extensive real estate holdings and a well-oiled trading and
arbitrage department. The Basses (Sid had three younger brothers,
Ed, Robert, and Lee) had first captured national attention in 1981,
when they expressed an interest in acquiring Marathon Oil Company;
Marathon had sold itself to U.S. Steel instead, and the Basses had
turned a pretax profit of more than $100 million when U.S. Steel
bought their Marathon stock. Other deals followed, and the Basses
had earned a reputation as aggressive asset players more concerned
with exploiting undervalued properties for quick profits than with
long-term investments—a reputation Sid Bass now claimed was un-
deserved.

He explained that although the Basses were known as short-term
investors, most of their investments were in fact long-term. They had
had a large stake in Church's Fried Chicken for years. And they were
venture capitalists who liked to build companies. They owned 27
percent of Prime Computer, which they had helped start in 1971. The
public, however, was unaware of many of these investments because
they had been made before the SEC began requiring investors to file
13D's. And since the Basses had not increased the size of these investments subsequent to the requirement, they had never had to file 13D's
revealing their position.

Like Saul Steinberg, the Basses had spent a lot of their money on
charitable projects that helped counterbalance their image as raiders.
Known as "the boys" in Fort Worth, they had restored their small
city's central business district, underwritten its symphony and museum, and even founded a local prep school. The City Center, two
massive black glass towers they had built, loomed over Fort Worth's
skyline, and the top floors of one, which served as headquarters for
Bass Brothers Enterprises, were laden with modern art.

It all sounded good to Ray Watson. In fact, the only thing Watson
disliked about his lunch with Sid Bass was the food. Soft-shell crabs.
It was the first time he had eaten soft-shell crabs, and it would be the

last (he thought they might have tasted better with ketchup, but there was none on the table). By the end of the meal Sid Bass had impressed Watson as smart, honest, and straightforward. Watson accepted his explanations for the various deals in which the Basses had earned their reputation as raiders. Even greenmail could be seen as simply a method of rationalizing assets; besides, the vast majority of the Basses' investments were passive. Watson decided to proceed with Arvida.

In the end, Disney's advisers reluctantly agreed. After all, there was no doubt that Sid Bass would be an invaluable ally in a takeover battle. He had deep pockets and overdraft checking privileges—handy in the event that emergency funds were required. He was also a buccaneer and a fighter. Forging an alliance with Sid Bass would send a strong signal to Saul Steinberg.

Negotiations began at eight o'clock the next morning at Morgan Stanley, with the Disney officers installed in one conference room and Sid Bass, Al Checchi, and Chuck Cobb in another. Peter Kellner shuttled between the two.

Disney had decided to make an initial offer of $175 million and to go no higher than $225 million, which Watson believed was Arvida's liquidation value. Sid Bass, Peter Kellner reported, would let Disney have Arvida for $300 million. The two parties were only $125 million apart. As the morning dragged on, Watson, Miller, and Bagnall wondered why the Bass Brothers team took so long to respond. Perhaps it was a negotiating tactic. Eventually Kellner returned to inform the Disney people that the other side was reconsidering.

"I've spent a half hour with them and they've come down to two eighty-five," Kellner said.

"We're sticking," Watson said.

Kellner left, then came back. "They don't really believe it."

"You'd better go back in and tell them that's it, and stay with them until they do believe it," Watson said.

Lunch was brought into the conference rooms. By midafternoon each side had inched away from its initial price, but they were still more than $100 million apart. At five o'clock Kellner appeared and said the Basses would let Disney steal Arvida for $275 million. Disney went up to $200 million—and stopped there. Though Watson had earlier agreed to go as high as $225 million, he had changed his mind:

Disney, he had decided, should offer no more than $200 million. For one thing, the Basses, ever the asset players, were probably more eager to sell than Disney was to buy. For another, Watson had become increasingly apprehensive about the lawsuits that Morgan Stanley had said were sure to be brought when any company with shareholders hostile to management made a dramatic and controversial move. The purchase of Arvida was certain to be controversial—if only because Walt Disney Productions had never before acquired another company. In his defense, Watson wanted to be able to show that he had gotten a bargain. So $200 million was the limit. Kellner carried this message back to the Basses, but he quickly reappeared.

"Ray, we're at an impasse," he said. "They don't believe you won't go any higher. You're going to have to tell them that yourself."

"Fine," Watson said. "Take me in there and I'll tell them."

Ron Miller, who, though he was chief executive, had deferred to Watson in all the negotiations, suddenly expressed concern. "Gee, Ray," he said. "Don't give away the company store."

"Don't worry," Watson said.

The Bass group was sitting calmly around a large table.

"Let me tell you why I'm here," Watson said. "Kellner tells me you don't believe we won't go above $200 million. I'm here for only one purpose, to tell you that that's it. That is the price.

"Now let me tell you why that is the price. I have a lot of confidence in you people as individuals. Chuck I've known for some time, and I think his team would make an outstanding addition to our company. But nobody at Walt Disney Productions really understands real estate except me. And I have to take full responsibility for this acquisition.

"I'm absolutely convinced, and I've been told this, that we're going to be sued over this no matter what price we pay. So I'm going to be sitting on a witness stand justifying this. And I can't justify anything above $200 million.

"Therefore, $200 million is the number, gentlemen. I'm not saying your property isn't worth more. I sure as hell hope it is worth more. I'm just saying we won't pay more. And if it's worth more to you, then you shouldn't sell it to us. You should keep it. I'll understand. I want you to feel comfortable with your decision."

"We'd like to think about it," Sid Bass said, and he and Al Checchi left the room.

Chuck Cobb then turned to Watson and started telling him about the contracts Arvida gave its top management. This struck Watson as a little irrelevant, even a little strange, given the significance of the deal at hand, but he nodded along with Cobb, and five minutes later Sid Bass and Checchi returned.

Watson had given his speech, now it was Checchi's turn. "We have a high regard for you, Ray," Checchi said. "We know your background, we even wanted to hire you some years ago."

Watson thought Checchi was praising his judgment only to disagree with it and that the Bass group would not sell for $200 million. Checchi proved him wrong.

"We accept the fact that your word is your bond and that you will not go higher than $200 million," Checchi said. "But we have partners. In Florida, Chuck Cobb is our partner and we don't do anything unless our partners agree." He turned to Cobb. "Sid and I have decided to sell for $200 million but only if you agree, Chuck. If you don't agree we'll leave the room, but if you agree we'll go along."

This put Cobb on the spot. He looked at Checchi, then at Watson, then back at Checchi. "Wait a minute," he said. "You're not going to negotiate with Ray?"

"No," Checchi said. "We believe him when he says this is the last offer. We've agreed to accept the $200 million. It's up to you, Chuck."

"Okay," Cobb said. He turned to Watson and picked up the thread of his earlier conversation about management contracts.

"Well, that's all very interesting," Watson said. "But what does it mean?"

"I guess we've made a deal," Checchi replied.

In the second week of May, Stanley Gold and Roy Disney picked up a rumor that the board of Walt Disney Productions had been summoned to an emergency meeting to approve an acquisition. If Disney obtained another company by issuing new stock, it would dilute the holdings not only of Saul Steinberg, but also of every other stockholder. On May 16, the same day the Arvida deal was negotiated, Gold drafted and Roy Disney signed a letter to Ron Miller, with copies to every other member of the board.

Dear Ron,

I am writing to you and each of the other directors of Walt Disney Productions about a matter of grave and urgent concern to our company.

I have been advised recently and continuingly that negotiations are currently underway between the management of Walt Disney Productions and another corporation that could result in a significant change in the ownership or control of our company. Such rumors have included, by way of example, Disney's acquisition of a company with substantial debt, an acquisition which could cause Disney to incur substantial debt, or issuance of significant new voting stock.

As I am sure you are aware, many of these restructuring tactics have come under severe public and regulatory criticism. If the maintenance of current management were its primary or perceived purpose at the expense of shareholders, such a restructuring would be especially detrimental.

I well understand the concern the Board might have at this time concerning the recent large purchase of Disney stock by third parties, but as a major stockholder I would like to respectfully caution the Board against any action made in haste, frustration, or fear that would basically alter the business resources, character, or structure of the business. I am particularly concerned that such restructuring might occur without obtaining shareholders' approval, regardless of whether the technical provisions of the Articles of Bylaws require such approval. Not to submit any plan for shareholder approval would not be fair or consistent with the best interest of the true owners of the company.

You are well aware of my family's deep and continuing interest in the welfare and success of Walt Disney Productions and the historic and emotional ties that bind us. It is within this context that I am sharing my views with you at this time.

Sincerely,
Roy

Neither Miller nor Ray Watson was unduly perturbed by the letter, though this was the first time anyone at the company had heard from Roy Disney since his resignation from the board. Making acquisitions was a prerogative of management, subject only to the approval of the company's directors. Moreover, the essence of the letter's advice was to avoid acquisitions that were not in the company's interest, and Miller and Watson certainly agreed with that.

The board meeting to approve the Arvida deal was scheduled for nine o'clock on the morning of May 17. Ray Watson, together with the other Disney executives, had flown back from New York the previous night. Before the meeting began, he discussed the presentations to be made to ensure that there would be no surprises. And there were none. Watson, Flom, and Kellner gave their views on the value of Arvida. Flom explained that Roy Disney's letter could be disregarded, since it was little more than an appeal to the directors to do their job well.

A few directors asked mild questions, but they tended to defer to Watson's judgment—he had the real estate experience, after all. The vote that followed would have been unanimously in favor of the deal had it not been for the abstention of Caroline Ahmanson, who was in the Middle East and had to listen to the discussion over a squawk box that kept fading in and out. The board also approved new compensation contracts for Disney's fourteen top officers similar to those given Miller and Watson at the previous meeting. It adjourned in time for lunch, after which Miller and Watson held a press conference announcing the deal.

Morgan Stanley still had much paperwork to do before the sale could be closed, but both sides had agreed that to save on taxes the two companies would "pool their interests" in order to avoid a reappraisal of Arvida's property, which had been purchased at relatively low prices decades earlier and which, because it had never changed hands, had never been re-evaluated at subsequent market prices.* Disney would issue Arvida as many shares as were needed to equal

---

*Also, had the two companies not pooled their interests and had the land been reappraised at current prices, Disney, when it came to sell the property, would not have been able to claim as large a profit.

a market value of $200 million. On the day of the announcement, Disney's shares were trading at $63.62, which would have meant issuing around 3.14 million shares. The deal, however, included what was called a "collar." The number of Disney shares to be given to Arvida's owners in exchange for their Arvida shares would ultimately depend on what happened to Disney's stock during the next twenty days, before the closing of the deal: If the stock rose, Disney would have to issue fewer shares; if it fell, more. And if Disney undertook another major transaction, such as another acquisition or the purchase of either its own or some other company's stock—moves likely to drive down the value of Disney's shares—Arvida had the right either to terminate the sale or to postpone the closing for another twenty days to reevaluate Disney's stock. Finally, there would be no stand-still, though not because of Sid Bass's objection. The reason was that when the interests of two companies were pooled, a standstill was prohibited by law.

Some companies spend up to a year mulling over possible acquisitions. Disney had discovered Arvida, examined it, and agreed to buy it in slightly less than two weeks. When the deal went through, Bass Brothers would end up holding some 5.9 percent of Disney's stock. Steinberg's holdings would drop from 12.1 percent to 11.1 percent. And the stakes of the other shareholders would likewise fall.

Stanley Gold and Roy Disney were outraged. They were opposed to *any* acquisition that would dilute Roy Disney's holdings. But Gold was particularly vehement in his disgust at the purchase of Arvida. In his opinion, the last thing Walt Disney Productions needed was a company that owned thousands of acres of land in Florida. After the Arvida deal was announced, a *Business Week* reporter called Gold for comment. "Disney needs those twenty thousand acres of Arvida land like they need another asshole," Gold said.*

The next weekend the Brain Trust assembled at Roy Disney's house in Toluca Lake to discuss the financing that Mike Milken and

*The editors of *Business Week* deemed this analogy infelicitous, and so when the article appeared the following week, Gold was quoted as saying, "Disney needs Arvida's twenty thousand acres like a hole in the head."

his group at Drexel Burnham had put together to enable Shamrock Holdings to attempt a hostile takeover of Walt Disney Productions. Shamrock would have to put up $200 million. As for the rest of the more than $2 billion needed, Milken had arranged for various other investors to supply the funds by purchasing junk bonds; to pay them back, Roy Disney would be required to sell off either Disney's film library or one of the two theme parks once the takeover was complete.

A maneuver that had seemed enticing in prospect seemed less so now that the specifics were in. For one thing, Roy Disney would have to borrow his share of the purchase price at prime interest rates, and that made Stanley Gold nervous. If interest rates went up three or four points within the next year his client would be saddled with towering debt. More important was the fact that he would have to, as Gold put it, "cannibalize the company" to pay off the other investors. It was an even worse prospect than having Ron Miller and Ray Watson continue to make acquisitions in their effort to deter Saul Steinberg. The Brain Trust decided against trying to acquire Walt Disney Productions. If they were going to go "all the way in," they would have to find some other means.

Late Sunday night, Gold and Frank Wells called Mike Milken at his home.

"The decision is no," Gold said.

"Do you have any objection if I now take on another client and try to do it for them?" Milken asked.

"None whatsoever," Gold said. Milken did not disclose the name of this other client, but as Gold hung up the phone he thought: You don't have to be a rocket scientist to figure out who it is.

8

RUMORS THAT Disney intended to ward off Saul Steinberg by making acquisitions had been circulating on Wall Street long before the announcement of Arvida. In fact, a certain trader had told a Reliance executive that Disney planned one acquisition a week. Another story was that Disney would issue one new share of stock for every share Reliance bought. By one theory, Disney's allies were spreading the rumors to try to frighten Steinberg off. According to another, Reliance was spreading the rumors because they helped justify a takeover by presenting Disney's executives as irrational and self-destructive. But despite the rumors, despite the fact that takeover talk had been in the air for two months, Reliance executives had, they maintained, made no decision to acquire Walt Disney Productions until Arvida. Prior to that, according to the 13D's Reliance filed, Disney was just a good investment. Now Steinberg wanted to know more than the documents could tell him. He ordered a site review and an investigation of the company's internal operations.

At once three of Steinberg's aides flew to Florida in Reliance's Boeing 727, chartered a helicopter, and conducted an aerial survey of the Magic Kingdom, Epcot, the undeveloped acreage, and Arvida's properties in the central part of the state. Members of the Reliance research staff tracked down former Disney executives and approached current employees in an effort to acquire detailed information about the company's management structure, operations, and morale. Reliance's research staff was capable of producing two separate analyses of a company, one evaluating it as an investment, the other as an acquisition. The investment analysis of Disney had been done more than two months earlier; now Steinberg wanted an acquisition analysis. Reliance had entered what its people called a takeover mode. In-house legal counsel Howard Steinberg ordered sweatshirts with a portrait of Mickey Mouse stenciled on the front and the words "I have a special fondness for children" printed on the back.

Had the purchase of Arvida served to put Steinberg off, Disney's stock would have fallen after the acquisition was announced, for Steinberg and the arbs who followed sheeplike behind him would have begun selling their shares, or as they put it on Wall Street, "closing out their positions." But Disney's stock did not drop after Arvida. It even went up a little. That might have meant that investors were expressing their approval of the Arvida acquisition. More likely, it meant that the arbs, smelling a battle ahead, were loading up on the stock even more heavily. In what had become a tired refrain, the Disney officers told each other there was no way of knowing.

The sense of impending combat was intensified late in May when *Forbes* magazine ran a cover depicting a mouse's ears rising into the scope of a rifle. "Knock, knock, it's Saul Steinberg," read the subhead of the accompanying article. "But even if the New York acquisitor goes away, there are other covetous acquisitors waiting outside the door. White knight, anyone? Enter the Bass brothers, as management begins to make its countermoves." The issue, dated June 4 but on the newsstands two weeks earlier, argued that Disney was worth "nearly $110 a share" and called the company "a giant and utterly legitimate tax shelter" because of depreciation on its amusement parks and amortization of the costs associated with its film library. After the *Forbes* story appeared, even small investors began stockpiling Disney in expectation of a takeover bid.

On May 21, the Disney executives returned once again to New York to meet with the chairman of Bally Manufacturing Corporation, the pinball game maker that had opened a casino in Atlantic City. Bally's management believed it was a takeover target, and had authorized Morgan Stanley to look for a white knight. But after discussions lasting two days, both parties agreed that the two companies had nothing in common. The fit wasn't there. Subsequent discussions with Binney & Smith petered out for the same reason: Disney could bring nothing to the crayon business.

At that point Peter Kellner mentioned Gibson Greetings. Ray Chambers, William Simon's partner in the leveraged buyout of the greeting card company, had continued to pester him about the terrific fit of Gibson and Disney.* The prospect of owning a greeting card company scarcely excited Ray Watson and Ron Miller, however, and they were prepared to pass it up when Miller received a call from the head of Disney's consumer products office in New York. He had heard that Disney's management was "talking to" Gibson, and he *was* excited. Gibson, he said, was an outstanding company; Disney should certainly consider it. So Miller summoned Barton "Bo" Boyd, the head of Disney's consumer products division, to New York to get his reaction; Bo Boyd, too, was immediately infatuated with Gibson.

One key to success in the greeting card business is to hold the copyrights to the characters that appear on the cards. Gibson controlled copyrights to the hugely popular Garfield the cat, Kirby Koala, and Sesame Street's Big Bird, to name three. But while Disney held the copyrights to its immense stable of characters, it had no card company. Instead it licensed Mickey, Minnie, Donald, Goofy, Snow White, and the rest of its creatures large and small to Hallmark. But Hallmark, understandably, devoted more energy to marketing cards for which it held the copyrights itself. If Disney owned Gibson, the card company could dedicate itself to promoting cards featuring Disney characters. And that would not only boost Disney's consumer product revenues, it would create a ripple effect for Disney's movies, cartoons, and theme parks by heightening the visibility of the characters. Gibson, for its part, would benefit enormously from the access to Disney's characters. In short, the two companies did, indeed, fit.

Phone calls ensued. Gibson's president, Thomas Cooney, who had participated in the leveraged buyout of Gibson along with William Simon and Ray Chambers, and who stood to make a sizable fortune from its sale to Disney, caught the next plane to New York from the company's headquarters in Cincinnati. There he joined Bo Boyd in waxing ecstatic about the "synergy" between Gibson and Disney—a term that was to emerge as the word of choice for Disney and Gibson

*Chambers and Simon thought Disney had such potential that they had even talked about doing a leveraged buyout of the company themselves, but, after crunching some numbers, had discarded the idea.

executives when describing the deal. Cooney, an enthusiastic man, even went so far as to liken it to the possibility of one plus one equaling three.

The Gibson deal proceeded with even more speed than Arvida. The Project Fantasy team at Morgan Stanley, giving Gibson the code name Koala Company, commenced an analysis. Within three days, Ray Chambers was invited out to the Burbank studio, to which Watson and Miller had returned.

As Sid Bass had done before him, Chambers spent much of the meeting selling himself—and William Simon—to the Disney executives. And as Sid Bass had done before him, Chambers impressed the Disney executives as straightforward. He also made the point that Simon, who sat on the boards of thirty-six companies and non-profit organizations, had the kind of clout on Wall Street and the connections throughout America that would make him an invaluable asset to Disney.

And then, though Gibson had come to the attention of Disney's management only three days before, Chambers started talking price. He said he and Simon would be willing to make an outright two-for-one stock swap, taking one share of Disney for every two shares of Gibson; since Disney was then trading at around $64, that would give Gibson shareholders the equivalent of $32 a share. Watson and Miller found this generally satisfactory, but they wanted to take a look at what they would be buying. Tom Cooney was consulted. He suggested that the Disney executives spend Memorial Day in Cincinnati; because Gibson would be closed for the holiday, they could tour the facilities without the embarrassment that might be caused if they encountered quizzical employees.

After Chambers departed from the studio, the Disney operators again arranged a conference call among the company's directors. At the recommendation of Joe Flom, the board approved another change in the corporate bylaws: From that day forward, the directors would be able to convene for special meetings on a mere twelve hours' notice.

That same day, May 25, Watson and Miller learned that a unit of Saul Steinberg's Reliance Group Holdings had sued in California Superior Court in Los Angeles to block the acquisition of Arvida by Walt Disney Productions, charging that it served no "proper or valid corporate purpose." And in a filing with the SEC, Steinberg formally announced that he might acquire as much as 49.9 percent of Disney's stock, that he had retained Drexel Burnham Lambert—the investment bank that the week before had been working for Roy Disney—and that he had held preliminary discussions with other potential investors. The move, Steinberg declared, was a reaction to Disney's proposed acquisition of Arvida, which was not "in the best interests of shareholders" and had made it impossible for him to remain "merely a passive investor." Hostilities had officially commenced.

Two days later, on the occasion of the marriage of Roy Disney's son, Roy P. Disney, whom everyone called Young Roy, to Linda Ross, Roy and Patty Disney were hosts at a reception among the lemon and orange trees in the backyard of their house. It was a very large affair —the Brain Trust was there in full force—but, the guests noticed, no one from the other side of the Disney family came. Not Ron and Diane Miller, not Sharon Lund, not even Walt Disney's widow, Lilly. The fact was that the only person from Walt Disney Productions who had been invited was Richard Morrow, a former director of the company and its longtime general counsel. He was a "Roy man," one of the very few still at the studio; he had also been a trustee of some of the trusts Roy O. Disney had established for his heirs.

Over champagne, Dick Morrow and Stanley Gold fell to discussing "the situation." "How soon before you guys will be working for Saul Steinberg?" Gold asked, only half joking.

"We're doing what we can," Morrow replied. "We haven't given up the ship."

Then, after some more banter, Morrow said wistfully, "Wouldn't it be nice if the family worked together again?"

Gold was feeling cocky. "If they really want to work with Roy," he said, "if they really don't want to be chased into Saul Steinberg's hands or somebody else's hands, you ought to have Ron Miller show up at my office at nine o'clock on Tuesday morning."

Morrow didn't seem to take offense at this impertinence. "I hear you," Morrow said. "I'll see what I can do about bringing elements together."

After the wedding, the Golds and some friends drove down to the Golds' condominium in Palm Springs, where they were going to spend the Memorial Day weekend. On Sunday night, Gold received a call from Arthur Bilger, a partner of Mike Milken's at Drexel Burnham, who confirmed that Drexel was now working for Saul Steinberg, that Milken had indeed sold Steinberg the very same financing package for a Disney takeover that he had prepared for Roy Disney. Now Steinberg had a proposition. Would Roy Disney join him? "Would you now take a piece of paper in this deal?" Bilger asked. "And, if so, would you trade it for a part of the company if the offer is successful?"

"We might consider it, we might consider taking it," Gold said. "But the only thing we would trade it for is the studio and the copyrights."

"If you're serious, come to New York."

The Golds returned home Monday night. About nine-thirty on Tuesday morning, Stanley Gold's telephone rang again.* The caller was Ron Miller. He had not appeared on Gold's doorstep at nine o'clock that morning, but he had done the next best thing. Gold, who had never spoken to Ron Miller before in his life, considered the call a victory.

"I understand you ran into Dick Morrow at the wedding," Miller said. "He says he thinks there's a basis for you and me to talk. If so, I'd be happy to get together—"

Gold cut him off. "I've got to catch a plane," he said. "I'm leaving town. I'll call you back before the end of the week and we'll arrange it."

Gold was about to fly to Cincinnati, from which Miller had just returned after inspecting Gibson, to attend a meeting of the board of governors of Hebrew Union College. But he did not exactly have to catch a plane right then. He was traveling in the private Shamrock jet, which departed at his whim, and he had no intention of leaving until later in the day. He just thought it wouldn't hurt Ron Miller to have to wait a little.

That same day Reliance filed a second suit against Disney over Arvida. This one, in federal court, charged that Disney was paying far

---

*Gold had a communications system that enabled the switchboards at both Shamrock and his law firm to route calls directly to the telephone in his study in Beverly Hills. The caller always assumed Gold was in the office.

too much for the Florida developer, that the deal was "a waste of corporate assets" undertaken by Disney's executives out of "a desire to entrench themselves." It also claimed that Bass Brothers Enterprises had "sold substantial income-producing assets" of Arvida when they bought the company. "Notwithstanding the diminished value of Arvida," the complaint went on, "[Disney's directors] agreed to pay substantially more for Arvida than Bass had paid only five months earlier, and . . . Bass would receive a premium of nearly 900% over Bass's actual cash outlay." Steinberg also announced plans to hold a proxy fight, saying he had "determined to seek the removal" of Disney's directors and was going to try to arrange a special stockholders' meeting to have them voted out of office.

This declaration of a proxy fight, coming only four days after the statement that Steinberg might make an offer for the company, struck Wall Street as a sign of confusion and weakness at Reliance. Why would Steinberg start soliciting proxies to oust Disney's directors if he planned to buy the company? Perhaps he had decided not to buy it after all. Some investors began selling Disney, which dropped almost $4 in one day.

Ray Watson and Ron Miller, however, took small comfort from this development, and they decided to plunge ahead with Gibson. The "synergy," after all, was irresistible. All that remained was to agree on a price, then sell the deal to the board and to the investment community.

It was raining when the Shamrock jet touched down at Teterboro Airport near New York on Wednesday morning. A car and driver were waiting there for Stanley Gold, who had interrupted his meeting in Cincinnati to pursue the Drexel Burnham offer. His first stop was the Wall Street offices of Fried, Frank, Harris, Shriver & Jacobson, the law firm Shamrock Holdings had retained earlier in the year. Gold wanted to discuss the Steinberg proposal with Herb Galant and Stuart Katz, another Fried, Frank partner working with Shamrock.

"What kind of deal can we cut?" Gold asked.

The lawyers reviewed the options, and, after some rough calculations, a decision was made: Roy Disney would offer Steinberg $350 million for the studio and the merchandising rights.

It had stopped raining by the time the car took Gold up to Reliance headquarters in mid-town off Park Avenue, where he was greeted by Lowell Freiberg, the Reliance treasurer and Steinberg's right-hand man. The two men talked for several hours. If Roy Disney, with almost 5 percent of Disney's stock (before the Arvida deal closed) were to join forces with Saul Steinberg, who owned more than 12 percent (before Arvida), they would together present a formidable block. Freiberg suggested that the two men become partners, with Shamrock investing in the shell corporation Steinberg was setting up to make the takeover, and receiving in exchange a preferred subordinated debenture that could be traded after the takeover for some of Disney's assets. But when Freiberg learned that Gold wanted the studio and the copyrights and merchandising rights for $350 million, his enthusiasm waned. "That's incredibly low," he said, adding that Reliance would probably want to keep the merchandising rights. "I don't really see that we're close enough to do very much."

Gold then went in to see Saul Steinberg himself. It was the first time Gold had met the financier, and despite the residual bad taste from the WICS litigation, the two men got along well enough. Steinberg was especially interested in the personalities and backgrounds of Ray Watson and Ron Miller.

About five minutes into the meeting, Robert Steinberg, Saul's younger brother, walked in.

"You're the only unfamiliar face in the place," Bobby Steinberg said. "You must be Stanley Gold."

"Yes," Gold said.

The younger Steinberg turned to his brother. "He don't look so tough," he said. "Why did we pay him so much in the last deal? We could have beat him."

Everyone laughed, and Bobby Steinberg put his arm around Gold to show there were no hard feelings. Then Gold and Saul Steinberg talked a little more about Disney, and Steinberg said they would get back to him if they decided to take him up on the $350-million offer for the studio, and that was that. With the matter still unresolved, Gold returned to Cincinnati for the last of the meetings at Hebrew Union College, then headed for Los Angeles. He was scheduled to see Ray Watson and Ron Miller at the Disney studio in Burbank at 9:00 A.M. on Friday, June 1.

Although it was Miller who had called Gold to set up the meeting, the session was held in Watson's office, and Watson did most of the talking. Gold began by reviewing the numbers his people had run on Arvida. The Basses, he said, along with Arvida's executives, had bought the company eight months before for something over $200 million—most of which they had borrowed. They had then stripped $70 to $80 million out of it to pay down the debt they had accumulated, which meant, he concluded, that Arvida was now worth $120 to $130 million.* Walt Disney Productions was paying way too much.

"It looks like a schmucky deal to me," Gold said.

Watson begged to differ. The deal had nothing to do with what had been paid for Arvida. Only two issues were relevant. First, the current liquidation value of Arvida was more than $200 million; Disney couldn't lose even if it simply turned around and sold the company's assets. Second, Arvida would provide the expertise to develop Disney's land in Florida and thereby boost earnings and, in the long run, the price of Disney's stock.

"It's a solid deal," Watson said. "Don't be paranoid, Stan, and see it just as an attempt to entrench management. Anyway, it's done. Now"—he moved to another subject—"why did Roy leave the board? I tried to make contact with him and he didn't respond." The fact that one side of the family opposed the executives running the company had certainly encouraged Steinberg, and Watson thought a takeover might be prevented if he could unite all the Disneys behind management. "What is it Roy wants?" he asked. "Why doesn't he come back on the board?"

"That won't solve anything," Gold said. Roy had been on the board a long time—almost twenty years—and nobody had ever listened to him. He had never gotten the company to do what he wanted it to do.

Watson pointed out that Roy rarely spoke up at board meetings. He had never made a motion that was overridden.

"Roy's not the kind of guy who stands up and is articulate at board meetings," Gold replied. Roy Disney had no training in law or public

---

*Arvida had sold a piece of property for around $70 million after the Basses took control but maintained it was in the normal course of business and not to pay off debt.

speaking or even business. But he had set forth his position in the letter he wrote when he resigned from the studio. There was nothing exotic about it; Roy wasn't crazy. But when he tried to push for changes at the studio, Card Walker had accused him of wanting to make *Deep Throat.*

Why didn't Roy come back on the board now and say those things, Watson asked. The directors would try to accommodate his views. They wanted him back.

Miller, who had been quiet up to this point, suddenly broke in. "Does Roy really hate me?" he asked. "I don't hate him."

"No, Ron, he doesn't hate you," Gold said. Roy had assured Gold that the stories circulating to that effect were untrue. But his client did believe that Disney ought to have first-class motion picture personnel and television personnel, and it did not.

"You don't even know Richard Berger," Miller said. "You don't even know how good Berger is."

"Wait a second, this is not a conversation about Richard Berger," Gold replied. Berger, he went on, might or might not be good, but he was not the kind of talent Roy Disney was thinking about, someone with the stature of Michael Eisner or Barry Diller or Frank Wells or Steven Spielberg or George Lucas. Berger, for whatever reason, had not achieved that rank. "You asked me what Roy thinks and that's what Roy thinks," Gold said. "It's not personal against you, it's not personal against Berger. That's what he thinks as a major shareholder of long standing in this company."

Before Miller could respond, Watson cut in to prevent matters from deteriorating further. "What will it take to bring Roy back on the board?" he asked.

"Roy's not coming back on the board by himself," Gold said. "He was a voice in the wilderness. He would have to come with other people as well who support his views."

"You mean increase the number of directors?" Watson asked.

"That's right."

"We'll think about it," Watson said.

After the meeting with Gold, Ray Watson flew to San Francisco, where the following night he was scheduled to give the keynote address at the annual conference of the Builders' Institute of America, a trade association for housing developers on the West Coast. He had planned to spend Saturday polishing his speech in his hotel room. Instead, he spent it renegotiating the Arvida deal.

Watson had kept the Basses informed of the Gibson discussions from the beginning. They had expressed concern about the price to be paid for Gibson but not about the advisability of acquiring the greeting card company. Later, Sid Bass was to become quite outspoken on the issue. That weekend, however, he was concentrating on concluding the immensely profitable sale of Arvida.*

Since Disney would issue new shares of its stock for Gibson, the value of the Disney stock already on the market could well diminish in value. That meant Disney would have to issue Arvida's owners a greater number of Disney shares in exchange for their Arvida stock, as required by the collar. But consideration of that could lead to a postponement of the deal, which neither side desired.

Watson had asked Morgan Stanley to reach an agreement in principle on Gibson before a Disney board meeting scheduled for Tuesday, and he wanted to be able to announce as well that management had closed on Arvida. Hence, he suggested to Sid Bass that the two sides drop the collar and simply assign a value of $60 to each share of Disney regardless of what happened to the stock in the near future. At that figure, Arvida's owners would receive approximately 3.3 million Disney shares.

"I want you to talk to your lawyer and I want your lawyer to talk to our lawyer so you don't think I'm conning you into accepting a cheaper price," Watson told Sid Bass. "Because if we end up getting sued, and we lose the suit, then you're going to lose the sale of Arvida. So we ought to be together. It will be a hell of a lot easier for us."

After conferring with his attorneys, Sid Bass agreed.

Early in the evening, Watson headed over to the Moscone Convention Center, where the Builders' Institute had arranged for him to give

---

*In some six months, the $20 million in cash that the Basses and Arvida's management had put up to buy the company was going to be turned into Disney stock worth more than $200 million—which works out, at an annual rate, to be a return on investment of around 2,000 percent. The $183.6 million in debt that Arvida had assumed in the original buyout would become the responsibility of Disney.

a press conference. He expected the reporters to ask him about quality in housing. Instead, all their questions concerned Saul Steinberg.

William Simon had begun his career as a trainee in a Wall Street brokerage house for $75 a week. Twenty years later, when Richard Nixon appointed him deputy treasury secretary, he was earning $2 million a year as head of the government bond department at Salomon Brothers. He had subsequently served as "energy czar" and then treasury secretary under Gerald Ford. When Jimmy Carter was elected president in 1976, Simon had returned to the private sector; in 1981 he had met Raymond Chambers, a former accountant at Price Waterhouse, and the two men had soon realized they could make money for each other by pooling Chambers's technical expertise with Simon's corporate connections. They had formed their own private investment bank, calling it Wesray Corporation after Simon's initials and Chambers's first name.

It was a timely association. Interest rates had peaked, the nation was slipping into recession, and many companies were undervalued—ideal conditions for leveraged buyouts. Wesray's first large purchase, consummated in 1982, had been Gibson Greetings. Since then, Chambers and Simon had used similar techniques to acquire some twenty other companies in everything from briefcase manufacturing to crude-, oil transport. The two financiers never ran these companies themselves; they knew nothing, after all, about greeting cards or briefcases. Instead, as in Gibson's case, the original management of the companies usually continued to operate them in exchange for up to 25 percent of the equity. By the summer of 1984, Wesray was one of the largest private conglomerates in existence, with sales of more than $7 billion a year, and Simon had become one of his country's most articulate—and vociferous—defenders of free enterprise. His book *A Time for Truth,* a best-seller for thirty weeks, celebrated an unrestricted market economy with almost evangelical fervor.

Rarely had William Simon been busier than he was that summer. As president of the U.S. Olympic Committee, he was in the midst of preparing for the summer games in Los Angeles; callers requesting appointments were told by one of his secretaries—he had several—that his schedule was "a mess" for the rest of the year. Nonetheless, as the largest individual shareholder of Gibson, he squeezed in a luncheon meeting on June 4 to discuss the company's sale to Walt Disney Productions. The Gibson stockholders had to decide on the price to charge for their shares prior to the negotiating session between the representatives of Disney and Gibson at Morgan Stanley, scheduled for that afternoon.

Ray Chambers had been talking to Disney about a value on Gibson stock in the range of $30 to $32 a share. But Bill Simon, who owned 22.8 percent of Gibson, and its president, Tom Cooney, who owned 5.7 percent, wanted at least $35 a share. William Kearns, a Gibson board member and a managing director of Lehman Brothers, Gibson's investment bank, had actually called Peter Kellner the week before to suggest a price in the $40 range.* "Save your subway fare if that's what you're thinking," Kellner had told him. "We aren't even in the same ballpark."

It went without saying that neither Disney nor Gibson was interested in a cash transaction. As in the Arvida deal, a cash purchase would deprive Disney of the opportunity to dilute Steinberg's holdings. And the capital gains taxes on a cash deal would be horrendous for Gibson shareholders. Moreover, Bill Simon, who already had plenty of money, was interested in a seat on the board of Disney, to which, as a large shareholder, he would be entitled.

Now, over lunch at the University Club on Fifth Avenue, Kearns conceded that $40 had been a bit greedy, but, he argued, Gibson could be sold to Disney for upwards of $35 a share—even though its stock was then trading at around $19. He based this evaluation on the fact that Gibson was heading for a year when, because of its earnings projections, it could command around $30 a share in a controlled auction (one in which only a few select parties are invited to make sealed bids). Disney should pay at least 10 percent more than that. The partners decided to shoot for $35 and settle for no less than $30.

After lunch Simon dashed off to catch a plane, while the rest of the group proceeded to Morgan Stanley to meet with the Project Fantasy team. Mike Bagnall and Bo Boyd were there for Disney.

---

*Lehman Brothers was a unit of the conglomerate known at the time as Shearson Lehman/American Express, which was referred to on Wall Street as Slamex.

Kearns opened with his argument that the stock was worth $35. Peter Kellner countered by pointing out that it was trading at little more than half that figure. The Gibson group worried about the value of Disney's stock. It had climbed on the strength of the takeover struggle. If Steinberg pulled out, it would fall.

Late that night, an agreement was reached. There would be a two-for-one stock swap. Disney would issue Gibson's owners some 5 million shares of Disney common stock—worth around $307 million at Disney's current price—in exchange for Gibson's approximately 10 million outstanding shares. But, like the Arvida deal, the Gibson deal contained a collar. At the lower end, if Disney fell to $50 or below, Gibson shareholders would receive .6 of a share of Disney for every Gibson share; at the upper end of the collar, if Disney climbed above $75 before the deal closed, Gibson shareholders would receive only .433 share of Disney per share of Gibson. The agreement also specified that if, for some reason, Disney decided not to acquire Gibson, the greeting card company would receive a $7.5 million kill fee.

A Disney board meeting had been hastily scheduled for the following afternoon. Boyd and Bagnall, Peter Kellner's team, and Gibson's Tom Cooney all flew out to Los Angeles to attend.

Saul Steinberg was uppermost in the minds of the directors. Although Steinberg had expressed an interest in acquiring Disney, he had no experience in outdoor recreation or movies or consumer products, and therefore, Ray Watson noted for the record, it was the unanimous opinion of the board that it was not in the best interests of Disney or its shareholders for Reliance to take over the company. Peter Kellner then gave a fairness opinion on the acquisition of Gibson, explaining why this acquisition *was* in the best interests of the shareholders. And Bo Boyd talked up the synergism between the two companies. Approval of the deal was unanimous. Then Watson presented the revised Arvida agreement to the board. Again, approval was unanimous, and Arvida's chief executive, Chuck Cobb, was made a board member. In less than three weeks, Disney had committed itself to investments in real estate and greeting cards worth more than $500 million, and had issued or agreed to issue roughly 8.5 million new shares of stock. Saul Steinberg's more than 12 percent investment in Disney would shrink to less than 10 percent when both deals went through. In addition, several major stockholders who would presumably vote with management and against Steinberg in any proxy fight would have been added to the roster.

As news of the Gibson deal spread through Wall Street, it was noted that William Simon, who had put up only $300,000 of his own money to buy his stake in the greeting card company eighteen months before, was personally to receive about 1.3 million Disney shares worth more than $70 million. That was what the former treasury secretary called free enterprise.

9

IT HAD BEEN several days since his meeting with Saul Steinberg, and Stanley Gold had yet to hear whether he would be invited to participate in the deal—or even whether Reliance was proceeding with an offer. So, early in the week beginning June 4, he put in a call to Mike Milken at Drexel Burnham. He tried to strike a casual note. "Well, what are we doing?" he asked. "Did I buy the studio? I mean, is Saul going forward?"

"We cannot communicate that to you at this point," said Milken.

Gold had the distinct sense that Steinberg and Milken were proceeding with an offer and that Roy Disney was not to be included.

On Wednesday, Gold flew to San José to inspect a small real estate project in which Shamrock had invested. As he walked through the San José terminal he was stopped by one of the airport employees.

"Are you Stanley Gold?"

"Yes."

"Everybody in the world is trying to get hold of you."

There were urgent messages for him to call Shamrock, his law office, and his home. "Everybody in the world" turned out to be Ray Watson and Ron Miller. Gold called them from the phone booth at the San José airport. The Disney executives wanted to inform him of the company's decision to acquire Gibson before he learned of it elsewhere.

Gold, who had never heard of Gibson, saw the acquisition as another attempt by Disney's managers to entrench themselves, to save their jobs by preventing a Steinberg takeover, but he kept his reaction to himself. "Okay, tell me everything I need to know," he said.

Watson explained the deal. It was not, he added, designed against Roy Disney. Management still want Roy back on the board, still wanted Gold to come and discuss terms for bringing him back.

Despite this disclaimer, Gold was outraged, as were the other members of the Brain Trust, to whom he immediately spread the word. For it was indisputable that, if Saul Steinberg's share of Walt Disney Productions had been reduced, so had Roy Disney's. Gold then attempted to reach Herb Galant at Fried, Frank. Galant was on vacation on the West Coast. He and his wife were driving up Route 1 from the Mexican border on their way to attend their son's graduation from Stanford. Gold arranged for himself, Roy Disney, Cliff Miller, Mark Siegel, and Frank Wells to meet Galant on Saturday, June 9, in Los Angeles.

Disney's executives had hoped that the acquisition of Gibson would induce Saul Steinberg to abandon his prospective takeover attempt. It did not. To the contrary, in fact: Steinberg told his associates that the deal eliminated any possibility of his dropping plans to make an offer for the company.

Steinberg and Mike Milken had decided they would need $2.4 billion to accomplish a takeover. Some of the money was to come from Reliance's investment portfolio and the banks it controlled. But Drexel Burnham would need to raise about $1.5 billion in "mezzanine," or second-level, financing from investors, most of which the investment bank would produce by placing junk bonds. The remainder—a substantial amount—would have to come from equity investors, people like Roy Disney who would be willing to commit large sums only in exchange for the right to buy certain parts of Disney.

As usual, the rumors on Wall Street were true: Drexel Burnham was indeed having trouble finding partners to invest in Steinberg's tender offer. Reliance had received more than a dozen inquiries from potential equity investors who were involved in businesses ranging from hotels to greeting cards; but a company seriously interested in becoming an equity partner needed to hire investment bankers and lawyers and conduct an independent study of Disney to bring to its own board. All that costs money, and the potential investors, concerned that Steinberg, with his propensity for greenmail, would eventually let Disney buy him out, were reluctant to go to the expense.*

It was Herbert Bachelor, head of Drexel's New York corporate finance department, who came up with the solution. Steinberg should entice investors by agreeing to pay them "commitment fees" equivalent to 1 percent or more of the funds they committed to the deal— whether or not the deal went through and the funds were used. Without necessarily having to put up real money, the investors could count on a real profit.

Early on the morning of June 7, Irwin Jacobs slid behind the wheel of his Rolls Royce Silver Cloud II and drove from his lakeshore estate to a modest yellow brick building next to an abandoned brewery in a blue-collar neighborhood across the river from central Minneapolis. Jacobs had acquired the building in his first hostile takeover. Although he had sold the company, Grain Belt Breweries, he had kept the building, which was now the location for Minstar, the corporation he used as his holding company. It was an unpretentious place, with fake leather furniture and bouquets of artificial flowers, but then Jacobs was an unpretentious, approachable fellow who—rare among tycoons—even answered his own phone.

Jacobs's casual style could be traced to his humble origins. His father, Samuel, had been a Russian Jewish immigrant who bought used feed bags from farmers, cleaned them, and resold them. Accompanying his father on bag-buying trips through the Midwest, Jacobs had gathered firsthand experience in the business technique he would later employ with such mastery: identify undervalued property, acquire it cheaply, and resell it quickly. At eighteen Jacobs, who had dropped out of college after three days, had made his first asset play, buying a shipment of skis at a U.S. Customs auction and selling three hundred pairs of them right outside the building for an immediate

*As part of its efforts to obtain the financing for Steinberg's tender offer, Drexel, on June 4, sent prospective investors sealed envelopes containing confidential information about the takeover bid. The envelopes were accompanied by letters warning each recipient that if he opened the envelope he would be in possession of "material non-public information" and thus prohibited, by federal law, from trading in the stocks of the company discussed within. When the tactic was revealed two years later it was criticized for providing recipients with a possibly irresistible temptation to trade on inside information, or at least to leak the information to others. Drexel maintained that it had taken adequate steps to safeguard against leaks.

profit of $7,800. Sixteen years later, in 1975, he and a Minneapolis banker named Carl Pohlad had acquired Grain Belt Breweries, then sold off the assets for a $4-million profit. A string of similar deals had earned him the nickname "Irv the Liquidator"; in addition, he had made a number of lucrative raids on such companies as Pabst Brewing Company, Kaiser Steel Corporation, and RCA.

After arriving at his office in the old brewery, Jacobs leafed through the *Wall Street Journal* and read about the Gibson deal. Trading in Disney had opened at $64.25. The stock seemed undervalued to Jacobs, and in what was for him just another relatively small market play, he called his broker Ronald Alghini in the Chicago office of Jefferies & Company and placed an order for two thousand call options on Disney, which would give him the opportunity but not the obligation to buy the stock at its current price some months in the future, when it might be trading at a much higher figure.

Later that morning Jacobs received a telephone call from Mike Milken at Drexel Burnham. Jacobs had heard of Milken, of course, but he had never talked to him before.

"I would like to speak to you about something," Milken said.

"What's the subject?"

"Disney."

"Don't tell me anything about it," Jacobs said. "But stay on the phone. I want to cancel an order that I have in."

Like most stock speculators, Jacobs had an abiding fear of lawsuits over, and SEC investigations into, charges of trading on inside information. Since no one really knew what the definition of inside information was—the term was so elastic, and the flow of information through the Street so ceaseless and informal—it behooved all investors to err on the side of caution. With Milken on hold, Jacobs called Ron Alghini again and told him to cancel the order to buy the Disney options. Then he got back to Milken. "Mike, okay, you can tell me. Before you tell me, I want you to know I just canceled an order. I want all this documented."

Milken said Drexel was arranging the financing for a tender offer Saul Steinberg intended to make for Disney.

"Do you want to put up twenty-five?" he asked.

"What is this, one of these deals where Saul is going to say he'll buy it and then he's going to sell his stock back?"

"No," Milken said. "Saul is committed to not selling his stock back."

Jacobs said he would think about it. The more he thought, the more he liked it. The junk bonds that Drexel was offering for the deal paid, as junk bonds always did, such high yields that Jacobs figured he could sell them with ease. Or, if he wanted, he could keep the bonds and rake in the cash. Either way, he couldn't lose. And there was the commitment fee if Steinberg did happen to sell his stock to Disney instead of going through with the takeover. That afternoon Jacobs called Milken back. "I'll give you $35 million," he said. "I like the deal."

Although Walt Disney had put his name almost everywhere he could, for many years the Disney studio off the Ventura Freeway at 500 South Buena Vista Street in Burbank had no sign. Crowds, Disney believed, belonged in theaters and amusement parks, not on sound stages and in executive offices. The company offered no public tours of the lot. Which didn't mean it was a drab, utilitarian place. The studio had low, unpretentious buildings painted in earthen pastels. It had benches and lawns, flower beds and walks. It had a barbershop and a post office.

At the center of the lot, on the corner of Mickey Avenue and Dopey Drive, stood the old animation building. When the studio was built in 1938, animation was the central activity of Walt Disney Productions, and Walt Disney and the other top executives had their offices there. Though the animators had outgrown the space and moved to other quarters in the mid-seventies, and though animation had long since ceased to be the studio's central activity, the company's executives still had their offices in the animation building.

In that quiet setting, as talk grew that Steinberg was trying to arrange financing for a tender offer, the Disney executives tried to maintain a semblance of normal life. On Wednesday, June 6, after giving Gold the news about Gibson, Ray Watson met with Jack Wrather, owner of the Wrather Corporation, to discuss the possibility of Wrather's selling the Disneyland Hotel to Disney. On Thursday,

Watson and Miller drove to the WED building in Glendale to review plans for the Joy of Life Pavilion, which the WED engineers proposed as an addition to Epcot.

But the minds of the Disney executives remained fixed on Steinberg. They believed they had strengthened their position with the Gibson deal, but they wondered if they had done enough. They monitored the company's stock constantly. A drop in the stock price would indicate that the acquisition of Gibson had discouraged Steinberg, as they had hoped would happen with Arvida. But the stock continued to climb. On Wednesday, the day the announcement of Gibson went out over the wire, it rose $1. By Friday it had climbed another $1. Wall Street was ignoring the Gibson deal, feeding instead on the rumor that Steinberg was finally piecing together his tender offer.

The Basses proved of invaluable assistance to Disney during this period. They had in fact put together a sort of informal "Save Disney" task force, and Ray Watson, with few sources on Wall Street, frequently telephoned Sid Bass and Richard Rainwater for information. They would hook up a speaker phone and bring in their well-connected arbitrageur, who would in turn pass along the latest hearsay. But they did more than just channel gossip to Burbank. At one point Watson became alarmed about a story that J. Willard Marriott Jr., of the Marriott Hotel Corporation, had joined in the Steinberg tender; the Basses had Al Checchi, a former Marriott executive, track down Bill Marriott, who was in Mexico, and get him to produce a statement that he had no intention of joining forces with Steinberg.

Unfortunately, other rumors kept cropping up. One especially disturbing story held that the Bass brothers themselves were "wolves in sheep's clothing"—that they had formed a clandestine alliance with Steinberg and planned to reveal their true intentions only on the day the formal offer was made. The Basses swore that such was not the case. "There's no way," Rainwater said. Reassured, Watson wondered whether Steinberg's associates were spreading the rumors to fan the interest of speculative investors like the arbs and to offset the rumor that Steinberg was having trouble raising money for his tender offer. The Basses, in fact, felt that he would fail. "Just ride it out, just ride it out," Rainwater told Watson. "But Ray," he added, "there's one thing you've got to look out for. Somebody like Steinberg, who has a very strong ego, who doesn't like to lose, may climb on a kamikaze plane and aim it at your corporation."

Watson wasn't sure what Rainwater meant. The message seemed to be that Steinberg was capable of destroying himself in order to destroy his opponents. It was a chilling thought.

Steinberg did not fail. By Friday, June 8, he had found his equity partners and formed a shell company called the MM Acquisition Corporation ("MM" for "Mickey Mouse"). Its stockholders were to be Reliance; Fisher Brothers Financial and Development Company, which was controlled by the Fisher brothers of New York, who were major real estate developers as well as old friends of Saul Steinberg's (they owned the building in midtown Manhattan that served as Reliance headquarters); and Tracinda Corporation, the privately held investment company run by Kirk Kerkorian, the shrewd Los Angeles financier who controlled casinos, hotels, and the MGM/UA studio.

Kerkorian had agreed to invest $75 million in MM Acquisition in exchange for a sixty-day option to buy Disney's studio, film library, and cable television channel for $447.5 million; the $75 million would be applied towards the purchase price if the deal was consummated.* The Fishers also agreed to invest $75 million, in exchange for the exclusive right to buy or lease fifteen thousand undeveloped acres around Walt Disney World and other property around Disneyland. The Fishers would be allowed to use the land only for hotels; moreover, Reliance would retain ownership of the land until they exercised their option, and would also retain control of the theme parks and the copyrights to the characters.

In addition to the equity investors, Mike Milken had lined up a second tier of investors who would receive junk bonds to be paid off when the specified Disney assets were sold to the Fishers and Kerkorian. These included individuals like Irwin Jacobs, but by far the

---

*An element of tension had marked the negotiations with Kerkorian. To begin with, Kerkorian's law firm was Wyman Bautzer Rothman Kuchel & Silbert, the same firm Reliance was using to sue Disney over Arvida. Kerkorian wanted Wyman Bautzer to represent him; with some grumbling from Reliance executives, Steinberg reluctantly consented. Then, the Reliance and Tracinda executives fell to arguing over who would control the Disney characters, and as a result the two sides never actually signed an agreement of intent.

largest of them was Financial Corporation of America, the savings and loan association Milken had originally approached on behalf of Roy Disney. FCA, which already controlled around 1 million Disney shares, invested $200 million in Steinberg's offer. To all of his investors, Steinberg agreed to pay commitment fees whether the deal went through or not.

On the morning of June 8, the directors of Reliance Holdings met in a conference room off Saul Steinberg's office. More than a dozen Reliance executives also attended. The research and legal staffs presented their final analyses. Some directors wondered how Disney would fit with Reliance—if indeed Reliance intended to operate the company. Several directors repeatedly raised the question of the public outcry that would certainly occur if someone like Saul Steinberg tried to take over an enshrined American institution like Disney. There was talk of motherhood, apple pie, and the flag. But in the end the directors decided the company was irresistibly attractive; the potential returns Disney would bring Reliance would more than compensate for any public uproar. The vote was unanimous in favor of the proposal.

That afternoon Kekst and Company, Steinberg's public relations firm, released to the financial news services a letter from Reliance to Disney's board informing it that on June 11, the following Monday, the MM Acquisitions Corporation would offer $67.50 a share for Disney (a mere $2.50 above the current trading price). As an inducement, it would raise the price by $4 if Disney canceled Gibson and promised to refrain from similar deals. Steinberg intended to make a tender offer for 37.9 percent of the shares of Walt Disney Productions, which would give him control of 49 percent of the company when added to the 11.1 percent Reliance already owned.

The morning of June 8 began normally enough for Ray Watson. At nine o'clock he met with the senior management committee and a compensation consultant named Bud Crystal to review the salary packages Disney's board had recently approved for the top executives. At eleven o'clock he saw the company's divisional heads and reviewed the corporate strategy he had outlined in the new business plan. That was followed by a meeting with an architect who was reworking a master plan for the studio property.

It was around noon on the West Coast when the announcement of Steinberg's offer came across the wire. Within minutes Watson's secretary was canceling his next appointments and Watson himself was on the telephone to Donald Drapkin, a partner at Skadden, Arps in New York who had assumed much of the work on the Disney account.

"Steinberg has made an announcement," Watson said. "Does that mean he will really do it?"

"He has to do it now," Drapkin replied. Once a tender offer was announced publicly, the acquirer had to proceed unless an agreement was struck with management. "Steinberg can't get out of it now without being in serious, serious trouble," Drapkin went on. "So you've got to say, 'It's been done. It's going to happen.' You're going to get the offer on Monday."

"Okay," Watson said. "Let's review our options."

A few minutes after the tender offer was announced, Stanley Gold received a call from Peter Ackerman, Mike Milken's associate at Drexel Burnham, who informed him that a group consisting of Saul Steinberg, Kirk Kerkorian, and the Fisher brothers had made a tender offer for Walt Disney Productions.

"Thanks for letting me know," Gold said. "Good luck." With Kirk Kerkorian willing to pay $447 million for the studio alone, Shamrock's $350 million offer for the studio and the copyrights had never had a chance.

Another brief telephone call took place shortly after the announcement, when Saul Steinberg called Irwin Jacobs in Minneapolis to thank him for investing in the deal. He was contemptuous of Disney's management and its acquisitions of Arvida and Gibson. They were, he said, nothing more than a defensive maneuver. Reliance had decided to make an offer for Disney to prevent it from undertaking further acquisitions. "I had to move because they would have kept doing this forever and ever," he said.

"Okay, Saul," said Jacobs, who was preparing to leave on vacation. "Take care of it. I'm going to Greece."

Later that afternoon Steinberg left Manhattan in his helicopter for his beach house in Quogue, an exclusive summer community on Long Island. It promised to be a warm, sunny weekend.

After Steinberg made his offer official, the speculative fever that had driven up Disney's stock suddenly broke. The New York Stock Exchange halted trading in Disney when the news came through; it closed just above $65 a share, where it had opened. But in off-market trades later in the day, the stock fell more than $1. Clearly some investors doubted the sincerity of Steinberg's offer and had decided to bail out before he could reconsider and accept greenmail, which would cause the value of their Disney stock to drop to considerably less than it was worth now. After all, no other financier in the world—*in history*—had greenmailed as many companies as Saul Steinberg. And the companies Steinberg did own and run were primarily devoted to the insurance business; not a lot of synergy there with the entertainment industry.

All that Friday afternoon, Ray Watson and Ron Miller were deluged with telephone calls. Reporters asked for comment. Investment bankers offered their services. Other chief executives hoped to explore mergers. Small shareholders wanted to know whether they should tender their stock to Steinberg. Arbs tried to warn the executives against paying greenmail. But as the pink message slips piled up on the desks of secretaries in the old animation building on Dopey Drive, the Disney executives remained closeted in Watson's office, hooked up via speakerphone with Drapkin, Joe Flom, and Peter Kellner in New York.

During the first stages of Steinberg's encroachment, Morgan Stanley had served as the primary adviser to Walt Disney Productions; the general strategy had been for Disney to try to deter Steinberg by aligning itself through mergers or acquisitions with other corporations. But now that war had been declared, now that Steinberg had finally announced his intent to take over Disney in a manner hostile to its management, the Skadden, Arps lawyers moved to the fore. The expertise of attorneys like Joe Flom and Don Drapkin lay in the actual battle.

Drapkin, one of the most skilled takeover attorneys at Skadden, Arps, did most of the talking on Friday. Watson found him extraor-

dinarily articulate, the most articulate of the advisers he had so far
encountered. Drapkin satisfied Watson's need to investigate, sometimes exhaustively, every option, and his lucidity provided the appropriate counterbalance to Joe Flom's occasionally murky utterances.*

The options Drapkin reviewed for the Disney executives were few
in number, however, and disappointingly familiar. (They were essentially the same choices Lazard Frères had put before Roy Disney and
the Brain Trust.) The team at Morgan Stanley had already drawn up
a list of potential white knights and had held exploratory talks with
some—from networks like ABC to studios like MCA/Universal—in
the event of just such an emergency. But the Disney management had
already decided (just as Roy Disney had) that it was essential for the
company to remain independent. Disney, and its unique culture,
might suffocate in the embrace of a conglomerate.

The crown jewels strategy was equally unattractive. Selling off the
parts of the company the raider sought would be a form of self-
mutilation, requiring Disney to get rid of its studio, film library, or real
estate. Similarly, a leveraged buyout by management could not be
accomplished without selling an essential component of the company
to pay off the debt that would be incurred. Just as bad, a poison pill
would require the board to arrange for the company to assume vast
amounts of debt if a raider bought a controlling interest in its stock.
Setting in place such a mechanism might deter the raider; but, if the
raider proceeded, it would cripple the company as surely as selling off
the theme parks.

Disney could always try to persuade the stockholders to refuse to
tender their stock to Steinberg, and the Disney executives favored this
tactic because it was democratic and fit the notion that the shareholders controlled the company. But Skadden, Arps and Morgan Stanley
were extremely discouraging about Disney's ability to succeed in a
campaign of this sort. They calculated that about 3 million of the
roughly 37.8 million shares of the company's stock now outstanding

---

*Like many in his profession, Drapkin lived for the adrenalin produced by takeover crises. His
office was lined with clocks given to him by clients in commemoration of deals done under the
pressure of time. "We're deal junkies, all of us," Drapkin once said of himself and his colleagues.
"If we don't have a million deals going at once, we start biting our nails. It's not just the money,
by any means."

were in the hands of arbs. Institutional investors handling stock portfolios for large pension funds, insurance companies, and brokerages
probably controlled up to three times as much as the arbs. Many of
these stockholders had loaded up on Disney shares in recent weeks
with one intent: to sell out for a quick profit if a takeover took place.
It would be hard to appeal to the sentimental instincts of such ruthless
traders; even if Disney occupied a fond place in their hearts, they
would always argue that they had a fiduciary responsibility to maximize profits for their clients.

There was only one other possibility: greenmail. For the past
several weeks, a gentleman whom Don Drapkin mysteriously refused
to name to the Disney executives, but who he said was close to
Steinberg and an extremely powerful figure in his own right, had been
calling Drapkin to hint that Steinberg was willing to settle. This
gentleman never mentioned greenmail. A word so coarse, so abomina-
ble never issued from his lips. But he had talked to Drapkin again and
again, each time to suggest in his discreet way that a settlement was
possible.

Disney's management thus had seven alternatives, including surrender to Steinberg. Seeking out a white knight, selling off the crown
jewels, or gutting the company in a leveraged buyout would all destroy
Disney in order to save it. A public campaign would be quixotic—like
sending Donald Ducks to shareholders. Poison pills and greenmail
were loathsome and cowardly, but to allow Steinberg to dismember
the company was inconceivable. Steinberg was legally committed to
making the tender offer on Monday. Watson and Miller had three
days in which to decide.

To investigate further the possibilities of a negotiated settlement,
Drapkin spoke that afternoon with acquaintances who had access to
Steinberg, including Robert Hodes, a director of Reliance and a partner in the law firm of Wilkie Farr & Gallagher. Hodes informed
Drapkin that nothing could be done at the moment. Earlier in the
week, Drapkin told his clients, Steinberg had been depressed over his
inability to put together the financing for a tender. Now that he had
done it he was euphoric, savoring his accomplishment and unprepared
to talk just yet.

But there was something that *could* be done, Joe Flom said, something that might make Steinberg more willing to come to terms. Disney could prepare a poison pill in the form of a self-tender. Watson and Miller were unfamiliar with the concept. Flom proceeded to explain.

Steinberg intended to make a two-tiered tender offer. He controlled slightly more than 11 percent of Disney's stock and, under the first tier, or "front end," of the tender, he was offering to buy an additional 37.9 percent for cash, which would bring his interest to 49 percent. The second tier, or "back end," which would become effective once the front end was complete, was an offer of assorted notes and bonds for the remaining 51 percent of Disney's stock. The back-end offer served as an incentive to stockholders. If they tendered during the front end of the offer, they would receive cash for their shares; if they waited for the back end, they would get not cash but a handful of notes and bonds of uncertain value.

That was the tender; the self-tender was the response. Once Steinberg completed the front end of his tender, Disney would make its own offer—to buy the remaining 51 percent of the company's stock for cash and retire it. To make the purchase, Disney would, of course, need to borrow funds. Thus, Steinberg would end up owning 100 percent of the company's outstanding shares, but he would have triggered Disney's accumulation of more than $2 billion worth of debt. The real purpose, of course, was to frighten Steinberg away and, secondarily, to discourage investors from tendering to Steinberg by offering to pay more for their stock in the self-tender—which would only occur, of course, once the front end of Steinberg's tender was complete.

Flom suggested that Disney's finance officer, Mike Bagnall, begin immediately to arrange financing from the Bank of America. There should be little difficulty, given the company's extended line of credit.

The decision had to be made over the weekend. "We don't have any time, gentlemen, for any more contemplation," Ray Watson said at the end of the day. "We're in a crisis mode."

That night Don Drapkin called Laurence Tisch. One of the most astute investors alive, Tisch and his brother Preston Robert controlled Loews Corporation, a holding company worth $13 billion. Though Tisch disdained hostile takeovers himself, because of his extraordinary power and connections he often appeared like some *deus ex machina* at the climax of corporate battles.* The previous winter, he had played a crucial role in settling the dispute between Gordon Getty and the Getty Oil Company—which had led to the sale of Getty to Texaco, which had increased Texaco's oil reserves, which in turn had convinced the Bass brothers to increase their investment in that company and subsequently to accept the premium for their shares that some had called greenmail.

One of Tisch's many friends was Saul Steinberg. When Drapkin got through to Tisch, he described the self-tender Disney was contemplating. Tisch then called Steinberg at the beach house in Quogue. It was eleven o'clock; Steinberg had just taken a shower and was preparing to go to bed. Drapkin had told him, Tisch said, that Walt Disney Productions was "out of control," that Watson and Miller refused to listen to the sage advice of Skadden, Arps and Morgan Stanley, that the Disney executives were bent on destroying the company in order to prevent Steinberg from acquiring it.

If Steinberg refused to sell his stock back to the company, Tisch said, then Disney would "do dangerous and stupid things." Its executives would commence a self-tender that would leave Reliance with total control of a company crushed beneath a mountain of debt.

If that was the case, Steinberg might well be forced to sell his stock back. He agreed to sleep on it.

The announcement of Saul Steinberg's tender offer, three months to the day after Roy Disney had resigned from the Disney board, gave a much sharper edge to the Brain Trust meeting scheduled already for the afternoon of Saturday, June 9, at the Beverly Hills home of Stanley Gold's law partner Mark Siegel.

After thrashing through the issues for several hours, the members of the Brain Trust isolated what they considered to be their two top priorities. The first was to keep Walt Disney Productions intact, to prevent Steinberg or anyone else from selling it off piecemeal. The

---

*In 1986, Tisch was named "acting chief executive" of CBS after he had acquired almost 25 percent of that company's stock and then persuaded the board to oust its chairman, Thomas Wyman. On Wall Street it was said that Tisch had been so shrewd in the CBS affair that he had managed to acquire control of the company without ever making an offer for it and therefore without having to pay a premium for its stock.

second was to prevent Disney's management from paying Steinberg greenmail, which, they believed, would weaken the company further, perhaps driving the stock down enough to tempt some other raider to launch a second attack. Raiders, spotting a vulnerable target, would pursue it as relentlessly as the wolves that spend days running a moose to the ground.

To avoid either of those fates for Walt Disney Productions, the Brain Trust decided to propose a leveraged buyout of the company. Since Roy Disney still did not have the resources to undertake one on his own, the time had come, the Trust agreed, for the Roy side of the family to forge an alliance with the Walt side, and therefore with Disney's management. They would all pool their resources and take the company private themselves. Together, they should be able to make a preemptive offer, one that would be high enough to prevent any other bidder, including Steinberg, from raising the stakes. And together they would have enough capital to avoid having to sell off too many of Disney's assets.

As the meeting drew to a close, Gold summed up. "We'll go to management and say, 'Don't pay greenmail. And don't sell to Saul; he'll cut it up. On the other hand, we don't need to crap on Saul by acquiring companies and running the stock down. It is now time to do a leveraged buyout. That way you'll get rid of Saul along with all the other shareholders. And you won't have done anything to hurt the company.' "

Gold called Ray Watson and arranged for himself and Frank Wells to meet the following day with Disney's chairman and with Ron Miller to discuss the proposition.

On Saturday, June 9, "Donald Duck" and his "one and only voice," Clarence Nash, were scheduled to return from their cross-country publicity tour and, in celebration of the very day on which Donald's debut film, *The Little Wise Hen,* had been released fifty years before, to lead a ticker-tape parade through Disneyland. At the rally, Anaheim Mayor Don Roth was officially to declare June 9 "Donald Duck Day." And, "because it wouldn't be a birthday party without presents," a Disney press release proclaimed, "children twelve years of age and under will receive a complimentary *Goin' Quackers* record."

Under normal circumstances, the chairman of the board of Walt Disney Productions might have been expected to attend the fiftieth birthday party of the company's most popular character. Instead, Ray Watson spent most of Donald Duck's birthday alone on the patio of his house in the hills above Newport Beach. Sitting at a redwood table with a portable telephone, he spoke first to Peter Kellner, then to Joe Flom, then to Don Drapkin, then to Ron Miller, then to various board members. Then he made the rounds again.

For the most part, Watson had managed to leave the pressures of the takeover battle at the office. Raised largely by his grandmother, who had run a series of boardinghouses in Oakland during the Depression, he had experienced hard times but had learned how to prevent them from tearing apart his private life. So he had not developed insomnia that spring, although occasionally he had awoken in the middle of the night thinking: My God, there are thirty thousand employees dependent on me; an entire institution is dependent on me. Nor had he fought with his wife or son. Still, on Saturday, June 9, Elsa and David stayed off the patio.

In the preceding weeks, Watson had come to think of the takeover battle as a chess game. Now Steinberg had put Disney in check; the game would be over if Disney made the wrong move. It was dreadful, yet in a way electrifying, as the calls caromed from Newport Beach to New York, to Encino, to Burbank, then back to New York, and back again to Newport Beach.

Watson informed the board members that late the night before, Drapkin, through Larry Tisch, had made Steinberg aware that Disney was considering a self-tender. None of the directors liked the idea of a self-tender. Watson didn't either. It was a bluff, and if Steinberg called it, Walt Disney Productions would self-destruct.

Nonetheless, Flom, Drapkin, and Kellner endorsed the idea. And the threat was a shrewd ploy, shrewder than Watson had at first realized. Drapkin had paved the way for it by suggesting to Larry Tisch, who then told Steinberg, that the Disney executives were "out of control," that they were willing to do anything, even destroy the company, in order to prevent Steinberg from acquiring it. This characterization of Disney's management was similar to the characterization of Steinberg as one who might "get on a kamikaze plane," that is, destroy himself in order to destroy Disney. Both were considerable exaggerations. The notion that Steinberg might "get on a kamikaze plane" may have originated either within Steinberg's camp or within the arbitrage community in order to alarm Disney's executives; or it may have been simply Richard Rainwater's expression of the uncertainty factor in the battle. Don Drapkin's description of his own clients as being out of control and preparing to make a self-tender was apparently designed, first, to alarm Steinberg and make him hesitate; Kellner believed it would cause Steinberg to walk away. Second, it would give him a pretext for accepting greenmail. It was an excuse with which he could defend himself to the arbitrageurs, who had bought large amounts of Disney stock in the expectation that this time Steinberg would carry out a takeover or drive the company into the arms of a white knight. If Steinberg sold his stock back to Disney for a premium, the arbs would be furious. Steinberg would look much better in their eyes if he could argue that he had had no alternative because Disney's out-of-control management intended to drown the company in debt.

Card Walker opposed the whole concept of the self-tender threat and of greenmail. It was most un-Disneylike, he thought. It was unethical. Once again he urged that the company carry the campaign directly to the shareholders. "We've got the culture of the company, the whole background, which we believe in," he argued. "We've got all these people who love Disney. We could win a vote."

So Watson called Joe Flom to determine one final time whether there was any possibility of winning the support of the shareholders. There was virtually none. Despite the fact that Disney was a unique company, a company that brought joy to millions of children around the world, a company that to many personified the American spirit; despite all this, Disney had less than a 1 percent chance of winning that sort of fight. All those millions of people who loved Disney didn't control Disney's stock.

Watson called Walker back. "Card, let me tell you what they're saying. I'm not saying they're accurate. I'm just telling you what they're saying. They're saying we can get in a train and we can load it up with Mickey Mouses and Minnie Mouses and Donald Ducks and Americana and we can go across this country and we can make speeches.

"I'm willing to do that, Card. I'm willing to get on that train, and I'll give a speech in every community in the country, because I believe in this company, and Steinberg has made the worst kind of tender offer. He isn't just somebody who says he's going to run the company better. He's giving Kerkorian the rights to the library and the Fishers the rights to the land. He's saying it's better dead than alive.

"So it would seem to be the easiest fight in the world to win based on who we are. We'll get tremendous turnouts at every station. They'll cheer me when I talk. And I'll even bring you along, Card, you're more inspirational than I am, and they'll cheer you. Unfortunately, none of those people are shareholders. Our stock is in the hands of arbitrageurs and people compelled to make money by what they consider their fiduciary duty, which is always a great excuse. So the Floms and the Drapkins are saying we can't win a fight. And they make a good case for it."

Card Walker still didn't like it. But he accepted it.

By the end of the day, Watson and Miller, together with Disney's advisers and the rest of its directors, had ruled out any action that would compromise the independence of the company or the integrity of its assets. Mike Bagnall was pressing ahead with preparations for the self-tender. And at noon on Sunday, Drapkin would begin negotiations with Reliance over the terms for buying back Steinberg's stock.

Paying greenmail would have its opponents, of course: the other shareholders, who would watch the value of their stock fall at the same time Steinberg was making a huge profit. Sid Bass had been quite vocal to Disney's management in his opposition to a greenmail deal with Steinberg, which would wreak havoc with the value of the Disney shares Bass Brothers was receiving for Arvida. As an alternative, Bass had suggested that Bass Brothers Enterprises buy out Steinberg's stock. But his proposal required the Basses and Disney to create a joint company, to which Disney would transfer some assets, such as the hotels in Florida, in exchange for some Bass Brothers bonds. In short, it involved transferring profitable parts of the company to the Basses. And even if Disney were willing to take such a step, which it was not, the joint venture sounded too complicated and time-consuming. Tomorrow was Sunday. The tender went into effect on Monday. No, under the circumstances, greenmail—and greenmail alone—provided Disney's management with the opportunity to keep the company whole and independent. So argued Joe Flom. Watson and Miller agreed. Greenmail was the worst option, except for all the others.

Saul Steinberg remained in Quogue on Saturday. And why not? The weather at the shore was beautiful. Steinberg's colleagues made a point of relaxing as well. Bob Hodes, the Reliance director and Wilkie Farr attorney, went sailing. Partly this was a negotiating ploy: Steinberg intended to make Disney come to him. At the same time, the whole exercise had become rather stylized. In the early days Steinberg and his associates had been exhilarated by the drama of pulling off massive deals under enormous pressure, but by the summer of 1984, he had engineered some twenty-five takeovers and attempted takeovers, and quite frankly the thrill was gone. Everyone knew pretty much what the outcome would be. After the obligatory posturing over the evils of greenmail, all that remained was to settle on a price for the Reliance shares. Steinberg trusted his people to work out the details.

Steinberg did call Reliance counsel Howard Steinberg and asked him to go to a meeting at noon the following day at the Wilkie Farr office of Bob Hodes. Don Drapkin and Alan Myers, another Skadden, Arps attorney, were scheduled to attend as well. And though the Reliance executives had not formally agreed to a buyback, nonetheless, in anticipation of that event, they set about estimating the expenses they had incurred in their takeover attempt. If there was to be a buyback, Disney would also have to reimburse Steinberg for all the money he had wasted in his effort to acquire the company.

10

SUNDAY WAS another clear, hot day. Early in the afternoon, Stanley Gold and Frank Wells drove out to Ron Miller's home in Encino to discuss the Brain Trust's proposal that the Disney family collaborate in a leveraged buyout of the company. Ray Watson came up from Newport Beach.

Miller, who at the time was still separated from Diane, lived in the old John Wayne house. It was a beautiful place, with a large veranda in the back and a broad, gently sloping yard. Watson, Wells, and Gold seated themselves around an outdoor table, while Miller served wine from his vineyard.

Despite some initial chat about the wine's charming bouquet, the meeting began uncomfortably. Gold had contacted Miller earlier to explain that Wells was accompanying him, but Miller was unclear about Wells's precise role, and Wells himself had never gotten around to calling his friend to explain his association with Roy Disney and Stanley Gold.

"I feel awkward here," Wells said. He told Miller that his main purpose was to serve as a bridge between the two sides of the Disney family. "If I can be helpful I can guarantee you, Ron, that I will certainly do whatever I can."

"Thank you," Miller said.

Wells went on to say that his old protégé Stanley Gold had asked him, as an experienced entertainment attorney and executive, to advise Roy Disney about the studio's value and related matters, but, above all, about ways to keep the company intact. If Miller was disturbed by the news that his friend Frank Wells had associated himself with the Roy side of the family, he concealed it admirably, and the meeting proceeded.

Stanley Gold wanted to know the Disney executives' plans regarding Steinberg's tender, but Watson and Miller felt they could confide nothing because neither Gold nor Wells, nor Roy Disney for that matter, was a member of the board. Instead, Watson turned the conversation to the question of Roy Disney's return to the board. His resignation had become an acute embarrassment: In the wake of the tender announcement, Walt's widow, Lilly, and his daughters, Sharon and Diane, had all issued statements supporting Disney's management and condemning Steinberg, but from Roy Disney there had been only silence.

In response, Gold and Wells outlined the Brain Trust's proposal for the two sides of the family to put the past behind them and, together with Disney's management—which included Watson—take the company private.

"We could write a Magna Carta that would make everyone happy," said Gold. "We wouldn't screw the shareholders, and we'd get Saul out of the picture." Gold believed that his proposal would satisfy Steinberg, who would be paid a premium for his shares; satisfy the other shareholders, who would receive the same price as Steinberg; and allow the studio to be run once again by the entire Disney family. As he talked, Watson got up every five or ten minutes to take phone calls. Wells and Gold figured they were related to the tender offer; they did not know that at that very moment, in New York, the lawyers were negotiating a price for the buyback.

"I urge you and Roy to sit down," Wells said to Miller. "I doubted that there would ever be an opportunity to do it, but by God there is, here, this Sunday afternoon. The company is being attacked by Steinberg, and here is a way to bring the family together."

"Don't greenmail Saul," Gold went on. "That's the worst thing. We've got a plan that beats greenmail. It includes you, Ray—not to be too discreet about it—and it's not even going to hurt Saul. We've got the perfect solution."

Watson did not think so. If the offer of reconciliation had come sooner, perhaps something could have been done. But coming now, it was completely impractical. With less than a day to reach a solution, Watson, who would say later that he felt as if he had a gun to his head, could ill afford to waste time on Gold's scheme.

"Stan, how many leveraged buyouts have you ever done?" Watson asked.

"One," Gold said, wishing he could give a larger number. "Starr Broadcasting."

"Well," Watson said, "my experts, including the Basses, who do a lot more of this and have a lot more knowledge than you, say now is not the right time. We just cannot do a leveraged buyout at this point."

As if to raise in turn the issue of Watson's and Miller's expertise, Gold launched into a diatribe against Arvida. Why had they bought the company? It was overpriced. Disney didn't need more Florida acreage.

Watson, who had grown a bit tired of the subject by then, cut Gold off abruptly. "You're talking about a field I know a tremendous amount about," he said. "I spent a career in it. I'll listen to you on anything else, but I'm not going to stand back and listen to you on this."

The conversation lasted two hours. Everyone found it inconclusive and unsatisfying, but late in the afternoon, as Gold and Wells climbed into Wells's Mercedes for the drive back to Beverly Hills, the two sides resolved to talk again. "Let's keep meeting," Watson said.

The atmosphere in Bob Hodes's corner office on the forty-seventh floor of the Citicorp Center was tense but subdued. Neither the attorneys for Skadden, Arps nor those for Reliance—everyone in the room was a lawyer—displayed any hostility or anger. Unlike the Disney executives, they did not see themselves as fighting for their lives. Nonetheless, there would be winners and there would be losers in the battle for Disney. And everyone hated to be associated with the losing side.

Drapkin told Hodes and Reliance counsel Howard Steinberg that this was the last chance they had to avoid catastrophe. He and his associates were booked on the last flight out of New York to California that night. There was a Disney board meeting the next day, and at that board meeting one of two things would happen. Either Disney's directors would consider a buyback—if terms could be agreed on—or they would consider a self-tender. So Reliance had to decide today. Disney was making a one-time offer.

Drapkin added that if Reliance's tender offer went through at $67.50 a share, Disney's offer in the self-tender for the company's remaining stock would be $80 a share. Hodes and Howard Steinberg stepped from the room to convey the terms to Saul Steinberg, who was still at the beach.

Was Disney serious? Steinberg asked. Would they carry out a self-tender?

The lawyers were uncertain. Disney's acquisition of Arvida and Gibson had shown that its management was determined to deny Reliance the company at any cost. There was certainly some risk that they would do it.

Saul Steinberg was less inclined than his lawyers to believe Disney would really self-tender. He thought perhaps they should proceed. After all, they had done all the work: made the analysis, raised the money, struck agreements with equity partners. And the investment was sensible. On the other hand, Larry Tisch had said that Disney was "out of control," that Morgan Stanley and Skadden, Arps could no longer contain their clients. Finally, Steinberg told his people to consider the possibility of selling—adding, in a remarkable echo of Ray Watson's feelings, that Disney had put a gun to his head.

Hodes and Howard Steinberg explained to Skadden, Arps attorneys that Reliance would consider a buyback at $85 a share, then quickly came down to $80 a share, the amount Disney had said it was willing to pay in the self-tender. Drapkin made an offer of $73 a share. After two hours of negotiations, the meeting broke up. An hour later Drapkin called Hodes and offered $75. That was better. At four o'clock the lawyers reconvened, this time at the Skadden, Arps offices on Third Avenue. Peter Kellner arrived and after some rapid calculations the two sides agreed on a price. Disney would pay Reliance $325.5 million ($77.5 a share) for its 4.2 million shares. That included $297.3 million ($70.83 a share) for Steinberg's stock, plus $28 million ($6.67 a share) to cover Steinberg's expenses, including his legal bills and the commitment fees he would have to pay to Kirk Kerkorian, the Fishers, Irwin Jacobs, and the rest of the investors. Excluding those expenses, Steinberg would make a profit of $31.7 million on the buyback, the difference between the price he had paid for his stock over the last ninety days and the price Disney would pay for it.

Drapkin called Watson with the details.

"How do we know their expenses are really $28 million?" Watson asked Drapkin. "What if they turn out to be $14 million?"

"We have to take their word for it," Drapkin said.

"Well, I don't understand that. I mean, how do we know we're not getting conned?"

"There will be lawsuits," Drapkin said. "They'll have to submit records."

Skadden, Arps had drafts of the papers already in its computer. Secretaries typed the specifics into their word processors, proofreaders examined the documents, and the computer printed them out. But as the printers began to thrash, the lawyers fell to bickering over conditions. Reliance wanted a "most-favored-nation" clause specifying that if another company bought Disney within a year for a price per share higher than that paid Reliance in the buyback, Disney would make up the difference. Skadden, Arps, for its part, insisted on a standstill from Reliance. Disney's attorneys also wanted standstills from Kirk Kerkorian, the Fishers, and Drexel Burnham. Hodes and Howard Steinberg said they could speak only for Reliance. Drapkin told Hodes there would be no deal without the standstills. Hodes and Steinberg said they should be able to work something out. Then Drapkin and Kellner left to catch their plane to Los Angeles.

Ray Watson did not return to Newport Beach that Sunday evening. Instead, he drove from Ron Miller's house to the small apartment Disney kept for its executives in Burbank near the studio. Joe Flom, Don Drapkin, Bob Greenhill, Peter Kellner, and their associates arrived in Los Angeles late that night. Watson called Drapkin at his hotel.

"We still don't have the standstill agreement from Drexel Burnham," Drapkin said.

"Just keep working on it," Watson said. "Tell them that unless we have the agreement we're not presenting the proposal to the board."

Then Watson turned out the lights. He didn't know how this business was going to be resolved, but he told himself that whatever happened, life would go on, the world would continue to turn. And on that self-counsel he was able to fall asleep.

At six o'clock on Monday morning, June 11, the security officer in the small guardhouse at the gate to the Disney studio waved the brown Cadillac the company assigned to Ray Watson into the parking lot. A crowd had already begun to gather in the conference room off Ron Miller's office. The Skadden, Arps attorneys were present with a battery of associates to do the stepping and fetching. So was the team from Morgan Stanley, who had brought their own attorneys from Shearman & Sterling because they knew that, as always happened when greenmail was paid, there would be lawsuits. The eleven board members were beginning to arrive. And several public relations agents from Hill and Knowlton milled about waiting to help manage the formal announcements and the uproar that was sure to follow.

Watson had prepared an outline of the subjects to be discussed. He reviewed it with Miller to make sure the minutes of the meeting would show that every issue had been presented and every option fully explored. He listed each of the Skadden, Arps attorneys and Morgan Stanley bankers he would call upon to address the board, the order in which they would speak, and the subjects they would discuss. Watson wanted to ensure that all the board members fully understood the situation and had an opportunity to express themselves.

Trading opened on the New York Stock Exchange at ten o'clock, seven o'clock California time. A half-hour before, Watson had the exchange informed that the directors of Walt Disney Productions were about to meet to discuss Steinberg's tender offer; they requested that the suspension of trading in Disney stock that had been instituted on Friday be continued. The stock exchange agreed.

Don Drapkin sat in a small office off the conference room speaking on the telephone with great agitation to one of Saul Steinberg's attorneys in New York. Everyone in the conference room could hear.

"Look," Drapkin said heatedly. "That is not the deal we had yesterday. You're reneging. I won't even recommend to my client that we take this to the board if that's the way you're going to be."

He put his hand over the receiver. "They can't get Drexel Burnham to agree to a standstill," he told the people in the conference room. "Drexel has never signed a standstill before."

Then, responding to the voice in New York again, he said, "Look, that's your problem. That's not our problem. Don't tell me you can't get them. If you want this transaction, you'll get them. We aren't going to go and con them into this. That's up to you. You said yesterday that you could get them. So *you* get them."

The voice in New York argued some more. Drapkin said, "No way will my client go for that. He's told me that."

Drapkin shouted over to Watson, "Ray, say something."

"There's no way," Watson said.

"Did you hear that?" Drapkin said into the phone. "He just said, 'NO WAY.' "

Drapkin was still negotiating with Steinberg's representative when Watson called the board meeting to order at nine o'clock. Sitting around the polished conference table were Chuck Cobb of Arvida; Philip Hawley of Carter Hawley Hale Stores; Ignacio Lozano, Jr., publisher of the Spanish daily *La Opinión* and a former U.S. ambassador to El Salvador; Samuel Williams, a senior partner in the law firm of Hufstedler, Miller, Carson & Beardsley; Richard Nunis, head of Disney's theme park division; Donn Tatum; Card Walker; Ron Miller; and Ray Watson. Hooked up on the speaker phone were directors Caroline Ahmanson and Robert Baldwin, the former head of Morgan Stanley. The attorneys and investment bankers took chairs ranged along the walls.

Watson began by reviewing the background of the tender offer, emphasizing the fact that Steinberg wanted to "dismember the corporation." He discussed each of the options available to the board, talked briefly along with Miller about the company's prospects for the future, then stated management's recommendation that the board reject Steinberg's proposal.

Peter Kellner took the floor. He said it was Morgan Stanley's opinion that Steinberg's proposal was inadequate and suggested that the board consider other options. He said the repurchase of Steinberg's shares, coming on top of the Gibson and Arvida deals, would cause Standard & Poor's and Moody's to revise Disney's credit rating downward, which would raise the cost of borrowing money. But Kellner believed this would have no material effect on the company in the long run.

Drapkin came in and said that they could get ten-year standstills from the Fisher brothers and from Steinberg, who would also as a matter of course drop his lawsuits and proxy fight. Drexel Burnham had agreed to a two-year standstill—its first ever—but Kirk Kerkorian absolutely refused to sign one. He preferred to see Steinberg go ahead with the tender, thus enabling him to acquire Disney's studio and library at a bargain price.

"It's the best we can do," Drapkin said.

The whole matter was thrown open for discussion. The board began to pelt Drapkin and Kellner with questions. Why not a proxy fight? What happened to the self-tender? How did you agree on the price? Are there *any* other options? No one in the room wanted to pay Steinberg greenmail, but no one could come up with a better idea. Even Card Walker was saying that, however despicable, it was the only choice.

The matter of greatest concern to the board, the one that nagged them the most, was that, if they swallowed their pride and offered Steinberg greenmail, there was nothing to prevent another raider from coming in and starting the whole process over again. Disney's advisers said the company had to take one step at a time. It had to wait and see what would happen next.

At six thirty that Monday morning a broker called Stanley Gold to say that the Street was alive with rumors of greenmail. He called again shortly before seven. Disney had requested that the stock exchange suspend trading in its stock; everyone was now certain the company would buy Steinberg out. Arbs were beginning to dump stock through third-market brokerage houses, such as Jefferies & Company in Los Angeles, that traded independently in Disney's stock.* Gold spent the rest of the morning at home talking to brokers and waiting for an announcement.

At 10:18 A.M. in Los Angeles an item by Reuters reporter John Crudele moved on the wire. Crudele quoted "Wall Street sources" who said

*Because Jefferies & Company and other third-market brokerage houses were not members of the New York Stock Exchange, they were not bound by the rules prohibiting members from trading in NYSE stocks outside regular trading hours or anytime trading was halted for special reasons.

Disney was "considering whether to buy back" its stock from Steinberg for about $77 a share. The story sparked a huge sell-off in Disney in the third markets, where its stock dropped almost $2 a share.

Before long the staff of the New York Stock Exchange was on the phone to Disney. The Exchange was losing money because of all the trading taking place in the third markets. When was the company going to make an announcement?

"Tell them we're not ready yet," Drapkin instructed a Skadden, Arps associate. "If they want to know why, say because we haven't reached a decision."

"They say they will open the market anyway," the associate replied.

"The New York Stock Exchange will have to take the responsibility then," Drapkin said. "We won't. We won't ask that trading be opened, we won't make an announcement, we won't explain what we're doing, until we have a decision."

The board then recessed, and the outside directors convened to discuss the matter without the potential bias posed by the inside directors, the managers whose jobs were at stake. They agreed that paying Steinberg greenmail would be considered unfair to the other shareholders. But, as one of the directors pointed out, if Steinberg's tender offer went through, the 49 percent of the stockholders who got in on the front end of the offer would do much better than the remaining 51 percent, including most of the small investors, who would see the value of their stock plummet. That was unfair too. The outside directors agreed to endorse the Steinberg buyback.

The full board reconvened. Phil Hawley said the outside directors would support the decision to buy back Steinberg's stock on the condition that Disney's management raise the company's earnings to the point where it would no longer be susceptible to raids. If that did not take place, Hawley said, the board would have to consider "other means" to realize the full value of the company's assets. In the ensuing scramble to issue a statement and gird for the inevitable backlash, few at Disney focused on what those "other means" might be.

At 3:23 P.M. Eastern time, the New York Stock Exchange reopened trading in Disney without the company's approval because of "significant trading" in the third markets off the floor of the exchange. Disney opened at $7 a share below its price on Friday when trading had been suspended. Less than forty minutes later, the Big Board closed; Disney's stock had fallen another $3.78. The company's announcement of the buyback came at 5:16 P.M. in New York, more than an hour after trading had stopped for the day.

After the board adjourned, Watson and Miller called Stanley Gold. They had not, Watson explained, informed Gold and Wells during their meeting the previous day of the negotiations then underway because it would not have been appropriate. "We didn't know whether it was going to be or not," Watson said. "We did what we thought we had to do."

Gold, as he put it later, came unglued. He gave his callers what he liked to term "Vintage Stanley Gold."

"What a stupid thing to do!" he shouted. "You're amateur night in Dixie. If you were going to greenmail him, why didn't you greenmail him sixty days ago when he owned only 5 percent and the stock was down ten points? Who advised you on this? I mean, you didn't have a plan, you didn't . . . you didn't . . ." Gold began to splutter.

"Calm down! Calm down!" Watson said. "We had to make the hard decision."

"You weren't there," said Miller. "It's easy to criticize."

"We still want to see if we can get Roy back on the board," Watson said. "Come and see us."

The Brain Trust scheduled an emergency session for that evening to discuss a response to the greenmail. Because Herb Galant of Fried, Frank was in Palo Alto watching his son graduate from the Stanford business school, they arranged to meet in the boardroom of KABL, a radio station Shamrock owned in San Francisco. Stanley Gold, Roy Disney, Mark Siegel, and Frank Wells all flew up from Los Angeles on the Shamrock jet. Cliff Miller was already in the city on other business.

Both Gold and Wells were personally offended by the fact that Disney had offered greenmail and Steinberg had accepted it. They believed they had proposed the perfect solution to the problem the day before when they suggested the two sides of the family join forces in a leveraged buyout. Miller and Watson had been cavalier in rejecting the idea and embarking instead on this disastrous course of theirs. It was time for the Brain Trust to take decisive action and issue Walt Disney Productions an ultimatum of its own. After several hours of conversation they decided to go to the company and demand several seats on the board and a management position for Frank Wells. If that failed, they would start a proxy fight to acquire the board seats; they might also sue Saul Steinberg to force him to return the greenmail.

Stanley Gold was to make some other moves before the week was out. One reason for his anger over the greenmail had to do with the plunge in the price of Disney stock that followed it. He had bought a lot of that stock for Shamrock over the last three months on margin —putting up only a percentage of the price in cash and borrowing the rest from his broker. When stocks bought on margin declined, the broker usually made a margin call, demanding more of the cash up front. The day of the greenmail, Gold was called by his broker, who said there was a $6 million margin call on Shamrock's Disney stock. The next day there was a $5 million margin call on the stock. The day after that, a $1 million margin call. Within three days Shamrock was forced to pony up $12 million to cover its position.

While Gold's emotional reaction to the dizzying decline in the price of Disney's shares and the resulting margin calls was predictable, his ultimate response was perhaps surprising. He recommended to his client that they buy more stock. If the company was undervalued before the buyback, he argued, it was even more undervalued now. Roy Disney agreed, and so from Tuesday, June 12, through Thursday, June 14, Shamrock acquired 100,000 additional shares of Walt Disney Productions—on margin.

Sid Bass was opposed to paying greenmail, but he was not opposed to receiving it. After all, less than three months before Steinberg sold his stock back to Disney, Bass Brothers Enterprises had made a $400 million profit when Texaco bought out their position in that company. And Sid Bass was a connoisseur of the asset play, able to appreciate the masterful execution, the pure artistry, of Steinberg's immensely profitable maneuver. On the day the buyback was announced, he called Steinberg in New York and said, with that faint trace of a Texas accent, "Congratulations, Saul—*you dirty dawg!*"

That same day, Irwin Jacobs had packed up his family and flown to Greece for a two-week vacation. On Tuesday morning, at the airport in Athens, he picked up a copy of the *International Herald Tribune* and read about the buyback of Steinberg's stock.

Jacobs had not actually given Steinberg $35 million. He and the rest of the investors, including Kerkorian and the Fisher brothers, had simply pledged funds to finance the tender in exchange for the commitment fee. Indeed, Jacobs would eventually receive a check from Steinberg for $570,412.48. But after performing some calculations, he determined that he had come out a loser in this particular venture. Canceling the call options on Disney stock the day Mike Milken contacted him had cost him a potential $700,000. "Oh well," Jacobs said later when reflecting on this development, "some days you win and some days you lose." He was a big boy.

The public outcry over the greenmail was deafening. Editorial writers, politicians, and shareholders heaped calumny upon corporate raiders and railed against the absence of regulations forbidding management to pay premiums to select stockholders. "Outrage Over Disney Buyout" was the headline on the front page of the Business Day section of the *New York Times* two days later. The article quoted Dean LeBaron, head of Batterymarch Financial Management, as saying, "This could be the last [hostile takeover] where greenmail will be tolerated." James Severance, investment director of common stocks for the State of Wisconsin Investment Board, called the behavior of both Steinberg and Disney "reprehensible."

While the outrage was general, its object depended on one's point of view. To much of the press and the public at large, Steinberg was the villain. In his article, titled "Steinberg's Was No Mickey Mouse Caper," Robert Knight of the *Los Angeles Times* wrote of the Reliance chairman, "It's too bad that this guy gets even a dime for scaring the socks off anybody who cares what happens to Disney, but at least he'll be out of the picture." At the time, Timothy Wirth, a Democratic representative from Colorado, was preparing a bill for Congress that would prohibit corporations from buying out stockholders at a premium of more than 3 percent unless a majority of all shareholders approved. In an article entitled "Holding Mickey Mouse to Greenmail," the *Christian Science Monitor* quoted a congressional aide as saying that " 'the Disney case provides some sense of urgency' to a bill that before had not drawn much interest." Following the Steinberg buyback Congress arranged to hold new hearings, at which raiders like T. Boone Pickens moralized against greenmail and investment bankers from Drexel Burnham defended junk bonds. It became an issue on a local level as well. The following year the New York State Legislature passed a bill outlawing hostile takeovers of companies headquartered in the state; the bill was vetoed by Governor Mario Cuomo.

But while the wrath of the public and the media was focused on Steinberg, the investment community tended to blame Walt Disney Productions. Lee Isgur, the analyst who followed Disney for Paine Webber, was quoted in the *New York Times* as saying of the Disney board, "They just folded. And that is sort of sad." By paying Steinberg greenmail, Disney had failed to treat all shareholders—including the arbitrageurs—equally and that had cost all shareholders—including the arbitrageurs—a steep paper loss.* As a result, Wall Street poured abuse on the company in its own inimitable fashion; by the middle of the week Disney's stock had plummeted another $7 to less than $46 a share. And it continued to fall.

---

*People like Stanley Gold insist with great irritation that there is no such thing as a paper loss: if a stock declines in value its owner is out that much money. However, to certain shareholders like Roy Disney, who had held much of his stock for years and had no immediate plans to sell it, such a temporary decline was likely to be somewhat less alarming than it was to arbitrageurs, who typically borrowed money at high interest rates to purchase their shares, and who planned to liquidate their holdings after a short-term run-up in the price.

PART · TWO

The Shake-up

11

BY JUNE 1984, Disney's animated feature *The Black Cauldron* was in the final stages of production. Described by the studio as its most ambitious animated project since *Pinocchio,* the film was based on Lloyd Alexander's five-volume fantasy series *The Prydain Cycle,* and revolved around the efforts of a boy named Taran to prevent the evil Horned King from gaining possession of the Black Cauldron, a magic vessel that could produce an army of supernatural warriors.

The studio had great hopes for *The Black Cauldron,* and had invested a huge amount of time and money in the project, which had been eleven years in the making and was to cost $25 million before it was complete. The movie contained 115,200 frames of film, and each individual frame took thirty-three steps to produce, from sketching the story and recording the dialogue through roughing out the animation, shooting it on film, transferring the drawings to cels and painting the cels and the background, to editing the film, recording the sound effects and music, balancing the color, and making prints for distribution. More than two hundred employees, including sixty-eight animators and assistant animators, working full time, had produced 2,519,200 individual drawings, and consumed more than four hundred gallons of paint and thirty-four miles of film stock. Though the most modern technology, such as video cameras and computer-generated animation, had been used, *The Black Cauldron,* in its painstaking detail, elaborate plot, and darkly mythic overtones, harked back to the Disney classics: It was the first animated motion picture to be shot in seventy millimeter since *Sleeping Beauty* in 1959. Ron Miller, under whose leadership at the studio the project had been conceived and produced, and who had seen a rough cut of the film, was excited about its prospects.

Meanwhile, *Splash* had established itself as the most successful Disney movie of all time; by the end of the company's fiscal year in September it would gross a record $69 million in theater rentals in the United States.* *Never Cry Wolf* was also doing well; to be reissued for the third time in less than a year that July, it would gross $25 million. The success of the two movies had more than compensated for the losses the film division had incurred during the previous year. Equally important, the films had helped revive Disney's flagging reputation— a reputation that had received another large boost with the announcement that *Country,* the Jessica Lange–Sam Shepard farm drama that was to be Touchstone's second release, had been chosen to open the upcoming New York Film Festival. It was a considerable honor for the studio, which was usually denigrated by the festival's *artistes* and *auteurs,* as well as for Ron Miller personally.

These developments might have been expected to rekindle investor enthusiasm for Walt Disney Productions, especially in light of the fact that total income for the company's third quarter, which ended June 30, was about $104 million, more than double the income for the same quarter of the previous year. Though that increase was in part the result of a $17 million contribution from Arvida, it was primarily due to the fact that the studio had gone from a loss of $32.2 million for the third quarter of fiscal 1983 to a profit of $7.7 million for the third quarter of fiscal 1984. But the success of *Splash* and *Never Cry Wolf,* the optimism about *The Black Cauldron,* the improved earnings figures that seemed to vindicate Ron Miller's leadership—all these normal barometers of performance had become virtually irrelevant to Wall Street. The financial press remained critical, the stock price showed no signs of the kind of recovery that might indicate renewed confidence in the company's future, and the talk about Disney's vulnerability persisted: Rumors abounded that new raiders were already gathering. Ivan Boesky and Roy Disney were both mentioned; Stanley Gold had let it be known that Roy Disney was accumulating Disney stock.

---

*In constant dollars, however, *Mary Poppins* was still Disney's largest-grossing movie.

Months before the takeover furor surrounded Walt Disney Productions, Morgan Stanley had invited a number of its senior clients, including Ray Watson, to accompany the investment bank's managing directors on a four-day raft trip down the Colorado River beginning June 14. Because Disney was in such turmoil, Watson had doubts about attending. But he needed a rest, and so he decided to go. On Thursday, June 14, he flew to Las Vegas; the group was to set out from there the next morning and return on Sunday.

After checking into his hotel, Watson touched base with the studio and learned that Phil Hawley had called him urgently. Hawley's outside public relations counsel was Brain Trust member Cliff Miller, and since the greenmail announcement Miller had conveyed to him in several conversations the depth of Roy Disney's alienation from the company. The information had disturbed Hawley. It was essential to get Roy Disney back on the board as soon as possible, he said when Watson returned his call. "Ray, it's very, very serious."

Watson agreed. "Let me go to work on it," he said.

Hawley believed it might be a good idea for Watson to return to Los Angeles immediately, but Watson decided against it. The expedition would last only through the weekend, and he had thought of nothing but Walt Disney Productions for months. He needed a change of scenery and some time to clear his mind. So he proceeded with the trip, but he arranged for the company to send in a helicopter and fly him out of the Grand Canyon if an emergency arose.

The group, which was almost equally divided between corporate executives and Morgan Stanley partners, including Peter Kellner, set off down the Colorado in five large rubber pontoons tied together. For four days they were completely out of touch with the rest of the world. Watson joked to Kellner that it was the first time he had seen him without his beeper. As the men floated downriver through the canyon, the history of millennia trapped in the layered walls put a bit of perspective on Watson's preoccupation with Steinberg and stock prices. He returned to Los Angeles refreshed and invigorated, prepared to put his company in order once and for all.

As soon as he arrived, he had Ron Miller call Stanley Gold and set up an appointment. Gold promptly appeared at the studio, and, after reiterating his complaints about Arvida, Gibson, and the greenmail, he spelled out the conditions under which Roy Disney would return to the board. There were two. The first was that the company would have to make directors of two of Roy Disney's allies as well.

Watson argued that three new members was too many. The board could accommodate Roy and one other. "Probably you, Stanley, though the board doesn't like you," Watson said. "You're too much of a lightning rod in this process."

The second condition for Roy's return, Gold said, was that the company give Frank Wells a senior management position. Wells would replace neither Watson nor Miller; he would be an addition to the team.

The Disney executives' reaction to this proposal was predictably unenthusiastic. "We'll think about it," Watson said.

Gold had scarcely returned to his office when Watson and Miller telephoned him.

"While we think Frank Wells is terrific, we just don't think it would work," Watson said.

"He's a friend of mine," Miller added. "I like him. But there's no spot for him."

Not only would a top position for Wells threaten Miller's control of the company; it would be difficult to explain to such Disney executives as Dick Nunis, the head of the theme parks. Nunis, Miller said, would interpret the advent of Wells as an indication that the company intended to emphasize films at the expense of the parks. "Nunis would absolutely leave the company if that happened," Miller said. "He is the most valuable guy in the company."

"Shit, then why don't you make him president?" Gold asked.

On that sour note the discussion ended.

Since it did not seem that Roy Disney would be returning to the Disney board after all, on Sunday, June 17, Stanley Gold called a meeting of the Brain Trust at Gang, Tyre & Brown. Roy Disney, Frank Wells, Cliff Miller, and Mark Siegel all came, as did Herb Galant and his Fried, Frank partner Stuart Katz.

Gold summarized the situation. First, the Brain Trust had set out to buy Disney, but they had decided that was too risky, and besides, it would have required splitting up the company. Next, they had approached management and the other side of the Disney family and proposed a joint leveraged buyout. That had been rejected. Finally, they had gone to the company and asked to be brought onto the management team. That too had been rejected. It was time for the Brain Trust to accept the fact that it was going to be impossible to work with Disney's management. They were now dissident shareholders. They were renegades.

Having thus defined their status, the Brain Trust resolved that Roy Disney should sue Walt Disney Productions to halt the Gibson deal. Simultaneously but separately, they would demand that the acquisition be put before the shareholders for a vote, a less hostile move than a proxy fight to oust the board, and one that would enable Gold to get the support of large shareholders without forcing them into open conflict with management. Nevertheless, if the shareholders voted against Gibson, the outcome would be interpreted on Wall Street as a vote against management's performance.

Stanley Gold had less than a week to prepare for the battle. Since the 100,000 shares of Disney he had purchased after the greenmail had put Shamrock's holdings at more than 5 percent, Roy Disney was required by the SEC to file a 13D within ten days declaring his intentions towards the company. The form was due at the SEC office in Washington by five o'clock Friday afternoon, June 22.

The fun began on Monday, June 18, when five attorneys from Fried, Frank in New York, summoned by Herb Galant, invaded the offices of Gang, Tyre & Brown, a small firm of some fifteen partners and associates. The Fried, Frank lawyers took over the desks of secretaries and paralegals. They camped out in the offices of firm members. They monopolized the telephones. They prepared legal papers, filings, and court motions. They drafted position memoranda.

In the middle of the week, at the height of the preparations, Frank Wells received a call from Ron Miller. It was the first time the two men had spoken privately since Wells had surfaced as a member of Roy Disney's Brain Trust, and the conversation did not go well.

"There are a lot of us here at the studio who are very disappointed in you, Frank," Miller said. He added that Wells had been denied a job at the studio not because he lacked ability, but because the timing was bad. A job at Disney in the future was a possibility—or at least it had been. Wells's decision to cast his lot with Roy Disney was viewed poorly by "the powers that be" at the studio.

Wells argued that Roy Disney and Stanley Gold had come to him, that he had always urged them to get the families back together. He had, he said, also insisted on two other things: first, that he would tell Ron of his association with Roy Disney, which was why he had joined Stanley Gold that Sunday at Ron's house, and second, that he would never publicly oppose Ron Miller. He reiterated that promise and then, hanging up the phone, reminded Stanley Gold of the condition he had laid down—that if there were a proxy fight, he, Wells, would not stand in public opposition to Miller. But Wells, who had, after all, been co-chief executive of Warner Brothers, who had, as well, been a partner at Gang, Tyre & Brown, the firm that had waged bloody legal battles with people like Howard Hughes, Louis B. Mayer, and Samuel Goldwyn, was not going to be embarrassed or intimidated into walking away from Roy Disney.

On the morning of Thursday, June 21, in an article that appeared in the *Chicago Tribune* and the New York *Daily News,* the financial columnist Dan Dorfman (who never had gotten his interview with Roy Disney) reported that sources had told him Roy Disney was preparing to launch a proxy fight against Walt Disney Productions. The leak did not disturb Stanley Gold, who believed it would only create chaos within Disney's management, chaos that he, Stanley Gold, would be able to exploit. Early that afternoon, Gold took a call from Watson and Miller, who always, it seemed, called together.

"Have you read the Dorfman column?" Watson asked.

"It's been read to me," Gold said.

"Are you really going to do all that?" Miller asked.

"Hey, wait a second," Gold said. "If you want to take my deposition, have your lawyers give me notice. I'm not going to tell you what we're going to do. I'm not going to tell you anything. If you want to know whether we think the place is being mismanaged, I think that was the sense of the message I was trying to send to you in our conversations and meetings."

"Well, could you come over?" Watson asked.

"Hey, lookit," Gold said. "I got my troops around. What's the sense of coming over? We've told you what we thought, where we stood. We don't seem to be anywhere close."

"I'm sure we could accommodate you." Watson said. But, he added, Gold's demand for three seats on the board would be more easily granted than the executive position for Wells.

So Stanley Gold drove through the Hollywood Hills to Burbank for yet another meeting with Ray Watson and Ron Miller. Because the Disney executives had specifically requested that Frank Wells not attend, Gold brought Mark Siegel with him. Don Drapkin was present to provide legal advice for Disney, since the matter involved the company's bylaws. Gold began with his by-then-familiar litany of complaints about Arvida and Gibson. But he and Roy were willing to put all that behind them, he said, if they could have four seats on the board.

Watson and Miller said they were willing to give Roy Disney three seats. Roy, whom they volunteered to make a vice-chairman of the company, would have one seat. Stanley Gold could take the second. The third could go to Roy's brother-in-law Peter Dailey or to Frank Wells. Neither Ron nor Diane Miller nor the other members of the Walt side of the family were particularly happy with this proposal. The Walt side had more stock than the Roy side, but had only one member, Miller, on the board; the Roy side would now have three representatives. Nonetheless, they endorsed the proposal for the sake of the company.

Gold, however, insisted once again on a management position for Frank Wells, and on this Miller was less flexible. Demoralization would sweep through Disney's second-tier executives if an outsider were placed over them, he said. They were all loyal employees who had devoted decades to the company; they all wanted to move up the ladder too. Dick Nunis in particular, he reiterated, would probably quit, and Nunis was too valuable to the company to risk that. The answer on Wells was no.

Gold then said that if the company was going to deny Wells a job, it should reconfigure the executive committee, which had almost the power of the full board and which met occasionally to approve management decisions. At the moment it consisted of Watson, Miller, Card Walker, and Donn Tatum. Gold demanded that Tatum and Walker resign in favor of an ally of Roy Disney.

At this point, both Gold and Watson wanted to review their

positions with their advisers. A board meeting was scheduled for nine o'clock the following morning, with committee meetings at eight-thirty. If Gold got to the studio by seven o'clock, and if they could reach an agreement, Watson said he would recommend it to the board.

It was after four-thirty when Gold and Siegel left the studio to brief the Disneys, Cliff Miller, and Wells, who waited at Roy Disney's house. Gold was running late. He was to be host at a dinner that evening to celebrate his daughter Jennifer's graduation from junior high school, and his call to inform his family that he would have to join the party at the restaurant had not been gladly received. He could not afford to fall any further behind schedule.

"I've got to go to this thing," Gold told the Brain Trust, after outlining the points that Watson and Miller were prepared to concede. "I cannot be late. My wife will divorce me, my kids will leave me. So I'm going to be at that restaurant at six. It will be a two-hour dinner. If anybody wants to see me, they can come to my house at eight."

All through the dinner Gold remained preoccupied with Watson's offer; he left the party alone at eight, and when he got home Mark Siegel was sitting on the front steps. They retired to Gold's study on the second floor, where Gold, who customarily drank grappa or Williams Pear Brandy after dinner, got out the grappa. For the next hour and a half he listened to Siegel's legal review of the Disney offer. Around ten-thirty, as Siegel was leaving, Frank Wells arrived. They consumed more grappa.

At midnight, Howard King, a Gang, Tyre & Brown litigator, and Michael Rauch, a Fried, Frank litigator, showed up. King and Rauch had been working all week against the SEC deadline on the papers Shamrock intended to file the next day to initiate the suit, and now they had learned that Gold had been at the studio trying to reach a compromise with Disney's management. They were not pleased. They had gone out to a Spanish restaurant, eaten paella, drunk wine, and decided at midnight to go to Gold's house and harangue him about negotiating with Watson and Miller.

"How the fuck can you goddamn settle this thing?" they wanted to know. "We can win it," they said. "We'll get issues, we'll get lawsuits. You've lost your nerve. You're absolutely selling the team out. We've worked our asses off. We've got a winner."

"This is the way to do it," Wells replied. "We don't want to ruin the company and split it apart with public fights."

"Get out of here, Wells," the litigators said. "Who needs you?"

The arguing and the drinking went on until two in the morning, at which point Wells and the litigators left; there was a conference call on the matter scheduled for 6 A.M. Gold went to his bedroom, setting his alarm for five.

"Hi," said his wife, who had not been able to sleep. "It was a *great* graduation party, wasn't it?"

"I'm sorry," Gold said.

"Is everybody finally gone?"

"No," Gold said. "I've got two secretaries in there typing up some stuff—"

"You've got people working in that damn study?"

"Just joking," Gold said, and turned out the light.

It was still dark when he awoke. After three hours of sleep he felt fine. All week he had worked late and risen early. Stanley Gold was operating on deal-induced adrenalin.

At six o'clock the team assembled at Gold's house. Herb Galant, connected by speakerphone from New York, seemed to have hundreds of points he wanted Gold to demand of the Disney management. Mark Siegel took them down as fast as he could write. Then, as the sun came up, Gold and Siegel sped over to Toluca Lake for a seven o'clock meeting with the Disneys, who agreed to drop the lawsuit if the company gave Roy Disney three seats on the board. It was unfortunate that Frank Wells could not be brought into the company, but that did not warrant a rejection of management's overtures. Wells had already insisted that he would not permit a settlement to hinge on whether or not he received a job.

There was, however, one condition on which Roy Disney was adamant: Card Walker and Donn Tatum would have to leave the executive committee. It was, quite simply, his revenge for the years when Walker had treated him with open contempt and sneered at his proposals for reform of the studio.

By eight o'clock, Gold and Siegel were at the studio meeting with Ray Watson, Ron Miller, and Don Drapkin. Gold gave a speech on the matter of Card Walker and the executive committee. Walker's resignation from the committee was symbolically important. It would announce to Hollywood and, more important, to Wall Street, that the studio was entering a new era, that Disney was no longer ruled by men bound to the past, men who, before reaching any decision, would invariably ask, "What would Walt have done?" Moreover, it would make clear that Roy Disney was returning to the board not simply because he missed attending the meetings but because he would now have a say in the running of Walt Disney Productions.

Although Donn Tatum had already volunteered to retire from the board if that would help, and Card Walker would certainly do almost anything for the sake of the company, Watson was reluctant to ask them to step down. The two men had both spent a lifetime serving Walt Disney Productions; their removal from the executive committee would be a slap in the face.

"It's a non-negotiable point," said Gold, though Frank Wells had urged him not to insist on it.

"Will you agree to a standstill if we give you this?" Drapkin asked, seeking to ensure that Roy Disney would refrain in future from accumulating stock with a view to a takeover hostile to management, or from engaging in a proxy fight.

"Will you give us a bylaw change assuring that you will never buy another Gibson or another Arvida without first putting it to the shareholders?" Gold asked in return.

"You're *not* going to give us a standstill?" Drapkin asked.

"I'll give you a standstill," Gold said. "Give me a bylaw change."

"We can't do that," Drapkin said. No management team would agree to such a humiliating restriction on its activities.

"I can't give you a standstill."

"Well, will you give us a little standstill?"

"Will you give us a little bylaw change?"

The two men both laughed at that point, but everyone realized that Roy Disney would not give the company a standstill and the company would not amend its bylaws.

Gold pointed out that they didn't have very much time to negotiate. He had to file with the SEC before two o'clock. "If we don't cut a deal we're going to have to announce to the public that we're at war," he said.

The corner of Mickey Avenue and Dopey Drive on the Disney lot is the site of the Animation Building, where Disney's executives have their offices. (*Paul Chinn/Los Angeles* Herald Examiner)

Walt Disney (right) and his brother Roy O. Disney in 1964. After Walt's death in 1966, Roy O. Disney became chairman of Walt Disney Productions. *(AP/ Wide World Photos)*

Walt's daughter Diane and Ron Miller, with two of their children, in 1956. At the time, Miller was a tight end for the Los Angeles Rams. He became head of the Disney studio in 1976 and the company's chief executive officer in 1983. (*Los Angeles* Times)

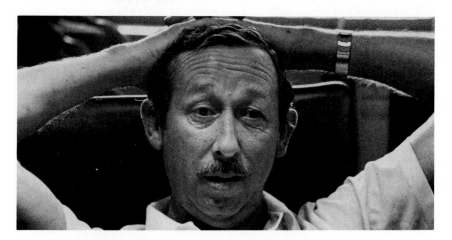

Roy E. Disney, Roy O. Disney's son and, before the takeover attempt, the largest individual shareholder of Walt Disney Productions. Roy quit his job at the studio in 1977, after a falling-out with management. In 1984 he resigned as a director and began exploring ways to force changes in the company. (*Penni Gladstone/Los Angeles* Times)

Card Walker (above) standing in front of a model of
Epcot, Disney's theme park for adults in Orlando,
Florida; and Donn Tatum. After Roy O. Disney's
death, they ran the company until Ron Miller,
Walker's protégé, assumed control. *(Steve Fon-
tanini/Los Angeles* Times; *Los Angeles* Times)

Stanley Gold, Roy E. Disney's attorney and financial adviser. While running Roy's holding company, Shamrock Holdings, he had engaged in a number of corporate battles—experience that prepared him for the fight with the management of Walt Disney Productions. (©*Max Aguilera-Hellweg)*

Saul Steinberg, who attempted the hostile takeover of Disney, in the office of his company, Reliance Group Holdings. *(Theo Westenberger)*

Drexel Burnham's Mike Milken in the firm's Los Angeles office. He put together the financing package for Steinberg's takeover bid. *(Steve Smith/ Wheeler Pictures)*

Arbitrageur Ivan Boesky bought Disney shares on the assumption that the takeover would go through. *(David Burnett/Contact)*

Ray Watson at Disneyland. Watson succeeded Card Walker as Disney's chairman soon after Ron Miller became chief executive officer. *(Ken Rogers)*

Don Drapkin, the partner at Skadden, Arps, Slate, Meagher & Flom who negotiated the buyback for Disney. *(Harry Benson)*

Bob Greenhill, a managing director of Morgan Stanley & Company, Disney's investment bankers. *(Joyce Ravid)*

Skadden, Arps's Joe Flom, Disney's senior legal adviser. *(Richard Sandler)*

Sid Bass, the Texas investor who sold Disney the Arvida Corporation, a
Florida real estate concern. By the end of 1984, after buying out Ivan Boesky
and Irwin Jacobs, he was Disney's largest shareholder. *(Rollin Riggs/Black
Star)*

Arvida's chief executive officer, Chuck
Cobb, who joined the Disney board after
the Arvida deal went through.

Former Treasury secretary Bill Simon (left) and Ray Chambers were the controlling shareholders in the Gibson greeting card company, which they arranged to sell to Disney. *(Michael Abramson)*

Financier Irwin Jacobs, who bought Disney stock when the price plunged after the buyback and then threatened a proxy fight to oust management. (*Minneapolis* Star and Tribune)

Ron Miller (above) and Ray Watson at the press conference announcing the planned acquisition of Gibson. Opposed by all the major stockholders, the deal precipitated Miller's ouster. (*Mary Frampton/Los Angeles* Times)

Roy E. Disney's intimate circle of friends and associates referred to themselves as "the Brain Trust." *Standing from left:* Patty Disney, Mark Siegel, Roy Disney. *Seated:* Stanley Gold (left), Cliff Miller.

Herb Galant of Fried, Frank, Harris, Shriver & Jacobson, the Brain Trust's legal adviser. *(Richard Sandler)*

Philip Hawley, Disney's most influential outside director. (*David Becker/Los Angeles* Times)

Dennis Stanfill, former head of Twentieth Century-Fox, was Hawley's candidate for chief executive officer of Disney. (*Robert Gabriel/Los Angeles* Times)

Michael Eisner, the Brain Trust's candidate for chief executive, with his family in the yard of their Bel Air house. *(Harry Benson)*

Frank Wells with his wife, Luanne. Wells, former co-chief executive of Warner Brothers, and a de facto member of the Brain Trust, was Eisner's running mate in the campaign to succeed Ron Miller. (*Craig Mathew/Los Angeles* Times)

Eisner, Disney's new chairman and chief executive, and Wells, its new president, on the Disney lot. *(©Max Aguilera-Hellweg)*

Watson asked if Gold wanted to be present at the board meeting. Morgan Stanley was giving a presentation on the Gibson deal. Did he want to see that?

Gold turned the offer down. "I don't think it's appropriate at this point," he said.

All the Disney directors except Phil Hawley were present when Watson convened the Disney board at nine o'clock. First on the agenda, Michael Diamond, an attorney with Skadden, Arps, advised the board on the twenty lawsuits that had been filed against Walt Disney Productions and its directors as a result of the Arvida and Gibson deals and the greenmail. The plaintiffs in such cases were often small shareholders represented by lawyers specializing in corporate litigation. The attorneys, who at times approached the shareholders about initiating the suits, would handle the litigation in exchange for 30 to 40 percent of any settlement. Diamond said most of the cases would be consolidated into one action, which was not likely to come to trial for several years, if ever; most suits of this kind were settled out of court. Nonetheless, Diamond recommended that the directors resist commenting publicly on the litigation. He also urged the outside directors to retain separate counsel. The board then moved on to the issue of Roy Disney's return.

The Brain Trust had been waiting for an hour in the Disneys' living room for word from the studio when the phone rang. Ray Watson wanted to speak with Stanley Gold.

"I can get everything, Stan," Watson said. "But can we leave Card and Donn on the executive committee? It hardly ever meets. It's cosmetic. Can't you just give me that one point?"

"Absolutely not," Gold said without consulting the others in the room, for he knew he was acting against the better judgment of Frank Wells. "We got no deal."

"Don't get excited," Watson said. "We're going to try it your way."

"Under no circumstances will I make the deal without that condition."

"I'll get back to you," Watson said.

.   .   .

In the boardroom, Watson asked Card Walker and Donn Tatum to leave, then explained Roy Disney's position. In order to entice him to return to the board, the directors would have to strip Tatum and Walker of their membership on the executive committee. The directors agreed.

Watson and Miller then faced the unpleasant task of informing Walker and Tatum, waiting in an adjacent room, of the board's decision. Watson tried to be as direct as possible. Both men knew how important it was for Walt Disney Productions to bring Roy Disney back on the board. But before returning, Roy was going to exact retribution for the ill treatment he felt he had received over the years. Watson had personally tried to persuade Stanley Gold to change his mind on the issue, but Gold had said it was non-negotiable. The board had no choice.

Tatum took it philosophically; Walker, while accepting the decision, did not hide his disappointment. "Ray, I think you caved in," he told Watson.

It was one o'clock, an hour before SEC regulations required Stanley Gold to file his 13D—a Fried, Frank lawyer was standing by at the SEC in Washington with the completed form—when the phone rang again in Toluca Lake. Stanley Gold took the call.

"We've got a deal," Watson said.

If the Brain Trust was not "all the way in," it had at the very least established itself as a force the company's management would have to reckon with. That night the Wellses and their son Kevin, the Golds, the Cliff Millers, the Mark Siegels, Roy and Patty Disney, their daughter Abby, and their son Roy Patrick and his wife, Linda, all met for dinner at Le St. Germain. The party was jubilant. But before the food could arrive, Roy Disney suddenly left the room; a few minutes later he was found crumpled in the hallway outside the dining room. He was as cold as ice. Stanley Gold thought he had suffered a heart attack.

"It's just a fainting spell," Patty Disney said. "It's his hypoglycemia."

At that point Gold himself started to feel dizzy. He made it through the restaurant door and then he too fainted.

The next day Gold explained his collapse to his friends by avowing that the loyalty of a lawyer to his client demanded that he pass out when the client did so. A week of subsisting on nervous energy had overtaken both of them. But a less reverent interpretation circulated as well. What had really happened, it was said, was that when Stanley Gold saw Roy Disney lying in the hallway, he had seen his horse go down, and he had gone down too—in horror.

12

AT EACH STAGE in Disney's travail, the company's officers believed they had solved a problem only to find that another issued from its solution. And so it was with Gibson. No one at Disney had ever expected the company's stock to fall as far as it had by late June; because of the collar on the Gibson deal, Disney would now have to issue Gibson's shareholders 6.2 million shares, 1.2 million more than they had expected to issue. As a result, Gibson's shareholders would control 15 percent of Disney's stock instead of the 13.7 percent originally anticipated; for Disney's other large shareholders, whose percentage holdings would be correspondingly reduced, it was not a happy prospect.

On June 26, less than a week after they had joined the Disney board, Stanley Gold and Peter Dailey flew to New York for meetings at The Interpublic Group of Companies, an international advertising conglomerate which, the year before, had bought Dailey's Los Angeles ad agency. Gold also had some business at Mutual of New York, which was financing a Shamrock broadcasting project.

Having checked into the Ritz-Carlton, Gold was relaxing in his room when the telephone rang.

"Stanley Gold?"

"Yes."

"My name is Sid Bass. Can I talk to you about something of joint interest?"

Bass Brothers Enterprises maintained an office in Rockefeller Center, a ten-minute walk from the Ritz-Carlton, and Sid Bass suggested the two men meet there at ten o'clock the following morning. Gold, who did not know Sid Bass, brought Peter Dailey along with him.

It was primarily a let's-get-acquainted encounter. Sid Bass wanted to make his views on Disney's real estate and theme parks known to the two new directors. Gold said he thought the company had paid too much for Arvida, but he didn't dwell on the subject. Arvida was a done deal. If you spent all your life talking about yesterday, tomorrow would catch you by surprise.

Then Dailey sounded Sid Bass out on the Gibson acquisition. He proceeded cautiously; since Bass had just made a killing on a similar deal, he might think Gibson was wonderful. But Bass agreed that Gibson was a mistake. It was an important revelation. Sid Bass and Roy Disney were at the time Disney's two largest shareholders, and they both opposed Gibson.

"Let me tell you about Disney's movie business," Gold said finally, preparing to plunge into a history of the studio and Roy Disney's views on its management.

"Oh, I'm not really interested in that," Bass said. "I wouldn't invest in movies to make money. It's too ephemeral for me. I'm a hard-asset man."

As had Stanley Gold, Irwin Jacobs, returning from his vacation in Greece, reasoned that if Disney had been undervalued at $53 when Saul Steinberg started buying its stock in March, it was even more undervalued at $47. A good investment, in other words, with little downside risk and a lot of upside potential. He explained his thinking to his associates, who liked what they heard, then asked a sympathetic Minneapolis banker if he could borrow some cash to make an investment; the banker agreed to lend him $4 million without collateral. Jacobs's associates called a few banks and cobbled together some loans of their own. And they all began to buy Disney.

Ray Watson, who from the outset had been feeling pressure from his shareholders on Gibson, and who was far less certain of the underlying value of the greeting card company than he had been of Arvida, had decided that, collar or no collar, Disney simply could not afford to issue more than 5 million shares of Walt Disney Productions to Gibson's stockholders. On the night of Friday, June 29, little more than three weeks after the Gibson deal had been hammered out, he called Ray Chambers. "We're going to have to renegotiate this," Watson said, and spelled out the company's dilemma.

Chambers disagreed. "A deal's a deal," he argued. "You're reneging on a deal."

Watson was unmoved. He was not presenting this as something for discussion, he said. When the original agreement had been made, the Disney executives had not known they were going to have to buy off Steinberg. The best they could offer now was a straight two-for-one stock swap: 5 million Disney shares for the 10 million shares of Gibson. If the Gibson shareholders refused to accept, Disney would exercise its right to cancel the deal and pay Gibson the $7.5 million kill fee.

"I apologize for all this," Watson said, "but it's too important for our company to let it slide."

"I'm very disappointed," Chambers replied. He hung up and called Bill Simon, who was in England. Simon was furious. An agreement was an agreement, a deal a deal. Once it was struck, you stuck. Chambers called Gibson's president, Tom Cooney. Cooney too was furious. Given the price of Disney's stock at the time, Gibson's shareholders stood to receive the equivalent of about $23 for each of their shares in a straight two-for-one stock swap—about $7 per share less than expected.

The next day Chambers called Watson at home in Newport Beach. He had talked to Bill Simon about abandoning the collar. Simon didn't like it. He was even less pleased at the idea that Disney would cancel the deal if he refused to go along. "Ray, he's outraged you would even suggest it," Chambers told Watson. "He's authorized me to give you his phone number in Europe if you want to call him."

Watson knew Simon slightly. During the seventies, they had served together on a corporation set up by Congress to oversee federal loans to new homeowners; since the Gibson agreement, Simon had called Watson periodically to express his enthusiasm for Disney and to explore the possibility of becoming a director. But Watson did not want to argue with him over this latest development and refused to make the call. He saw no reason, he told Chambers, to make a long-distance call to Europe so he and Bill Simon could compare notes with each other on who was the most self-righteous. He didn't expect Chambers to be sympathetic. He was informing him that in the best interest of its shareholders Disney had to take this step, and Chambers and Simon would have to deal with that. "We're prepared to announce on Monday the cancelling of this transaction unless you agree to our terms," he said. "That's what you have to decide."

All that weekend Ray Watson was once again on his patio in continual conference via the portable phone with Ron Miller in Encino and Don Drapkin in New York. Drapkin in turn was negotiating with the Gibson lawyers and investment bankers.

The Gibson people argued that their company was having an even better year than anticipated, and that therefore Disney should grant them some concessions. At one point Watson was called by Bill Kearns, the Lehman Brothers investment banker who was on the Gibson board. There was no way Lehman Brothers, which had to write a fairness opinion on the sale, could recommend the revised deal to Gibson's shareholders, Kearns said. It wasn't fair to them.

"You're going to do what you have to do," Watson replied. "I respect you. If you need to turn this down, you need to turn it down. I don't have a problem with that. That isn't going to change my mind."

By the middle of Sunday afternoon, Watson was convinced that the Gibson deal would collapse, that it had "cratered," as the investment bankers liked to say. So sure was he that he called Ray Chambers to say he would compose a press release complimenting Gibson and announcing that both parties had agreed to terminate the sale. He also called Stanley Gold, who was hosting a barbecue for family and friends in his backyard.

"It looks like Gibson's dead," Watson said.

"Terrific!" Gold replied. "Wonderful! That's marvelous news. It's going to make Roy happy. It's going to make Sid happy."

Watson admitted that he was relieved, adding that perhaps now they could get on with the business of running the company. He told Gold that Bill Simon and Ray Chambers had complained bitterly about the fact that Disney was backing out of the agreement.

"You want to blame it on me?" Gold said. "I'll be the bad guy."

"No. No," Watson replied. "I can take care of it."

Stanley Gold was jubilant. He had been sitting around eating barbecue and an important issue had been decided in his client's favor. He called Roy Disney, who was on vacation in Hawaii.

"They've dropped the Gibson deal."

"Well," Roy Disney said. "We have accomplished something."

An hour later, as Watson was writing his press release, he received another call from Don Drapkin in New York. Ron Miller was also on the line. Drapkin had first called Miller and convinced him it was possible to salvage the deal, providing he and Watson were willing to soften their position ever so slightly.

"They want to make it," Drapkin said. "You can get a compromise, but you've got to pay some sweetener over and above your position."

Watson reminded Miller that consumer products were not his field. "*You* have to decide how much further you want to reach," he said.

"I can't decide," Miller said.

"Well, do you want to compromise?" Watson asked.

"Yes," Miller said.

"What do you think, Ray?" Drapkin asked.

"I'd stick with the original proposal. That's the only way there is with me. But if you do that, the deal is dead wood." Again, Watson said he would defer to Miller.

Inexperienced in such matters, Ron Miller found it hard to judge the numbers on Gibson and decide for himself whether or not it was a good deal. He relied, perforce, on his advisers, and both the Morgan Stanley investment bankers and the Skadden, Arps attorneys advocated the deal, as did Bo Boyd of Disney's consumer products division. Miller told Drapkin to see what kind of compromise could be reached.

Complicated discussions ensued between Drapkin and Ray Chambers, talk of escrow accounts and open-ended agreements. In the end, Chambers said he would accept a two-for-one stock swap if Disney paid Gibson's shareholders an additional $30 million in cash—an amount equal to Gibson's projected earnings for 1984. At one o'clock Monday morning, an agreement was reached.

. . .

At 6:15 A.M., little more than five hours after Gibson had been renegotiated, Stanley Gold took a phone call from a broker.

"Did you see the news on Disney?" the man asked.

"Read it to me," Gold said, not wanting to reveal what he knew in case the broker was probing for inside information.

He expected to hear the announcement that the deal had been canceled, but the story merely described some minor amendment to the transaction. Gold couldn't believe his ears. The broker then quoted an analyst as saying that this might mean a further decline of 40 cents a share in Disney's stock. Gold thought: 40 cents? In his view, Disney was overpaying on Gibson by *$150 million*. That was more likely to send the stock down $5 than forty cents. The analyst was an idiot.

Gold dialed Hawaii. "I hate to tell you this, but it's back on again," he informed Roy Disney.

After hurrying to the office, he put in a call to Ray Watson. Watson failed to return it, and as the hours slipped by, Gold stewed. He was a director, a member of the executive committee, and the lawyer for Roy Disney, who was one of the company's largest shareholders and the son of its cofounder. Yet the chairman of the board of Walt Disney Productions was ignoring his calls. His sense of outrage mounting, he sat down and drafted a letter.

Watson finally returned Gold's call late that afternoon.

"How could you let me hang out there?" Gold asked. "All that business, Ray, about cooperating with us and getting along with us and asking for our guidance is just baloney. You don't mean it."

Watson reacted with equal indignation. "What do you think you're doing, running this company? I have to consult with you on everything?"

"You consulted with me on Sunday," Gold said. "You told me there was no deal. Now, you can't convey bad news to me?"

Gold had not yet sent Watson the letter, and so he read it over the phone.

Dear Ray,

Monday's news that the Gibson Greeting transaction was proceeding (albeit in a slightly altered form) came as a disappointing surprise. . . .

I urge you to reconsider this transaction. I have explained my substantive objections to it and would be happy to do so to the entire board, if you would call a meeting. Although you have been advised by your counsel that a Board Meeting is unnecessary (with which advice I disagree since the form of the transaction has changed from one of all stock to one of part stock and part cash) I would have hoped that you would have welcomed advice from your Board Members (to say nothing of an executive committee meeting to discuss this matter). I want you to know that because of the changed nature of the transaction, including the expenditure of $30 million cash, without Board approval or Board discussion, I do not believe that management has the authority to complete this transaction.

I would appreciate receiving from you by messenger copies of all written agreements relating to the Gibson transaction; all correspondence concerning it; and a full description of any oral agreements with Gibson principals or relating to this transaction. I regret that my first correspondence with you since becoming a Board Member has to deal with such a highly charged subject; however, I would be less than frank with you if I did not express my unhappiness with the transaction on its merits and the shabby way it appears to have been pushed through the Company this weekend without my ability to know of it or comment on it.

Kindest personal regards.

Very truly yours,
Stanley P. Gold

By the time they hung up, both Gold and Watson were openly angry. Gold believed he had been betrayed. Watson believed Gold was trying to interfere in areas that were the proper responsibility of management. Watson also saw that the reconciliation he had worked so hard to effect between the Walt side and the Roy side of the Disney family might well collapse.

.   .   .

Even though the changes in the deal made the acquisition of Gibson somewhat more favorable to Walt Disney Productions, a number of prominent stockholders now joined Stanley Gold in agitating against it. Sid Bass called Ray Watson personally to complain.

"The price is too high, Ray," he said. "Bailing out for $7.5 million was the cheapest thing Disney could do. I tell you, Ray, you're making a mistake to go through with it."

"I have nothing to indicate that this is a mistake except your opinion," Watson replied. "We've gone through the analysis. I've got a board that put itself on the line to vote for it. How can I go back and say it's a mistake?"

It seemed to Watson that his answer annoyed Sid Bass. But Bass, who had promised never to interfere in the management of the company, often seemed to get a little irritated when Watson failed to follow his advice. As Watson had told him on one occasion when Bass had complained that Disney's chairman wasn't listening to him, "I think the only problem is that your definition of listening is obeying."

Ray Watson firmly believed that the Gibson decision was a management prerogative. He also had the opinion of Skadden, Arps that the Disney board did not need to meet again to confirm the deal, although the terms were slightly different from those already approved. Nonetheless, in an effort to defuse the growing opposition, Watson arranged for Morgan Stanley to give its by then well-rehearsed presentation on the greeting card company to the Basses and to Roy Disney's Brain Trust. The meeting took place on July 6 in one of the small theaters at the studio.

Though Watson had tried to persuade Ron Miller to take the lead in promoting the Gibson deal, Miller, uncomfortable speaking to groups of any size, preferred that Watson open the meeting. "I know you all think we wanted to acquire Gibson as a defensive maneuver," Watson said. "And now that the threat is over we ought to give it up. But that's not the reason."

Peter Kellner then made the presentation, which was a fully orchestrated affair with blown-up greeting cards, freestanding graphs, and a plethora of numbers. He spoke glowingly about the marketing possibilities for Disney's consumer products division and about the "synergy" between the two companies.

The dissidents were unmoved. Stanley Gold pointed out that the essence of the greeting card business was copyrights: If you owned those, the rest was easy. So why buy a greeting card company when you could create your own? Besides, Gold said, he had "run some numbers." The value of Gibson was precisely $162 million; Disney was paying almost twice that.

Gold's suggestion that Disney start its own greeting card company struck Disney's advisers as naïve. It could take years to build a market position like Gibson's from scratch.

Then Sid Bass got up. He too thought Disney was paying too much for Gibson. The greeting card company wasn't worth more than $150 million. Even if it were, Sid Bass said, the perception in the marketplace was that Disney was paying too much, and that was going to hurt the price of the stock. Disney ought to cancel Gibson, and use the money to repurchase some of its own stock.

Bob Greenhill of Morgan Stanley offered a lengthy discussion of multiples and premiums and the full valuation of Gibson, pointing out that Disney would have to pay cash to buy back its stock, whereas the Gibson deal was primarily a noncash transaction. For Disney to buy up a block of its own stock at that time would be a mistake.

The debate continued during a lunch Stanley Gold and Sid Bass had with Ray Watson and Ron Miller, but no one's mind was changed.

"Sid, it was a great meeting," Watson said as Bass and Gold prepared to depart.

"It *was* a great meeting," Sid Bass replied. "It just came out wrong."

Stanley Gold drove Sid Bass to the airport. That morning, he had met Bass's plane, and because of the rush hour traffic it had taken them more than an hour to reach Burbank. Over the course of these two rides, they had discovered that they had more than Disney in common; despite their contrasting personalities, they liked each other. It was the beginning of an alliance.

The objections Gold and Bass raised to Gibson all had to do with price and fit and value and strategy. These were all matters of business. But one of their major objections, which they had not mentioned to

Disney's management, had nothing to do with multiples or premiums or even greeting cards. Quite simply, they did not want William Simon to control approximately one-sixth of Disney's stock. A thin man whose thick glasses magnified the size of his eyes, William Simon possessed a notoriously forceful personality. In a 1983 profile in *Newsweek* magazine, he was called a "gorilla" who could be "brutal" to subordinates. A profile the following year in the *Wall Street Journal* — in which Simon complained of being called "a gorilla in the press" —also mentioned his "brutally demanding nature." Yet another profile a year later in *Business Week* said Simon's "demanding" nature had once earned him the nickname "Bad Bill" among his subordinates. As one of Disney's largest shareholders, Simon would inevitably demand to be made a director. He would then probably attempt to dominate the board. And neither Sid Bass nor Stanley Gold wished to see center stage occupied by Bad Bill.

On July 12, Ray Watson had lunch with Roy Disney. To ensure privacy, they ate at the Lakeside Golf Club near Shamrock rather than at the studio commissary. The object of the lunch was to enable the two men to get a feel for each other, not to debate Gibson; although they had known each other for ten years, they had never really talked.

"Tell me what the problem is, Roy," Watson said when they sat down. "Give me a little bit of history."

Disney explained his objections to the operation of the studio.

"You never spoke up at a board meeting," Watson said.

"I don't find it comfortable to talk at meetings like that," Disney replied.

"In that case," said Watson, "you should come to me directly, so we don't find ourselves in a situation where you resign and no one knows why. It was a big mystery. It caused all of us trouble."

Disney then described his unhappy relationship with Ron Miller and with the Walt side of the family in general, and his doubts about Miller's ability to run the company.

"But you've made a commitment to work with him," Watson pointed out. "You can't tell until you work with him."

"I'm willing to work with him," Disney said.

Watson suggested that Roy and Ron have lunch with him in the studio commissary to show some unity in front of the employees. There was a lot of speculation that the two men were at each other's throats, and that wasn't healthy for the company.

"I agree one hundred percent," Disney said.

They lingered at the table for two hours, and as Watson drove back to the studio, he began to believe that maybe the trouble was over.

The following day, however, he received a call from Ronald Gother, a lawyer with Gibson, Dunn & Crutcher, who represented Walt Disney's widow, Lillian Disney, her daughter Sharon Disney Lund, and the Disney trust. Gother wanted to review the Steinberg buyback, and the Arvida and Gibson deals. Essentially, he wanted to find out for his clients what was going on at the company, because his clients were not being informed. They had seen their stock fall some twenty points in less than a month, and all they knew was what they were reading in the papers, which was almost entirely critical. They were also concerned about Roy Disney's return to the board.

Watson had assumed that Ron Miller was keeping the Walt side of the family abreast of developments, but apparently Miller's separation from his wife had created a gap in communications, and, despite her public proclamations, Lilly Disney's support for Ron Miller had wavered. In fact, Gother said, Lilly Disney had become so upset and confused during Steinberg's takeover attempt that at one point she had thought of selling her stock in the company.

It would be catastrophic if the Walt side of the family suddenly turned against management, and through Gother, Watson tried to allay their fears. He explained that the decision to bring Roy Disney back on the board was an attempt to reconcile the two sides of the Disney family and to provide some much-needed stability to the company. Lilly Disney and her daughter needn't worry that he was going to dominate the other directors.

Because of its unorthodox practices, Jefferies & Company, the Los Angeles brokerage house through which a number of arbitrageurs had sold Disney shares when the New York Stock Exchange halted trading in the stock, was a firm with strong ties to the maverick fringe of the investment community. It was through Jefferies' Chicago office that Irwin Jacobs had placed his order for Disney call options the day

Mike Milken approached him about participating in Steinberg's tender, and when Jacobs began acquiring stock in Disney in late June, he did it through Jefferies. By mid-July Jacobs had scooped up some $10 million worth of Disney, and the Minneapolis investor's purchases were naturally a matter of considerable interest to the head of the firm, Boyd L. Jefferies himself.*

A close friend of Stanley Gold—Gold, after all, was another maverick—Jefferies was well aware of Roy Disney's position in Walt Disney Productions, and during a conversation with Gold, he suggested that his old chum contact Jacobs. The same day, Gold put in a call to Minneapolis. He and Jacobs wasted little time on formalities.

"Why are they pursuing this Gibson deal?" Jacobs asked.

"You're talking to the wrong guy if you want an answer to that question," Gold said, then ran through his complaints about Gibson and described the Morgan Stanley presentation. He told Jacobs that he had valued Gibson at $162 million and that Sid Bass had said it was worth $150 million. Management was paying *twice* that much for it. Jacobs agreed it was outrageous. The two men decided to get together soon.

Gold had also been in touch with Ivan Boesky. Much of Boesky's large stake in Disney had reportedly been bought late, after the price of the stock had surged to $60 a share in takeover speculation, which meant that his losses were even more severe than others' when it subsequently declined. Hence, while many arbs had sold their Disney stock after the buyback and eaten their losses, Boesky had hung on, hoping that another takeover attempt would drive the price back up. Not surprisingly, Boesky, too, was against the Gibson acquisition.

So Gold called Ray Watson to say that now four of the company's largest shareholders—Roy Disney, Sid Bass, Irwin Jacobs, and Ivan Boesky—opposed Gibson. Watson reiterated his position that acquisitions were issues to be decided by management and the board. Gold urged Watson to listen to the people who owned the company.

"Have you discussed this with Sid Bass?" Gold asked.

Despite their confrontation the weekend the Gibson deal was renegotiated, Watson and Gold enjoyed each other in an adversarial

*Jefferies was among those subpoenaed in the insider-trading scandal in the fall of 1986.

sort of way. They could kid around. So, to avoid another argument about stockholder rights, Watson attempted a diversion. "You ever had a discussion with Sid Bass?" he asked. "In a discussion with Sid Bass, he comes into your office, he tells you what he wants you to do, he leaves two guys to make sure you do it, and then he walks out. That's how a discussion with Sid Bass goes."

Gold burst into laughter. He thought that was hilarious. Watson had succeeded in sidetracking him, but only temporarily. For by the middle of the month, Wall Street had started to display renewed interest in Walt Disney Productions. From a low of $45.25 shortly after the buyback, its stock had risen more than $5 as speculation about a second raid gathered momentum, fueled by the unhappiness of the institutional investors with Gibson and by rumors that, once again, someone was "taking a position" in Disney.

For Ray Watson, matters were complicated now as they had not been during the fight with Saul Steinberg, by the dispute among the directors over Gibson. Not long after Watson had assured Stanley Gold that no board meeting was required to approve the revised Gibson deal, he received a call from Don Drapkin. Some disagreement existed at Skadden, Arps; the firm was unable to produce an opinion letter supporting the legality of the deal without such a meeting, and hence was reversing itself. Board approval *was* necessary.

The meeting, on July 16, was the most difficult and divisive the Disney directors had experienced thus far. Although the atmosphere was cordial, it was obvious to everyone that the board was split in its support of management. Watson, Card Walker, Donn Tatum, and Phil Hawley spoke in favor of Gibson. Ron Miller said nothing. The four new directors all opposed the deal. Chuck Cobb argued against it on price; although his view seemed to echo that of the Basses, he insisted he had reached his conclusion independently. Stanley Gold, Roy Disney, and Peter Dailey seconded Cobb's points, adding that, whatever the price, the deal would dilute the holdings of current shareholders and made no business sense. None of this was new, and Gibson passed on a vote of nine-to-four. But the united front the board had presented through Disney's earlier trials was gone.

The directors' vote was not made public, however, and the following day Ron Miller and Roy Disney declared their solidarity by lunching together with Watson in the Disney commissary. Nothing of great moment transpired, but the three men avoided awkward subjects, and it was heartening to the staff to see the main representatives of the two sides of the Disney family sitting amicably together.

The longed-for return to business as usual lasted no more than twenty-four hours. On July 18, the very day after the solidarity lunch, articles in the *New York Times* and the *Wall Street Journal* reported that Jefferies & Company had acquired some 1.2 million shares of Walt Disney Productions, roughly 3.5 percent of the company's outstanding shares. More than half of those shares were being held for unidentified customers of the First National Bank of Minneapolis—and everyone knew who lived up there. Stanley Gold called Watson that morning. According to an "unconfirmed rumor," Irwin Jacobs was going to file a 13D on Disney, announcing that he had almost 6 percent of the company's stock and that he had bought it for investment purposes.

"If you're going to do anything about Jacobs, you should do it right away," Gold said. "You should call him. If you're going to have Disney buy him out, or whatever, you should try to get rid of the problem early on."

Jacobs filed his 13D later that day. He and four associates had acquired 5.9 percent of the stock of Walt Disney Productions, which made them for the moment the company's largest shareholders, with more stock than either Roy Disney or the Basses. As expected, the purchases were described as "an investment." There would be "no present attempt" at an unfriendly takeover, but, Jacobs said, he and his associates might buy more stock in the weeks ahead.

Disney was again "in play." As before, Peter Kellner and Joe Flom advised the company to wait and see what developed; Jacobs, after all, had declared no hostile intentions. And so, once more, the company was in a "reactive mode."

And as before, others—besides Sid Bass and Stanley Gold—began trying to tell Ray Watson how to run his business. All too often, he would pick up his phone and there would be some arb on the other end of the line, managing to sound both sanctimonious and threatening.

"You wouldn't buy back a shareholder's stock at a premium again,

would you?" one asked. "You wouldn't treat the shareholders un-
equally, would you?"

"Sir, I can't tell you what we would or wouldn't do," Watson said,
and hung up. He supposed arbs served some ecological function that
justified their continued existence. But then so did sharks, jackals,
hyenas, and vultures. And that didn't make those beasts any less
repulsive.

13

ON JULY 23, before Ray Watson had the opportunity to take Stanley Gold's advice and call Irwin Jacobs, the Minneapolis investor called him. They began by bickering over Gibson.

"You should reconsider the Gibson thing," Jacobs said.

"I won't," Watson replied.

"The deal isn't sound."

"Gibson has a lot of synergy with Disney."

"Why would you go ahead when you have so much opposition?" Jacobs asked. "You don't have to worry about Steinberg and the Reliance Group anymore. Why don't you just cut the transaction off?"

Watson said it was too late.

Jacobs persisted. "You're overpaying," he said. He argued that instead of the roughly $300 million Disney was widely understood to be paying for Gibson—a sum based on the market value of Disney's shares when the acquisition was announced—the company was actually paying about $430 million: $30 million in cash, plus about 5 million shares of Disney stock, which, Jacobs pointed out, the company itself had valued at some $78 apiece by buying back Steinberg's stock for that price.

"You should cancel the transaction or put it to a shareholders' vote," Jacobs said.

"There's no reason," Watson replied. "It's not required to go to a shareholders' vote."

Jacobs recounted all the arguments cited by Sid Bass and Stanley Gold to make the point that Disney was overpaying for Gibson.

"Look, every one of those arguments was presented to the board,"

Watson said. "They've heard them all, Irwin." Watson saw no reason now, merely because Irwin Jacobs had bought some stock, to go back to the board another time. After all, the Gibson transaction had been public information when Jacobs bought his stock. "If you thought it was bad for the company, why did you buy the stock?" Watson asked. "I mean, that's a decision you have to live with, not me."

Jacobs said he had learned from Stanley Gold that the board had split in its vote on Gibson.* Watson said that was true but irrelevant.

"Are you telling me it's a done deal?" Jacobs asked.

"Yes, it's a done deal," Watson said.

Jacobs called Watson back twice that afternoon, but Watson was out having his deposition taken for an SEC investigation into rumors that some investors in Disney had acted on inside information about the Steinberg buyback.† When Jacobs called again the following morning, however, Watson took the call. At least Jacobs, unlike Steinberg, was willing to talk.

Jacobs reiterated all the points he had made the previous day.

"I urge you to take the matter to the shareholders," he said.

"The board has considered it *three* times, Irwin," Watson said. "In my view, the shareholders elect a board to make these decisions."

"You'd better reconsider, or I'm going to talk to some shareholders myself and find out what they think about Gibson," Jacobs said. "The shareholders should vote on it."

"It's not an issue for the shareholders to decide," Watson said again.

"Look, if you will call off the Gibson deal, there is nothing to fight over," Jacobs said. "But my associates and I would be very happy to help in the restructuring of this company. Clearly you're not capable of running the thing."

Not surprisingly, by the time they hung up, Ray Watson had

---

*Much to the chagrin of the investment bankers and lawyers advising Walt Disney Productions, director Stanley Gold had been discussing the board's deliberations with a number of investors. Gold felt he was merely conveying to the company's large shareholders the results of the board's vote, which was not confidential.

†The rumors arose from the fact that the June 11 Reuters story that Disney would buy back Steinberg's stock had moved four hours before Disney's official announcement and the sell-off of Disney shares in the third market while the New York Stock Exchange halted trading. The rumors were not substantiated, and the SEC never charged anyone.

developed a pronounced dislike for Irwin Jacobs. He did not believe Jacobs really cared about the business logic of Gibson, only that the acquisition would dilute his holdings. But he had known when he bought his stock that it was going to be diluted by a pending acquisition. Thus, to Watson, Jacobs was behaving hypocritically.*

Shortly after speaking with Watson the second time, Irwin Jacobs made good on his threat to contact other shareholders. He called Stanley Gold. "I'm thinking of a proxy fight over Gibson," Jacobs said. "Will you join me?"

Gold was reluctant. He, Roy Disney, and Peter Dailey had just gone on the board, and they had done so knowing that the Gibson transaction had been approved. "It would be a little inappropriate for us to yell and scream at management in a public forum about an issue that's already been decided," Gold told Jacobs.

"But if I put it to a shareholders' vote, how will you vote your shares?" Jacobs asked.

"When it comes to that, we're going to vote our own economic interest," Gold said. "Our interest is to see the Gibson deal scuttled."

Jacobs also called Sid Bass, who said he wanted to discuss the matter in person. So the following day Jacobs flew to New York and spent several hours with Sid Bass in a suite at the Pierre Hotel. Since the two men had never met, they spent much of the time on the generalities of investments and investors, buybacks and takeovers. But they also discussed calling a special meeting of Disney's shareholders. Jacobs said he was seriously contemplating a suit against the board. Sid Bass said he would support Jacobs in every possible way. The wide-ranging conversation lasted until late in the afternoon; it was a good head-to-head, and the financiers and their retinues left with warm feelings.

Irwin Jacobs passed the next day, Thursday, July 26, in a lengthy conference with his attorneys at the law firm of Weil, Gotshal &

---

*Watson's dislike of Jacobs intensified later when he learned through depositions that Jacobs had taped their telephone calls and played them back to his associates in Minneapolis. Watson regarded this as an underhanded invasion of privacy; indeed, it was illegal in some states. Jacobs, for his part, professed not to understand the fuss over the tapings. "There was no malice intended," he said. He was simply making it possible for his associates, who also had substantial holdings in Disney, to hear for themselves the position of the company's chairman.

Manges, which had offices in the General Motors building, three blocks down Fifth Avenue from the Pierre. In order to call a special shareholders' meeting to vote on Gibson, Jacobs was required by California law to obtain the support of the owners of at least 10 percent of Disney's stock. He felt sure he had it. Though Stanley Gold and Roy Disney would not go public, Sid Bass had said he was "outraged" by the company's decision to proceed in the face of the opposition, and had promised his support. Ivan Boesky had called to say he was opposed to Gibson. An arbitrageur at the brokerage house of L. F. Rothschild, Unterberg, Towbin had also expressed concern.

Jacobs began by trying to solidify his backing with Sid Bass. Just the day before, Bass had told Jacobs he would do anything to help. But when Jacobs called, Sid Bass said no.

"How can you sit there and watch this happen?" Jacobs asked.

"We just aren't the type of people who stir up those kinds of problems," Sid Bass said. "But we will support you if you can get the deal blocked."

"Come forth, for God's sake," Jacobs pleaded.

"No," Sid Bass said. "I just can't do it."

Jacobs called Ivan Boesky.

"Let me think about it," Boesky said. "I'm thinking favorably about it, though." Later, Boesky called Jacobs back. "I've checked with my lawyers, and I don't want to get mixed up in this thing," Boesky said. "I'm going to have to stay out."

As the day wore on, and the rejections mounted, Jacobs realized that none of the major stockholders would join him in a fight. They all wanted Jacobs to make the move, take the heat, shoulder the expense. He was getting great closet support for *that.* He was reminded of a guy going into battle with all these soldiers hiding behind him saying, "Keep going, keep going. We're right here with you." Meanwhile he was the one drawing the fire.

Jacobs was particularly irate about Ivan Boesky; Boesky, he figured, owed him one. After the greenmail, the arb had watched his Disney stock drop from the sixties to the forties; now, because Jacobs's purchases had reawakened speculative interest in Disney, the value of Boesky's shares had climbed back into the mid-fifties. But would Boesky commit to the proxy? No. Jacobs decided never to have anything to do with Ivan Boesky again. He would say hello to him on the street, but Boesky could forget any deals.

By the end of that long day, however, Jacobs had been able to convince one stockholder, a large institution, to join in his suit. With the 6 percent of the stock he and his associates controlled, that meant he had the approval of more than the 10 percent of the shares he needed to call a shareholders' meeting and attempt to vote out the directors. Jacobs decided to issue an ultimatum to the board of Walt Disney Productions. They could defy it at their peril.

Ray Watson, Ron Miller, and Mike Bagnall were also in New York on July 26. In fact, they were less than ten blocks away, in the conference room at Morgan Stanley, discussing the possibility of a joint venture with a large entertainment company. The project, however, which had been conceived years before, and which came to nothing, was only one of the matters that had brought them to New York.

In the wake of the Steinberg buyback Walt Disney Productions had been publicly excoriated, especially in the financial press. Unhappy from the outset with the advice it had received on public relations from Dick Cheney of Hill and Knowlton, Disney's management, perhaps inevitably, felt the firm had failed it. Before leaving Los Angeles, Ray Watson had called Cheney's arch-rival, Gershon Kekst.

The call had taken Kekst by surprise. "You do realize I work for Saul Steinberg," he said. Kekst had in fact helped draft Steinberg's letter to Disney's director making the tender offer.

"Yes," Watson said. "I presume he hired you because you're the best in the business. We're coming to New York. Can we meet with you?"

"Of course."

It was a sweet victory for Kekst. The opponent of one of his foremost clients, crushed in a recent battle, was coming to him for advice. Moreover, that opponent had been represented by Dick Cheney of Hill and Knowlton, a firm that would not even consider Kekst for a job when, as a young man, he had first tried to break into public relations.

At the meeting, in Kekst's swank Madison Avenue offices, the PR

agent advised the Disney executives to concentrate on the press and
the financial community. Watson mentioned that Disney was still
receiving critical coverage about the golden parachutes that weren't
really golden parachutes at all; the issue had created tension among
Disney employees, particularly those executives who had not received
new compensation contracts.

"Our PR guys said, 'Let's send a letter off to everybody,' " Watson
told Kekst.

Kekst suggested that a better way to resolve this and other such
matters would be actually to meet with employees and answer their
questions. It was easier that way to reassure them that top management was looking out for their interests.

This struck Watson as thoughtful advice, and Walt Disney Productions hired Kekst and Company, even though the agency continued to represent Saul Steinberg, and even though Hill and Knowlton's contract with Disney remained in effect and Hill and Knowlton's
staff continued to labor on behalf of the company.

For the Disney executives, the most difficult part of their stay in
New York was a series of encounters with the research analysts who
covered the company for brokerage houses. One by one, the analysts
—people like Harold Vogel of Merrill Lynch, Lee Isgur of Paine
Webber, and David Londoner of Wertheim & Company—were invited to Morgan Stanley to discuss Disney's performance and its
prospects. The analysts were uniformly harsh in their criticism. They
were angry over the Steinberg greenmail and upset over the pending
Gibson transaction, both of which they said had driven down the price
of Disney stock. They were recommending that their clients sell
Disney.

There was nothing Disney could do about the greenmail, but
Watson tried to explain the rationale behind Gibson. He described the
synergy. The analysts remained unconvinced. Their clients were primarily institutional investors, asset managers at banks, and traders at
brokerage houses. Such individuals had little interest in long-term
investments; their job was to provide the best short-term returns on
the investments of *their* clients.

Maybe in five years Gibson would turn out to be a good transaction, one of the analysts told Watson. But right now his clients were

all so angry over the drop in the price of the stock that there was nothing he could tell them that would make them happy. "I don't think you're going to get over that hump," he said.

The analysts saw the greenmail and the Gibson deal as symptoms, and the condition producing these symptoms, they believed, was weak management—Ron Miller in particular. "We're angry at management and I'll define management as you, Ron," one of the men said to Miller. At least part of the company's vulnerability, as the analysts saw it, was due to the weakness in the motion picture division. It was a "drag on the company," and Miller, as chief executive, had to take the blame.

Miller protested that a turnaround was in progress, as evidenced by the success of *Splash* and *Never Cry Wolf.* But the analysts were unmoved. The stock was down thirty dollars from where it had been the year before, and the period of its decline coincided roughly with Ron Miller's tenure as chief executive; that was all that mattered.

Ivan Boesky was a gaunt man with sharp features and gray hair, whose vested black suits and white shirts gave him a rather funereal appearance, and whose appetite for work was matched only by that of Mike Milken at Drexel Burnham. Rising before five o'clock in the morning, he was driven by limousine from his Westchester estate to his Wall Street office in time for breakfast meetings. He spent his days at a desk surrounded by banks of telephones, computer consoles, and a microphone like a disc jockey's that connected him to any of the more than a hundred traders who worked for Ivan F. Boesky & Company. Although he ate little and drank less, Boesky scheduled dinner meetings on most evenings, then was chauffeured home around midnight, where he read corporate reports for two hours before going to bed. Two hours later he rose to repeat the cycle.

Rumor had it that Ivan Boesky owned about 4.9 percent of Disney's stock—the maximum amount he could acquire without having to disclose his position to the SEC. The word on the Street was that he had not bought more because he was embarrassed to reveal his bad judgment on the takeover: Before Irwin Jacobs had arrived on the scene and driven the stock up somewhat, he had reportedly been down about $15 million, and that had made him nervous.

He had telephoned Ray Watson at regular intervals, even though Watson usually refused to take his calls; he had also called Stanley Gold, who was much more forthcoming. Gold was so forthcoming, in fact, that Boesky invited him to dine at the Beverly Hills Hotel, in which Boesky's wife, Seema Silberstein, had a controlling interest. They met on July 26, the same day that Watson and Miller talked to the analysts at Morgan Stanley and Irwin Jacobs conferred with his lawyers.

"Is the Gibson deal going to go through?" Boesky asked. "What do you think of it?"

"I'll tell you what I've told Irwin Jacobs and what I've told everyone else," Gold said. "I don't like it, but it seems to me like it's going to go through. The board has voted on it."

Boesky wanted to know what Gold thought Disney's management would do in the event that Irwin Jacobs made a takeover bid. Gold thought greenmail could not be entirely ruled out, but the Steinberg buyback had created such a furor that the Disney executives would be extremely reluctant to attempt it again. This led to a broader discussion of Disney's management. Both men expressed reservations about Watson and Miller, particularly Miller. They were the same doubts voiced by Irwin Jacobs and by Sid Bass.

On Friday, July 27, Irwin Jacobs dispatched his ultimatum to each of the directors of Walt Disney Productions.

Dear Members of the Board,

As you know, my associates and I own approximately 6% of the outstanding Common Stock of Walt Disney Productions ("Disney"). I am writing to the Board of Directors to express my strong opposition to the proposed acquisition of Gibson Greetings, Inc. ("Gibson"), which I have already communicated to your chairman, Raymond Watson. It is my understanding that other substantial stockholders have also advised you of their opposition to the transaction.

Our reasons for believing that the Gibson transaction is wasteful and highly detrimental to the company and its stockholders include the following:

As we understand it, Disney would pay one half share of Disney stock plus $2.90 in cash for each of the 10.3 million shares of Gibson. Based on the price of $77.85 per Disney share which you authorized paying last month for the Disney shares held by Reliance Financial Services Corp. ("Reliance"), the total cost to Disney of the Gibson transaction is approximately $430 million and the cost of each share is $41.83.

Gibson is not worth that much. The present major shareholders of Gibson bought 100% of Gibson in 1982 in a "leveraged buyout" in which their total investment was $1,000,000. Gibson's book value on March 31, 1984 was a mere $68,073,000 or $6.61 per share. Gibson's 1983 earnings were $22 million or only $2.16 a share. Hardly enough in either case to justify a $41.83 per share payment.

You authorized the Gibson transaction when Reliance had obtained a substantial block of Disney stock and was rumored to be seeking control of Disney (and just before it announced a hostile takeover of Disney), and the transaction was perceived by the investing community as a defensive measure.

I am advised by Raymond Watson that Disney has the right to decline to consummate the transaction by paying $7.5 million in "liquidated damages." We consider $7.5 million a price worth paying to terminate this transaction.

Mr. Watson has also advised me that several members of the board—including directors who own or represent substantial amounts of stock—strongly oppose that transaction and in fact have voted against it.

Under these circumstances, we wish to reiterate our request to Mr. Watson that the directors terminate the Gibson transaction. At the very least, we believe that you would be grossly abusing your authority and discretion as directors unless you first comply with your duty to obtain stockholder approval before proceeding with the Gibson transaction which would dilute the ownership interests of all present Disney shareholders by approximately 15%. We, therefore, request that the board convene a special meeting of stockholders as promptly as reasonably possible, to vote on the Gibson transaction and that the board abide by the wishes of the stockholders as expressed in the vote at the meeting. That is the only responsible way to deal with an issue that has divided the board and would substantially dilute the holdings of present stockholders and has aroused strong opposition from major stockholders.

Please advise me by Monday, July 30, 1984 whether the board intends to comply with this request.

Very truly yours,
Irwin L. Jacobs

A number of Disney's directors were out of town and so failed to receive their copies of the letter before the deadline. Stanley Gold never got his. Ray Watson was away and had to have his secretary read it to him over the telephone.

On Saturday, July 28, Ray Watson headed north with his wife and son for a long-planned stay at Stanford Camp, a collection of cabins on Lake Tahoe run by Stanford University, where visitors were offered the opportunity to relax, hike, talk to students, and take in the odd lecture.

While Elsa drove, Watson sat beside her writing a memo to himself on a yellow legal pad. He had carried back from New York a vivid impression, conveyed to him by the analysts, of the anger and resentment on Wall Street over the decline in Disney's stock among both institutional investors and arbitrageurs. Few if any of them would be likely to support management in a proxy fight, should Irwin Jacobs start one.

In other words, Walt Disney Productions was still in crisis. Despite Arvida, despite the buyback, despite Gibson, the company remained frighteningly vulnerable. The question was, what could be done to guarantee survival? Watson wrote:

Disney's primary support historically comes from the Disney family and the institutional investors. Today that support is at best precarious. The Disney family is seriously split in their support, and the analysts suspect this. Roy Disney's resignation from the Disney board confirmed what many had long suspected. Few knew of the split between Card Walker and Roy but the resignation was seen as a clear vote of no-confidence for Ron. This was followed by the separation of Ron and Diane. The marriage difficulties indicated erosion of support from the Walt side. When all of this was put in the same crucible with the investment community's suspicions that Ron got the job more because of who he was married to than for what he had done, then any kind of bad business news made the company vulnerable. . . .

[The investment community] knew little of Ron when he was made CEO, they have seen little of him since, and they are judging his performance on the buyout decision. The negative of that act in their minds was not balanced by the image of a strong leader. . . .

Thus their view is that we are a rudderless boat caught in a violent storm. . . . We need to resolve the [Ron Miller] issue as soon as possible. Perceived lack of leadership hurts all alternatives.

"A rudderless boat caught in a violent storm." That was Wall Street's perception of Disney. It hardly mattered any longer whether the perception was accurate. Perceptions so often created their own reality on Wall Street. If brokers thought the market was going to go up, they would all place buy orders, and then the market *would* go up. If they thought a company was mismanaged, they would sell their stock in it, the stock's value would fall, and the remaining shareholders would take this as an indication that the company *was* mismanaged. A simplification, perhaps, but that was how Ray Watson saw the market's behavior with regard to Disney.

On Monday, July 30, Irwin Jacobs filed suit against the directors of Walt Disney Productions to block the acquisition of Gibson Greetings. His object was not so much to win his case in court as to increase the pressure on the Disney executives, draw public attention to the dispute over Gibson, and mobilize shareholder support for the upcoming proxy fight. It was Jacobs's opinion that Morgan Stanley and Skadden, Arps always tried to lawyer their opponents to death; he decided to outdo them. "I don't care what it costs," he told his attorneys at Weil, Gotshal. "Bring in all the lawyers necessary."

Weil, Gotshal put fifty-two lawyers on the case, in Washington and Los Angeles as well as New York. They filed interrogatories and gave notices of deposition to everyone involved with Disney and Gibson, from Card Walker and Stanley Gold to Ray Chambers and Peter Kellner. They "triple-tiered" those depositions, holding as many as three at once rather than conducting them sequentially, the normal process. In two days they deposed twenty-one individuals. The bill for the two weeks of legal work that ensued came to $3 million. Irwin Jacobs paid it all himself.

Shortly after filing the suit, Jacobs received a call from Saul Steinberg. The two had not talked since the day of Steinberg's tender announcement, though Steinberg had sent Jacobs the check for his commitment fee of $570,412.48 along with a letter saying the payoff was "better than a heartbeat." Now Steinberg was calling to laud Jacobs for his position on Gibson. He was not offering to help in any way—he had signed a standstill preventing that—but he did encourage Jacobs to stand firm against Disney's management.

Jacobs thought he would rib Steinberg a little. "Saul, you should be the last to call," he said. "You sold out to them for greenmail."

"Irwin, it was blackmail," Steinberg said. "They had me in a corner and there was nowhere for me to go."

Ray Watson spent too much of his vacation at Stanford Camp on the telephone. Since his cabin did not have one, incoming calls were taken at the main office. One of the students would trot down to the cabin with the message, and Watson would hike back up to the main office to return the call. Thus inconveniently he not only "received" Irwin Jacobs's letter of July 27 to the Disney board; he subsequently conferred several times a day with Don Drapkin and Peter Kellner about possible responses to Jacobs's suit. The two advisers calculated that Jacobs had the support of enough shareholders to call a special meeting—and he might even be able to win a vote on Gibson.

One day a student appeared at Watson's cabin door. "You have an emergency call," he told Watson. "They're holding on."

Watson was reluctant to get on the phone without knowing the identity of the other party. It could be an arb or a reporter. He asked the student to go back and take a message. Fifteen minutes later he walked up to the office. "Can you tell me who it was who called?" he asked.

"No," the student said. "They got angry and hung up."

It could have been anyone: Stanley Gold, Ivan Boesky, Dan Dorfman. But Watson suspected it was Irwin Jacobs. He decided Jacobs was the type to get angry and hang up if Watson didn't come running.

Another day Stanley Gold called to urge Watson to drop Gibson and pay the $7.5-million kill fee. "Get rid of Gibson and you take the wind out of Irwin's sails," Gold said. He also recommended that Watson meet Jacobs. "It's not a matter of liking him," he said. "You don't have to like him. But he's a man of substance. He can launch a proxy fight costing five million dollars with some very good lawyers. Face reality."

"We've made a decision," Watson said. "It's a good deal."

"It's such a good deal it's going to have your ass and Miller's ass out of the company," Gold retorted. "You've put together the impossible coalition. Irwin Jacobs, Sid Bass, Ivan Boesky, and Roy Disney couldn't agree on where to have dinner tonight. But you've given them an issue that's brought them all together. You've got to stop Gibson, Ray."

"Some of the directors hate the idea of backing down before Irwin Jacobs."

"It ain't Irwin Jacobs," Gold said. "It's your own team. It's Roy Disney. It's Sid Bass. Those guys aren't on the outside. They're on the inside."

All during the week Watson conducted an excruciating debate with himself over the Gibson deal. It was true Walt Disney Productions had decided to acquire the company during their attempt to ward off Saul Steinberg, that without Steinberg, Gibson would never have materialized. But that hardly meant it was an ill-conceived acquisition. In fact, Watson believed, it was good business for Disney; it represented the aggressive management style the company should have displayed long ago. The synergy was undeniable, and so were the long-term values. Gibson and Disney fit. "Without Steinberg we wouldn't have acquired Gibson—but we should have," Watson kept saying to people.

There were other factors to be considered as well. Once an agreement had been struck, Disney's credibility was at stake. As Ray Chambers had said, a deal was a deal. If management reversed its stand on Gibson—after weeks of advocating it—people would begin to wonder, even more than they had already, what was going on at Disney. What were guys who couldn't even make up their minds about a simple acquisition doing running a Fortune 500 company? To squelch the deal, moreover, would be seen as an admission that it had been undertaken for no other purpose than to forestall Steinberg, and that, given management's insistence to the contrary, would be embarrassing. Even worse, canceling Gibson would give the impression that Disney had allowed itself to be bullied by Irwin Jacobs. If Disney yielded on Gibson, what would Jacobs demand next? It was hard to imagine that he would quietly return to Minneapolis. And conceding Gibson would only encourage Sid Bass and Stanley Gold and Ivan Boesky to believe they, too, could intimidate Disney's management. Thus, management's authority would be further eroded and the widespread perception that Disney's executives were weak would be hardened. And that could well tempt yet another raider.

On the other hand, the Gibson issue refused to go away. It continued to divide Disney's board. Major stockholders were in open revolt. Jacobs had already sued and was preparing a proxy fight. Watson had tried to tell the dissidents that, whatever they thought of Gibson, the deal was done, a decision had been made, and the company was moving forward. But the shareholders had refused to drop the matter. There might have been no fight had Gibson not been a company bought less than two years earlier for $1 million in cash and had its largest shareholder not been "Bad Bill" Simon. But those were the facts. Simon's $300,000 cash investment in Gibson was going to turn into $70 million worth of Disney stock. And Simon would become Disney's dominant shareholder. Disney's current shareholders intended to prevent that from happening.

Gibson had turned into a mess, and Wall Street blamed management for the debacle. Instead of appearing decisive for sticking with Gibson despite all the opposition, Disney's executives were said to be childishly intransigent, unable to acknowledge that they had made a mistake. That they would be condemned as childishly indecisive if they changed their minds did not alter that reality: Since Sid Bass and Stanley Gold and Irwin Jacobs were not going to give up, persisting with Gibson would only fuel the hostility against Disney on Wall Street and prolong the paralysis that gripped the company.

By the end of his week's "vacation," Watson had made his decision. Gibson had to go. More important, the management issue had to be resolved.

14

B Y JOINING THE board of Walt Disney Productions, Roy Disney, Stanley Gold, and Peter Dailey had committed themselves to working with management, though they were still of course free to express independent views. Hence, in part to promote Roy Disney's proposals for the company, but also to get more of a feel for the place himself, Stanley Gold had arranged appointments with Disney's divisional heads. During the month of July, he had met with Jim Jimirro, the head of the Disney Channel, with Dick Morrow, the general counsel, and with Richard Berger, the head of production at the studio.

Berger told Gold that he believed Disney would best be served by a larger but still relatively modest production schedule; he intended to put out six to eight pictures a year. Gold said his client had much larger ambitions. Roy Disney wanted the studio to return to what he believed was its rightful place as the "wellspring" that gave the parks their reason for being. He wanted Disney to produce up to twelve pictures a year, which would place it in the ranks of Hollywood's major studios. He no longer wanted Disney to be an afterthought in the movie industry. He no longer wanted it said that in Hollywood there were the six studios and then there was Disney. Berger said that sounded wonderful. But he wondered whether it was possible.

On Friday, July 20, Gold met with Ron Miller in the chief executive's office. Despite the Jacobs threat, Miller was in a good mood over the success of *Splash,* and also the word-of-mouth on *Country,* which was probably the most serious and politically controversial film ever made at the studio, dealing as it did with the bankruptcy of a small farm and the disintegration of the family that owned it. Miller and Gold had a pleasantly rambling conversation. But the object of the meeting had been for Gold to find out whether it was possible for Roy Disney, who wanted to get back into the family business, to return to the studio in some capacity. Miller was perfectly willing to discuss the matter, but in the end, he said he saw no real place for his cousin-by-marriage in the company just then.

On Saturday, August 4, in his dual role as Disney director and attorney for one of the company's largest shareholders, Gold spent the day in his backyard with Richard Rainwater, the man who worked side-by-side with Sid Bass on the Basses' major investments. A convivial man of Cherokee Indian and Lebanese descent, Rainwater had helped Sid Bass formulate the Bass brothers' basic investment strategy, which involved identifying and then putting money behind the best executives in a given business. Rainwater was interested in Roy Disney's reasons for insisting on changes at the company. Was he motivated primarily by economic considerations, or by an emotional desire to strike back at Ron Miller and Card Walker?

"No, there is substance in what Roy wants," Gold said. "He believes in creativity."

Talk about creativity made Rainwater edgy. Like Sid Bass, Richard Rainwater was a hard-asset man, uncomfortable, from an investment point of view, with the entertainment industry. It was just so unreliable. Only after Gold had given some economic reasons for such an innovation as regular Sunday-night Walt Disney movies on television—free advertising for the theme parks, promotion of the trademark—could Rainwater see the point.

Gold provided Rainwater with a capsule history of the company. Under Walker and Miller, he maintained, the emphasis had shifted away from the studio.* A new leader was necessary to revitalize the whole company by restoring the primacy of the film division.

"Well, if you know this business so well, who should be running Disney?" Rainwater asked.

"There are lots of people who might run it," Gold said. "One of the guys you ought to talk to in terms of quality executive talent is Frank Wells."

"Okay," Rainwater said. "Where can I meet him?"

---

*This was not entirely so; the shift had actually begun under Walt Disney in the 1950s. But Walker and Miller had certainly encouraged it.

"Where will you be?"

"Nantucket." Rainwater, who had worked for the investment bank Goldman, Sachs & Company before joining Bass Brothers, spent summers on the island, a popular retreat for brokers, bankers, and corporate chieftains. He was flying there the following day.

From a chair in his backyard, Gold tracked down Wells, who was in the Rocky Mountains. "What are you doing for the next couple of days?" he asked.

"Not much. What do you have in mind?"

"I want you to see Richard Rainwater."

"Fine. Where do I find him?"

Gold gave Wells the address.

Since early summer, when athletes in Los Angeles for the Summer Olympics had taken over the UCLA track, Stanley Gold and Frank Wells had been doing their jogging along a course that ran from Coldwater Park up through Franklin Canyon to Mulholland Drive. It included a steep straight climb the two men nicknamed Character Hill; Stanley Gold never made it to the top, but Frank Wells usually did.

By this time, Wells's involvement with the Brain Trust had tapered off. Though Gold still kept him apprised of developments at Disney, he had been rejected for an executive position by Ron Miller when Gold, Roy Disney, and Peter Dailey had joined the board, and he was still under contract at Warner Brothers. Now it once more seemed that an opportunity might arise for him to go to work for the company.

Wells flew to Nantucket immediately, and over the next three days he and Richard Rainwater got acquainted. They found they were both decisive by nature, with little tolerance for those who dithered, and cosmopolitan in perspective, equally comfortable with balance sheets and wine lists. And they both liked to run. So Wells and Rainwater jogged along the sandy back roads of Nantucket. They exchanged ideas, talked business philosophy, and analyzed the entertainment industry. Then they flew back to the West Coast together on one of the Bass brothers' jets.

"What did you think?" Gold asked Wells during their first morning run after Wells's return.

"Damn smart," Wells said. "Those guys are damn smart."
Later in the day, Gold called Rainwater.
"What did you think?"
"We're making some progress," Rainwater said.

On Monday morning, August 6, Ray Watson had breakfast at the California Club in downtown Los Angeles with Disney director Phil Hawley. An articulate man with silvery hair and what reporters called movie-star good looks, Hawley was a pillar of the Southern California establishment. He sat on the board not only of Disney but of Arco and the Aspen Institute; he belonged to the Bohemian Club and was a member of the Business Roundtable. He was an exemplar of conservative virtues, an upstanding family man with eight children. He had been on Disney's board longer than any of the other outside directors; he was also a man who had just defended a company against a hostile takeover.

An acquisitive executive, Hawley had turned Carter Hawley Hale Stores into the nation's sixth-largest retail chain by buying such upscale emporiums as Neiman-Marcus and Bergdorf Goodman. But about the time the battle for Disney got underway, Leslie Wexner, chairman of The Limited, a smaller specialty chain in Ohio, had launched a takeover bid for Carter Hawley Hale. Hawley, advised by Skadden, Arps and Morgan Stanley, had fought off Wexner by issuing 1 million preferred shares convertible into 37 percent of the company's equity to General Cinema Corporation—a variation of sorts on Disney's attempt through acquisitions to increase the number of its shares and thereby dilute Saul Steinberg's holdings. Hawley had also given General Cinema an option to buy his profitable Waldenbooks division —making Carter Hawley Hale less attractive by selling one of its crown jewels. The company had emerged much weaker from the fight, but it had emerged independent, and thus it was logical that Watson would bring his concerns about Disney's future to Hawley.*

During their discussion Watson avoided the subject of Gibson, an acquisition Hawley favored. Instead, speaking generally, he summed

---

*In late November 1986, The Limited attempted another hostile takeover of Carter Hawley Hale. Carter again thwarted the bid, this time by spinning off the rest of the company's crown jewels —Neiman-Marcus, Bergdorf Goodman, and Contempo Casuals—into a separate corporate entity.

up for Hawley the conclusions he had set down in his memo to himself on the drive to Stanford Camp. Walt Disney Productions was in the most desperate of straits, Watson said. It was seen as a rudderless ship caught in a violent storm. Once again, the company needed to review every option, from seeking a white knight to undertaking a leveraged buyout. Even more urgent, Disney needed to address "the management issue."

Hawley understood. "I agree with you, Ray," he said. "Let me think about it and I'll get back to you."

That same morning, Irwin Jacobs, who was preparing to fly to Los Angeles, called Stanley Gold.

"I'm going to be on the Coast for a few days," he said. "We've never met. Why don't we get together?"

"Sure," Gold said. "I can't do it on Wednesday because your lawyers are inconveniencing me for my deposition."

Jacobs got a kick out of that.

"Let's get together Thursday morning for breakfast," Gold said.

Jacobs said he was staying at the Beverly Wilshire.

"Let's do it at my house," Gold said. "There'll be some privacy. I have a very nice patio with a garden."

A few hours later, in yet another declaration of solidarity between the two sides of the Disney family, Stanley Gold had lunch with Card Walker in the commissary at the studio. Given the bitterness between Walker and Roy Disney, no one at Disney had thought Stanley would ever have the nerve to ask Walker to lunch, and no one had thought Walker would accept if Gold called. But Gold had, and Walker did. Gold made no apologies for orchestrating Walker's ouster from the executive committee, nor did Walker express regret for his behavior toward Roy Disney over the years. All that was history. Gold and Walker were pragmatists. Neither wished to waste time in recriminations. Instead they chatted about the studio, about Roy Disney's inclination to increase production and his perception of the need for a new creative head. They agreed the jury was still out on Richard Berger. Both men found the meal productive, even enjoyable. Word of it spread rapidly through the studio.

. . .

Stanley Gold arrived at the Beverly Wilshire at 7:15 on Thursday morning for his breakfast with Irwin Jacobs. He sipped a cup of coffee as he waited in the dining room. When Jacobs had not appeared by 7:45, Gold called his room.

"He left for a breakfast appointment," Jacobs's wife told Gold.

Soon it was eight o'clock. Gold was outraged, then furious. He had been stood up by Irwin Jacobs. Who the hell did Jacobs think he was? Gold drove home.

"Boy, Daddy, you're in trouble," Gold's daughter Jennifer told him when he returned. Jacobs had arrived at the house promptly at seven thirty.

"Daddy, was he *angry*," Jennifer said. "He finally made me call him a taxi because he had let his driver go."

And then Stanley Gold's daughter looked up at him and smiled. "Daddy, you're on your own," she said. "I sold my shares to him at a profit."

Such a precocious kid. Gold tracked Jacobs down, apologized for forgetting where they were to meet, and sent champagne to Jacobs's suite. The two men finally got together later in the day at the downtown Los Angeles office of their mutual friend Boyd Jefferies.

"Will you publicly support my suit?" Jacobs asked.

"That wouldn't be proper for us," Gold said, and restated the position he had taken the last time he and Jacobs spoke. "In spirit we're supporting you, but we can't come out against management."

"Well, if it comes to a vote, how are you going to vote?"

"I've already voted once against Gibson as a board member," Gold said. "I'll vote against it as a shareholder if I get the chance."

It was the best Jacobs could get.

Having decided to cancel Gibson, Ray Watson was determined to receive certain concessions from the stockholders in return. He asked Stanley Gold to schedule a meeting of some of the dissidents at two o'clock on the afternoon of August 10 at Gang, Tyre & Brown. Gold agreed on the condition that Ron Miller not attend. Watson consented. Sid Bass's lieutenants Richard Rainwater and Al Checchi flew in from Fort Worth. Brain Trust members Cliff Miller and Mark Siegel were also present.

The meeting began on a hostile note. Watson had become somewhat frayed by the months of fighting, and he had been further irritated in the past few weeks by the public ridicule to which the shareholders were by then subjecting management. Criticism was one thing, sneering another. Watson had heard that Al Checchi in particular had made snide remarks on Wall Street, calling Disney's management "dumb," saying management didn't know what it was doing, heaping scorn on management's "stupid" decisions. So once the men had gathered in the Gang, Tyre & Brown conference room, Watson turned to Checchi.

"Al, I'm glad you're here so I can say something to your face," he said. "I've heard the caustic comments you've made about management, and I presume that includes me. Al, if we're going to get along, the one thing you're going to have to learn about me is that I don't mind criticism. You just phone me up or you come and see me and you tell me right to my face whatever you think. But I don't want ever to hear it again secondhand. That's the one thing I won't tolerate. If you have the guts to say something about me you'll say it to my face. If you don't have the guts to say it to me, then shut up."

Checchi didn't say much, and the rest of the room became rather quiet as well. But they all put that uncomfortable moment behind them when Watson made his announcement.

He was prepared to drop Gibson, he said. But he needed something he could take to the directors that would give him the ammunition to get the transaction canceled. He couldn't just walk in and say, "Well, let's cancel it." The atmosphere was too bad for that. "You've got to give me something," he said again, "and it's called a standstill." Watson wanted Richard Rainwater and Stanley Gold, representing Disney's two largest shareholders after Irwin Jacobs, to pledge to support the company's management so it could present a united front to Jacobs and with any luck put an end to all the fighting and the harassment.

"Maybe we can work it out," Gold said, but Rainwater demurred. "Sid Bass is philosophically opposed to standstills," he said.

This struck Watson as moral posturing. After all, as he remembered it, the Basses had practically agreed to a standstill when they wanted to sew up the Arvida deal, although in the end the specific form the merger took—a pooling of interests—had precluded one.*

"You know, I put my reputation on the line for you guys when we bought Arvida," Watson told Rainwater. "Everybody was afraid of you. I'm the one who decided to move on it because I knew you and I know real estate. Now I'm the guy who's on the line, and it bothers me that you aren't reciprocating. I need you to show me that what I said about you—that you're honorable and trustworthy and would make good shareholders—that what I said about you is true."

"We don't have any problem with the standstill," said Checchi. "It's Sid Bass."

On the following Monday, August 13, Watson met with Don Drapkin, Peter Kellner, and Ron Miller in the Disney boardroom. Standing in front of a blackboard, he listed the pros and the cons of dropping Gibson. Then the group worked out an estimate of how the shareholders would vote in the proxy fight that Jacobs had arranged to be held the following month. If the institutional investors voted against Gibson—which was highly probable, given the message Watson had gotten from the analysts—and if the arbs, and the Basses, and Roy Disney all voted against Gibson, management would lose. The deal had to be abandoned.

There was no argument. Kellner said he would explain Disney's decision to his partners at Morgan Stanley. Drapkin would talk to Joe Flom, who believed the company should not appear to surrender to the piratical demands of Irwin Jacobs. "But Ray," Drapkin added, "you've got to get the standstill."

The next day, Watson met Stanley Gold and Al Checchi at the studio at nine o'clock in the morning to thrash out a standstill agreement. It was an immensely stressful day for Watson. His sister-in-law's husband, one of his best friends, was having a cancerous lung removed, and Watson was plagued by the fear that his friend might not survive surgery.

The haggling began immediately over terms. Would the standstill be for six months or ten years? Gold, aggressively representing the

*The Basses insisted that they were never prepared to sign a standstill on Arvida.

interests of his client Roy Disney, tried to wring concessions from Watson—even though the standstill was supposed to be the concession Gold granted in order to procure the cancellation of Gibson. Gold said it was no longer enough to terminate Gibson. He demanded a complete change in management.

"There's no way, Stan Gold, we can make that part of the package," Watson said.

Gold insisted that Ron Miller resign.

"You've got to concentrate here on Gibson," Watson argued. "If we start mixing in other issues, we're going to compound the problem. I won't discuss it."

Checchi said he wanted to work out the terms for a standstill and then present them over the phone to Sid Bass, who was in Europe. Although Sid Bass was "philosophically opposed" to a standstill, he might agree, just this once, if the terms were generous enough. Stanley Gold thought this was a waste of time. Sid Bass, he said, had stated again and again that he would never sign a standstill. This was all a farce.

At one point Gold became so impatient that he stormed out of the room. He was prepared to sign a standstill alone if Watson would link up with Roy Disney to oust Ron Miller from the company. But that opportunity would be lost if Watson persisted in trying to secure standstills from both groups. When Gold returned he asked to meet Watson alone.

"You're not going to get anywhere with the Basses," Gold said to Disney's chairman after they sat down in an unoccupied office. "They're not going to give you a standstill."

He urged Watson to declare himself a partisan of one faction or another, either Ron Miller and his supporters or Roy Disney and the large shareholders. As Gold saw it, Watson was sitting on the fence, trying to please everyone by remaining uncommitted but in reality pleasing no one. "Ray, you're going to have to figure out what camp you're in," he said.

Once again, Ray Watson, a man known for his equanimity and tolerance, lost his temper. "Stan Gold, let me tell you something," he said. "You have just stepped across the line with me. Ray Watson is in nobody's camp. Ray Watson is Ray Watson. I am my own man.

I am going to do what I believe is right, and I resent the implication that you would even think any other way."

"Okay, okay," Gold said. "You misunderstood me. All I meant was that you're never going to accomplish anything by indecision."

"I don't want any more conversation ever again about camps," Watson said.

By day's end, Watson had reached agreement on a two-year stand-still with Stanley Gold, and Gold had dropped his demand for a wide-ranging change in management. In return, the standstill would provide that Disney's executives would seek the approval of the directors loyal to Roy Disney before undertaking major transactions such as acquisitions or stock buybacks.

Checchi, however, tried without success to sell a similar package to Sid Bass. "I just can't turn him around, Ray," Checchi finally said, handing the phone to Watson. "You'll have to talk to him."

Watson got on the phone. "Sid," he said, "I'm not going to go through all the arguments. You've heard them all from Al. I think it's the key to getting the board to agree to cancel Gibson. And it's very, very important to me. But if this is a moral principle, I'm not going to argue it with you. That you have to decide for yourself."

"Ray, that's the issue with me," Sid Bass said. In his view it was a fundamental tenet of capitalism that shareholders—the owners of a company—had to be free to do what was best for the company, and that could include getting rid of management. They should never bind themselves to support a group of executives, who, in the end, were there to serve the shareholders. Watson said he understood.

And that was that. There would be no standstills. The entire day had been for nothing.

As the session broke up, Checchi asked Watson if they could talk alone. On their way through the executive suite, Watson's secretary stopped them.

"You got a phone call, Ray," she said. "Your brother-in-law is fine."

Filled with relief, Watson led Checchi into his office.

"Ray, I wanted to say something to you," Checchi said. "I've thought about what you said to me the other day, and I want to apologize. I was wrong and I want you to know I appreciate your saying what you did."

The board meeting to consider Gibson for the fourth time was to be held on Friday, August 17, and Stanley Gold and Richard Rainwater spent Wednesday and Thursday attempting to change the minds of the nine Disney directors who supported the acquisition. They divided up the board. Gold saw Card Walker and Sam Williams. Rainwater spoke to Caroline Ahmanson. In the afternoon they switched lists. Cliff Miller, who handled public relations for Phil Hawley as well as Roy Disney, was asked to call the Carter Hawley Hale chief executive.

    The argument the two men made was based on simple arithmetic: So many large shareholders disapproved of Gibson that management would probably lose the proxy fight now scheduled on the issue. And even if management won, the discontent of such a large block of shareholders would mean continuing instability and perhaps provoke another takeover attempt.

Ray Watson also spent the two days lobbying. When the negotiations with Checchi failed to produce a standstill agreement, he had decided that Gibson must be canceled even without one. Disney, in its weakened state, could not endure a proxy fight; the shareholders had to be mollified at all costs. Not only did he have to persuade the directors to vote against Gibson—after months of urging them to endorse it— but he also had to enlist the support of Joe Flom and of the Morgan Stanley bankers, whose recommendation to the board would be crucial.

    That would not be easy. Peter Kellner, who was back in New York, had called Watson to say that Morgan Stanley had held a partners' meeting and voted to recommend that Disney proceed with Gibson. Despite the possibility of losing a proxy fight, the investment bankers still felt that Disney's executives had already decided to acquire the company and that they—and their advisers—would look bad if they reversed their position.*

---

*It should perhaps be noted that Morgan Stanley was to receive a fee of approximately $3 million if the deal went through. That figure, about 1 percent of Gibson's sale price, was a standard fee. If the deal "cratered," the fee would be much less.

Watson was furious. "You know, Peter," he said, "you're out here, we go through the argument, you agree with me, then you go back and you have some sort of invisible meeting with your partners at which I'm not even present, and I then get this call that you've all taken a vote. I resent that on something this critical. It's your job to get them turned around."

Watson also spoke repeatedly to Joe Flom, finally convincing the Skadden, Arps attorney that Disney would lose the proxy fight. Flom then talked to Bob Greenhill at Morgan Stanley, and Greenhill reluctantly agreed to argue for the cancellation of Gibson at the board meeting.

Meanwhile, Ray Chambers was exercising all of his considerable suasive resources to convince Disney's chairman to hold fast. He called Watson several times. "We're willing to deal with the Basses," he said. "Bill Simon will be the greatest director you ever had. He wants to go on the board. He knows corporate America, he knows the politicians. Isn't it terrible they're putting that pressure on you, Ray?" He added, "I know you'll stand up."

The morning of the board meeting, Watson and Gold had breakfast at a restaurant in Beverly Hills. By then Watson believed a majority of the directors supported his position, and he urged Gold not to get excited at the meeting, to remain calm, to refrain from behavior that would incite the other directors. Gold said the board knew where he stood. He and Rainwater had been lobbying the directors.

This news alarmed Watson, who feared some of the directors might vote to continue with Gibson for no other reason than that Gold and Rainwater opposed it.

In fact, Gold went on, he had an appointment to talk to Phil Hawley after breakfast. He wanted to discuss two issues: Gibson and Ron Miller.

Watson's alarm increased. Gold might provoke Hawley. Watson and Hawley had already discussed the Ron Miller issue. Hawley's wife, Mary, was a friend of Diane Miller's, and Hawley was reluctant to agree to any measure that might suggest Roy Disney had seized control of the company. If Gold barged in and demanded Miller's head, Hawley could well back off from his tentative agreement that the company should reconsider its management team.

"Do you object if I go too?" Watson asked Gold.

"Not at all," said Gold, a little amused by the request. "What do I care?"

At the meeting in Hawley's office on the top floor of the Bank of California building in downtown Los Angeles, Gold made his usual arguments about Gibson. Hawley listened politely without committing himself.

Then Gold said, "Look, I came down here for this stuff, but I also came down to meet you. We have this common friend, Cliff Miller, and he thinks highly of you."

"Well, we will continue to think about Gibson," Hawley said. And then, abruptly, he changed the subject. "What do you think of Ron Miller's management of this company?"

"I think it stinks," Gold said.

"You can't talk to Phil Hawley like that!" Watson said, appalled. His worst fears were confirmed.

"I'm sorry if I insulted you, Mr. Hawley," Gold said. "But you asked a question and I gave you my answer. If you want me to lie to you, I'll play you violins."

"It's all right," said Hawley. "I understand."

"What are you suggesting about Ron Miller?" Gold asked.

"I have grave doubts about his management," Hawley said.

"You know Ron Miller isn't the CEO anyway," Gold said. "Ray is, really."

Hawley agreed that Watson was Disney's *de facto* chief executive. Ron Miller had, perhaps without even being aware of it, abdicated his position. Lacking the experience to make decisions on corporate strategy, he had done little more than endorse the decisions Watson had made. Hawley added that the outside directors had been discussing the matter among themselves for some time. Card Walker, he said, had imposed Miller on the board without seeking its consent; as a result, the directors had little vested interest in the chief executive, and their confidence in him had dwindled.

"We have to address the issue," Watson said. "How do we do it without slinking around behind Ron's back?"

The three men agreed that at the upcoming board meeting, they would recommend that the outside directors form a committee to review management. To be fair, before the board met, one of the three of them would have to explain to Miller why this committee was being formed. For Stanley Gold to do it would be in the worst possible taste. Watson said that if he broke the news, Miller would feel he had been stabbed in the back by a confidant and ally. Thus the unpleasant task fell upon Hawley.

The talk turned to possible replacements for Miller.

"Let Ray Watson be the CEO," Gold said.

Watson said he thought the suggestion inappropriate under the circumstances.

"People tell me you have someone you like very much," Hawley said to Gold. "Someone you're backing."

"You mean Frank Wells?"

"Yes." Hawley was aware that Gold had urged Watson and Miller to hire Wells in an executive capacity during the negotiations for Roy Disney's return to the board.

"I think he's terrific," Gold said. "I'd like you to meet him."

Hawley agreed, adding that he too had someone who he thought was pretty capable: Dennis Stanfill.

"I'd like to meet him," Gold said.

At two o'clock, Watson opened the board meeting. The directors looked tense, and an air of desperation seemed to him to fill the room.

"I still think Gibson is a great deal for the company," Watson began. "I have always been in favor of it for economic reasons, not just as a defensive maneuver. But the issue is tearing the place apart. It will clearly cause a proxy fight. In order to avoid that and to bring peace to the company, we ought to give it up. Although on the merits it's a good deal, it's better for the company to drop it and go forward together."

Bob Greenhill of Morgan Stanley, who had been unable to attend the meeting in person, spoke over the squawk box, urging the board to cancel Gibson. Joe Flom followed Greenhill with the same argument. Phil Hawley spoke. He didn't want to cancel Gibson, he said, but he would vote to do it.

The actual vote was thirteen to one to cancel. Robert Baldwin, the retired chairman of Morgan Stanley, refused to concede.

Immediately after the vote was taken, Watson took the floor again. Just cancelling Gibson was not going to save Disney, he said. The company was in serious trouble. Like the others, he had heard it said that management had made its recent decisions in order to protect itself. This was not true. Watson had always believed the company was more important than management. Now he wanted to have a committee of the outside directors appointed to look at all the alternatives, from leveraged buyouts to white knights, from changing management to maintaining the status quo. If anybody had an issue he wanted studied, he should put it on the table.

Ron Miller agreed. "I think we should look at everything," he said. Phil Hawley had been unable to speak privately with Miller about the formation of the management committee, and Miller apparently failed to grasp its significance.

The outside directors scheduled a meeting for September 6, two weeks away, to review the situation. When the board adjourned, Hawley asked Miller if he could speak to him privately. Miller wanted Ray Watson to join them. "I'd just as soon talk to you alone," Hawley told him.

When the two men were together in Miller's office, Hawley said he had no official report to make to the chief executive, but his telephone had been ringing off the hook with people who had questions about Disney's management, and he wanted to prepare Miller for what he thought would come from the management committee's study. He believed, he said, that the study would result in the board's asking for Miller's resignation, although he had not been officially told to tell Miller that or, indeed, to tell Miller anything.

It was a stunning blow. Miller immediately left the room and returned with Ray Watson. Then, as Watson and Hawley sat in pained silence, Disney's chief executive cried. It was several minutes before he could speak. When he regained his composure, he turned to Ray Watson.

"What should I do?" he asked.

"I think you ought to get a lawyer to protect your interests," Watson said. "Because you're too good-hearted a guy, Ron, you're liable to give away rights you have. If in fact you are severed from the company, you ought to make sure you get what's fair and just for you."

"You know, maybe it is over my head," Miller said to Hawley. "I don't know."

And then Ron Miller left the studio. Watson stayed, for there was still much to be done. Walt Disney Productions had to issue a press release; the company, it said, had canceled Gibson because the transaction had created a "contentious atmosphere" among the shareholders. In addition, the publicity department had arranged for several reporters to interview Watson by phone. Soon, he found himself defending the decision to cancel Gibson to the same journalists to whom he had advocated its acquisition. That was difficult, though less difficult than the call he had to make to Ray Chambers.

Chambers, however, proved quite civil. Disney had made its decision. Nothing could be accomplished by berating Watson. "I'm very disappointed," he said.

"Ray, you've acted like a gentleman throughout this whole thing," Watson said. "I feel bad about the fact that to some degree we've jerked Gibson around. But we did what we believed we had to do in the best interests of Disney."*

Watson got home at nine o'clock.

"Ron Miller called," his wife told him. "He asked if you were home, and when I said no he hung up without another word. I think he's upset."

"I know what he's upset about," Watson said. After briefly recounting the day's developments, he returned Miller's call.

Miller was angry—very, very angry. "Why didn't you defend me?" he asked Watson. "All you said to me was 'You ought to get a lawyer.' You didn't defend me."

That charge took Watson by surprise. "Look, Ron," he said. "I wasn't there when you had the conversation with Phil Hawley. When I walked into the room you broke down and at that moment I was not quite sure who had said what to whom."

Miller made no response to this. "Why didn't you defend me?" he asked again.

"Ron, I'm sorry," Watson said. "I really am sorry."

Miller hung up.

---

*Although the acquisition fell through, and Gibson's major shareholders failed to make the enormous profits they had anticipated, Gibson itself did not fare badly. In addition to the $7.5 million kill fee, it received the exclusive rights to merchandise Disney characters on greeting cards.

15

STANLEY GOLD BACKED out of his family's long-standing plans that weekend to make their annual trip to the Running Y Ranch, owned by Shamrock, near Klamath Falls, Oregon, to attend the Ashland, Oregon, Shakespeare festival. In fact, Gold hardly paused to celebrate the collapse of the Gibson deal. There was no time. The opportunity to install new management at Walt Disney Productions had finally presented itself.

After the board meeting, Gold called Frank Wells with the news of Ron Miller's imminent departure, and they met Sunday night to talk over developments. Sitting in Gold's study drinking grappa, Wells suggested they invite Michael Eisner to join them and bring him up to date. For some time, the rumor had been making the rounds that Eisner and Barry Diller, who had run Paramount Pictures together for the past eight years, transforming it into the most consistently successful studio in Hollywood, were about to part company with it.

Gold found Eisner's number and Wells made the call. Eisner said he would be by in about an hour; before he could come over he had to take his kids to Baskin-Robbins for ice cream.

Barry Diller and Michael Eisner had first gotten to know each other as young programmers at ABC. After dreaming up the concept of the made-for-television movie for the network, Diller had been named chairman of Paramount in 1974 at the age of thirty-two. He had hired Eisner, who was Diller's age, as president two years later.

During the reign of Diller and Eisner, Paramount's movies had included *Saturday Night Fever, Ordinary People, Raiders of the Lost Ark, Urban Cowboy, Star Trek—The Motion Picture, Reds, An Officer and a Gentleman, Terms of Endearment, 48 Hours,* and *Friday the*

13th and its three sequels. Because of the success of such films, Paramount's revenues had risen from $100 million in 1973 to more than $1 billion in 1984, while earnings more than tripled. Since April 1984, when *Terms of Endearment* had won five Academy Awards, the two men had been profiled in *Newsweek, Business Week,* and *New York* magazine, which, in a July 30 cover story by Tony Schwartz, called them "Hollywood's Hottest Stars."

Despite this enormous success, however, there was tension between Paramount's two highest-ranking executives and the new management of Gulf & Western, the New York conglomerate that owned the studio. On February 19, 1983, G&W founder Charles Bluhdorn, a tempestuous, opinionated man, had died of a heart attack; he had been succeeded as chairman by Martin Davis, the company's president and Bluhdorn's protégé.

Davis—whom *Fortune* magazine featured in an executive roundup headlined "America's Toughest Bosses"—moved quickly to consolidate his control of the company. Although he had won his job with the help of the Bluhdorn family, he attempted to undermine the influence of Bluhdorn's widow, Yvette, a board member who controlled four million shares of G&W stock.* Davis had Yvette Bluhdorn's direct telephone line from her home to the corporate headquarters disconnected, and her chauffeur-driven limousine cancelled. He also began to restructure the corporation Charles Bluhdorn had built. Selling off companies and eliminating more than a hundred executive positions, he created three divisions, including Entertainment and Communications, which he named Diller to head. And while Davis was just as hard-driving as his predecessor, he was reserved in manner; under his direction, Gulf & Western assumed a more formal, more bureaucratic atmosphere.

Michael Eisner had enjoyed a good relationship with Charles Bluhdorn, who, whenever the impulse seized him, would call the Paramount president directly rather than go through Eisner's boss, Diller. Eisner, however, hardly knew Martin Davis at all, since, when Bluhdorn ran the company, Davis was precluded by the corporate structure from participating in Paramount's affairs. And under the

*Coincidentally, Yvette Bluhdorn's attorney was Stanley Gold.

new corporate structure Eisner had no direct access to Davis; Diller, who had apparently been unhappy when Bluhdorn ignored corporate channels to talk directly to Eisner, made sure of that.

Diller was a balding bachelor whose pals included Warren Beatty and Mike Nichols. Serious and intense, he concentrated more on Paramount's business side and played the pessimist when reviewing projects. Eisner was a casual man with an effusive personality who was devoted to his three sons and his wife of seventeen years. He tended to focus on the creative side and played the enthusiast. The relationship between Eisner and Diller was a complicated one. Although their fights were legendary, they were on many levels close, and during the Bluhdorn years they had regularly shared their feelings about G&W's management, about their jobs, and even about their personal lives. But after Bluhdorn died and Davis succeeded him, Diller seemed to Eisner to turn inward, to hold himself aloof. And not only was he keeping Eisner and Davis apart, but Eisner heard that behind his back Diller was damning him with faint praise, leaving Davis to understand that Eisner was of decidedly secondary importance at Paramount. It did not take long for Eisner to become discontented with Diller's behavior and with his lack of access to G&W's top management. Eisner's alienation increased when he learned that he was the source of some discontent himself; for Davis let it be known that, despite Paramount's success, he was dissatisfied with the studio's performance.

Soon enough, distorted accounts of these problems spread through the entertainment industry. By the time the Motion Picture Academy declared *Terms of Endearment* best picture of the year, the relationship between Eisner and Diller, as well as between Paramount's top officers and the management of Gulf & Western, was believed to be so soured that "Hollywood's Hottest Stars" were said to be on the job market. And indeed, Diller, whose contract with Paramount expired in September, had secretly been approached by Marvin Davis, owner of Twentieth Century-Fox (no relation to Martin Davis), to run that studio. For his part, Eisner, who had been approached a year earlier by Ron Miller about coming to Disney, thought the studio's takeover turmoil might offer him an opportunity. An acquaintance of Roy Disney's—both were on the board of the California Institute of the Arts, founded by Walt Disney—he had asked Roy that spring about possibilities there. Roy had responded warmly and Frank Wells had later let Eisner know that if things broke the right way there might be a place for him. In July, Roy called Eisner in Middlebury, Vermont, where he was visiting his children at summer camp, and again expressed interest in having Eisner come to Disney. Now, in mid-August, with no improvement in his relationship with either Davis or Diller, Eisner had begun actively looking for another job.

A tall man with close-set eyes, receding black hair, and a generous grin, Michael Eisner was often described as engagingly naïve, even childlike. He certainly possessed childlike enthusiasms for commercial entertainment as well as almost unswerving commercial instincts. On that Sunday evening, after he had finally arrived at the Gold house, he stayed late into the night talking excitedly not about the problems at Disney and Ron Miller's impending ouster, but about making movies. Acting as if he were going to begin running Walt Disney Productions the next week, he spilled out ideas for films Disney could produce. He named directors and actors he would bring to Disney. He wanted the studio to get back into television. It could produce sitcoms, Saturday morning cartoons, and made-for-television movies. It could even rent the animated classics to the networks.

Gold explained to Eisner that he was in no position to offer him anything. He said the committee was reviewing Ron Miller's performance. If, as expected, Miller were asked to leave, the board would begin to consider candidates. Dennis Stanfill, the former head of Twentieth Century-Fox, had been mentioned by Phil Hawley, Gold said. However, he wanted the board to consider Wells and Eisner, either individually or as a team, with Eisner concentrating on creative affairs and Wells handling the business end.

"What do we do?" Eisner asked, half in jest. "Do we submit résumés and then wait to see if they call us?"

Gold said he would schedule interviews.

Ron Miller put in a brief appearance at the studio the Monday after the fateful August 17 board meeting when he had been told that in all likelihood he would be asked to resign. Hearing that he was in the building, Watson called him.

"Can I come up?" Watson asked.

"Why not?"

"Hi, *friend*," Miller said sarcastically when Watson entered his office. He then accused Watson of being a "traitor." Not only had Watson failed to defend him, Miller said, Watson had betrayed him, conspiring behind his back with the other directors to arrange his ouster.

"Ron, I'm sorry you feel that way," Watson said. "I don't know what's going to happen, but there are various things you could still do with the company, and I wish you would think about those."

But Miller was not interested in independent production contracts or other arrangements. He seemed to Watson to be consumed with rage.

"Well, I'm sorry about how you feel," Watson said again, and walked out.

Miller departed almost immediately for his place in Aspen. And he left behind him a vacuum. Since his resignation had yet to be officially requested by the board, much less submitted or announced, Watson could tell no one on the lot what had transpired. None of the top managers, from Mike Bagnall in finance to Richard Berger at the studio, knew that for all practical purposes Ron Miller no longer ran the company. Watson told them that Miller had gone on vacation, which they found somewhat odd. "What's Ron doing going on vacation at a time like this?" Bagnall asked. Watson made an excuse, and from time to time people like Bagnall called Miller in Aspen to conduct business. It was a charade, but Watson and the other directors feared for the company if yet another rumor, particularly one concerning the chief executive, began to circulate. Rumors had wreaked enough havoc at Disney already.

Watson himself maintained a normal routine as part of the pretense. He kept an appointment with Malik Ali, who was in charge of the minority enterprises connected to Walt Disney World. He talked to Sam Williams and Card Walker and Donn Tatum. On Tuesday, he met with John Baity, the lawyer Ron Miller had retained. Watson made it clear that Miller's resignation was a foregone conclusion. The only subject for discussion was the terms for his departure.

Although Irwin Jacobs had dropped his suit and his proxy fight when the Gibson deal was canceled, he and his associates were still

Disney's largest shareholders, and their intentions remained ominously vague. But Jacobs had said he wanted to meet Watson—an improvement over Steinberg—and after conferring with Disney's lawyers and PR people, Watson decided he had no reason to keep the visit a secret. So on Tuesday, August 28, Ray Watson showed Irwin Jacobs around the Disney lot and had lunch with him in the studio commissary, in full view of all the employees.

Like Sid Bass and Ray Chambers, Jacobs was intent on selling himself to Watson. He told Watson about his childhood. He said he had learned from his father that his most important asset was his reputation. "It's worth more than money and everything else," Jacobs said. He explained that he had been unjustly tagged as a liquidator; sure he'd liquidated a couple of companies, but that was in the past. Watson listened and said little. There was, after all, nothing to be gained by offending major shareholders.

After lunch, Jacobs drove off in a limousine, and Watson returned to his office, where he had an important meeting scheduled with Ron Gother and John Baity. Gother was the attorney for Retlaw who also represented Lillian Disney and Sharon Disney Lund. Baity, in addition to representing Ron Miller, looked after Diane Miller's Disney stock. He also handled tax matters for Walt Disney Productions.

Watson had invited the two men to the studio because he wanted their views on a management slate that their clients could support. He was determined that the company not go through another period in which one of the Disneys was unhappy about its management; he also wanted to impress upon the lawyers the importance of alleviating the tensions between the Walt and the Roy sides of the family, tensions complicated by Lillian Disney's erratic support for Ron Miller. When Ron and Diane Miller had separated, her support for Miller had waned. Now, just as Miller was about to leave the company, he and Diane had gotten back together. Gother reported that Lillian Disney was once again backing her son-in-law.

Watson said that Ron Miller was not the issue. Miller was no longer the chief executive, he would not return as the chief executive, and the Walt side of the family would have to accept that. In any case, the time had come to stop supporting individuals and to start supporting the company. "I no longer want to hear about what's wrong with

Roy or with Stan Gold or with anybody else, or even about the arguments between the two of you," he told the lawyers. "This company is the heritage of your clients, and you have to find a way to get together with Roy's side of the family and show a solid front. I don't know how you do that, but you do have to do it."

The attorneys agreed to try their best.

After leaving the Disney lot, Irwin Jacobs called Sid Bass from Los Angeles and briefed him on the meeting with Watson. Watson seemed like a nice person who meant well, Jacobs said, but he was in way over his head. Sid Bass agreed. Then he called Watson.

"Just got a report about your lunch with Jacobs," he said. "He likes you and he thought it was a good meeting. And the reason he likes you is he doesn't think you're going to do anything crazy."

Stanley Gold had arranged for Ray Watson to meet Michael Eisner that weekend, and on the afternoon of Saturday, September 1, Watson drove from Newport Beach up the San Diego Freeway to Eisner's home in Bel Air, a stark white mansion he had bought with a $1.25 million loan from Paramount. Eisner seemed slightly house-proud, and Watson, thinking of Tom Wolfe's book *From Bauhaus to Our House,* joked that the place reminded him of Gropius. Eisner and his wife, Jane, caught the allusion and laughed. Then the two men settled into chairs in the living room, and, after describing his own background and his perceptions of Disney's strengths and weaknesses, Watson asked Eisner to talk.

Eisner said he had always wanted to work at Disney, and he told Watson why. The son of a successful New York lawyer, Eisner had grown up on Park Avenue, attended Lawrenceville prep school in New Jersey and Denison University in Ohio, paid his dues with entry-level jobs at NBC and CBS, then joined ABC, where in 1969 he was put in charge of the network's Saturday morning children's programs. ABC was then in last place in the Saturday morning ratings. Undaunted, Eisner had set to work, proposing a cartoon series about a group of young black musicians called the Jackson Five. He followed that with a cartoon show on the Osmond Brothers. ABC leaped to first place in the Saturday morning ratings.

Eisner told Watson that during those years he had watched a lot of Disney cartoons. He thought Walt Disney was an entertainment genius. Walt Disney Productions, he said, offered him an opportunity, unavailable at any of the other studios or at the networks, to produce a special variety of entertainment—family entertainment. Eisner loved family entertainment.

But there was also a pragmatic reason for moving to Disney, Eisner said. He drew a rough chart on a piece of paper and handed it to Watson. The chart showed a line climbing ever more steeply upward from 1977 to the present. Paramount's earnings, Eisner explained, had grown from $40 million in 1977 (the year after Diller named Eisner president) to $145 million in 1984. Marty Davis wanted that line to keep going up; Eisner didn't think that kind of growth was sustainable. A studio could do twelve to fifteen movies a year, not twenty-four. The business was precarious. There was no way he and Diller could achieve what Gulf & Western thought they could achieve. The implication was that Disney, an independent studio, a company that had always been in the entertainment business, understood that.

Eisner added that he was also attracted to Disney precisely because the studio had been performing poorly. "You guys are on the mat," he said. "If I go somewhere I want to go to a place that's on the mat and build it up. That's how Paramount was when I came in. That's how ABC was when I went there."

Ray Watson thought Michael Eisner was the most impressive man he had met in the entertainment business. He was articulate and imaginative, and he had the wonderfully unabashed enthusiasm for popular entertainment that was essential for a company like Disney. Eisner also understood and appreciated the Disney culture, the Disney values. He was even a family man. Walt Disney would have loved him.

The following day, Watson drove to Beverly Hills to see Frank Wells, who provided a striking contrast to Eisner. Intense where Eisner was relaxed, Wells was a lawyer and businessman, a deal maker. "I love the business of business," he told Watson. Walt Disney Productions needed solid and professional business direction. Wells could provide that. He also enjoyed the support of some of the major stockholders. He did not, however, have Eisner's creative firepower.

Wells himself acknowledged that. At the end of the meeting, Watson told him the company was only looking for one executive, and Wells said, "Then get Eisner. You need creativity more than anything else."

Watson agreed. After he left, Wells called Eisner. "You got the job," he said.

Watson believed Disney needed to find a successor to Ron Miller immediately. He could not keep up for long the pretense that Miller was on vacation, concealing the fact that no one was running the company. Disney was more vulnerable at that moment than it had been at any time in the past year. Thus, although he had not yet seen Phil Hawley's candidate, Dennis Stanfill, on Labor Day, the day after he met with Wells, Watson sat down at the Apple computer in his study and wrote a six-page memo to the board.

In it he urged that the directors hire Michael Eisner as president and chief executive officer of the company. Eisner's primary responsibility would be to revitalize the studio. Watson also proposed that he himself remain in his current position as chairman of the board to oversee the development of Disney's real estate, though he made it clear that he was willing to step down as chairman or even to leave management altogether if the directors decided that was best for the company. The memo suggested nothing for Frank Wells or Dennis Stanfill.

Disney's outside directors, who were scheduled to meet on Thursday, September 6, to review the company's management, received Watson's memo early in the week. Their reaction was decidedly cool. Phil Hawley, Bob Baldwin, and Caroline Ahmanson believed Eisner lacked sufficient corporate experience. Eisner might be president of Paramount, but Paramount was a subsidiary of Gulf & Western, and he was not on the G&W board. One of the biggest complaints about Ron Miller had been his lack of sophistication in financial matters and his awkwardness when dealing with corporate veterans like Disney's investment bankers, its lawyers, and its outside directors. No one said Eisner would not be different; perhaps he would. But he did not have the track record to prove it, and in light of what Disney had been through in the past seven months, the company could not afford to take the risk. The directors, however, recognized Eisner's unusual talent, and asked Watson to find out if he would accept any position other than chief executive officer.

On September 5, Watson again drove to Bel Air for another talk with Eisner. This time, however, he brought with him an attorney named Joe Shapiro; Eisner's lawyer, Irwin Russell, attended as well. Watson started out by asking Eisner if he would be interested in becoming chief operating officer of Walt Disney Productions. Would he take the number-two slot?

Eisner was adamant. He wanted Ron Miller's job, he said, and no other. He suggested that he be made chief executive and that Watson remain as chairman. "The same relationship you had with Ron," Eisner said, which was exactly what Watson himself had in mind. The two men even discussed—and agreed upon—the compensation Eisner should receive if he was given the job.

In the evening Watson called Eisner at home to tell him that he was going to recommend that the board name him chief executive. "I've got a pretty independent board," he added. "They might ask for an interview or for time to study the issue. But I'm very impressed with you. I'm going to try to put it to bed."

That same night, Stanley Gold and Roy Disney met to discuss Watson's memo. It was not a complete victory: Although Eisner was on board, Wells had nothing. Wells was naturally disappointed, but, putting his own ambitions aside, he insisted that they embrace Watson's proposal. Landing Eisner was more than the Brain Trust had expected to accomplish just one month ago. "If we can get that," Gold agreed, "let's take it. We'll worry about getting the rest later."

At 8:00 A.M. on September 6, the outside directors of Walt Disney Productions gathered at the studio. Much to everyone's surprise, Ron Miller was also on the lot, closeted with Erwin Okun, Disney's vice-president for corporate communications, preparing a paper defending his tenure at the company.

After being served coffee, the directors retired to the boardroom, where Ray Watson opened the meeting. "You know your charge because I have talked to each of you individually," he told the directors. "It is the serious consideration of whether Ron Miller should remain as chief executive of this company. Let me tell you that Ron is here, and he would like to address this body." Watson then left the room, shutting the door behind him, and a sober, even grave mood settled on the nine directors ranged around the conference table. A drastic decision was about to be made. Its consequences would be immensely painful both for Ron Miller and for Walt Disney Productions.

But the directors were candid with one another. They quickly reached the consensus that Ron Miller should not continue as chief executive officer, then reviewed various methods of resolving the matter. Should Miller resign without comment? Should Disney offer him an independent production contract? Miller *was* a member by marriage of the Disney family. Should the company compensate him over and above the terms of his contract? What sort of public statement was required? After three hours of discussion, Hawley called Watson.

"We would like to meet with Ron," Hawley said. "Can you get hold of him?"

"Sure," Watson said. "He's upstairs."

Watson called Miller. "Ron, they would like to meet with you."

"Well, I haven't finished my paper yet," Miller said. He and Erwin Okun were still at work.

"I don't think it has anything to do with the paper," Watson said. "I think they just want to meet with you, Ron."

When Miller entered the boardroom, he was in control of himself, but his hurt and his anger were evident to the directors, some of whom tried to avoid his eyes and all of whom sat in silence.

"Don't you have something to say to me?" Miller asked the group. "Aren't you men?"

No one responded.

"I'm very disappointed in this," he went on. "I've given my life to this company. I've never worked anywhere else. And I've made progress with this company. I think I've taken great strides in leading it as far as it has come. I feel like this is a betrayal."

Miller then addressed the directors individually, telling each one how disappointed he was in him. When he came to Roy Disney, they glared at each other but said nothing. Then Miller turned to Stanley Gold. "Don't you have anything to say, Stanley?" he asked. "You talk so much all the time. You're really the ringleader of this."

Gold looked down at the table and, like Roy Disney, said nothing.

It was finally Phil Hawley who took the floor after Miller had finished. "As you know, we are considering the matter of whether or not you ought to be relieved or asked to resign," he said. "We understood you wanted to make a comment about that before the deliberation is completed. If you have said all you have to say, we will vote."

When Miller left, the outside directors unanimously agreed to recommend that the full board ask for his resignation. Shortly thereafter, the paper that Miller and Okun had written was delivered to the room. In a conciliatory tone, Miller described all he had accomplished while chief executive. Though he had been on the job only a year and a half he had started to turn the company around—as the most recent quarterly figures confirmed. He had established the new Touchstone label, which had released Disney's biggest movie ever. He and Ray Watson had acquired a real estate company, Arvida, that would enable Disney finally to develop the seventeen thousand acres of Florida land that had lain fallow for a decade. The company was moving close to an agreement with the French government to open a Disneyland in France, which would certainly be a phenomenal success. Miller pleaded that he be allowed to retain his position. The total lack of animosity in the letter, as well as its assumption that his dismissal could be averted, provided a striking contrast with Miller's bitter speech to the directors.

The full board of Walt Disney Productions, with the exception of Ron Miller, convened at eleven o'clock the following morning and after very little discussion unanimously called for Miller's resignation. Then one of the directors asked if Watson wanted to discuss his recommendation that Michael Eisner replace Miller. All of them had Watson's memo on the table before them. It was the only briefing paper they had received.

Phil Hawley, however, demurred. The directors had just had to remove one chief executive. They should not hire a second in haste. Other directors agreed. Card Walker had forced Ron Miller upon them just eighteen months before—and look what had come of that. They intended to proceed more deliberately this time.

"Okay," Watson said. "Fine."

Stanley Gold was flabbergasted. He had expected Watson to nominate Eisner, for the board to discuss him a bit and then vote him into office. Gold had thought they were going to be able to walk out of the meeting and announce that Disney had a new chief executive. Now the whole matter had been tabled.

Phil Hawley then recommended that a screening committee be created to interview the candidates for chief executive. It was to consist of Hawley, Ray Watson, Stanley Gold, and Sam Williams, the outside director who was a partner at Hufstedler, Miller. Hawley told the board he thought it was essential that the new chief executive have "corporate experience." Caroline Ahmanson and Bob Baldwin agreed.

Michael Eisner had spent the previous day in the belief that on Friday he would be named the new chief executive officer of Walt Disney Productions. He had an appointment at ten o'clock that morning with Martin Davis, who was in Los Angeles on his first trip to the Coast since becoming head of Gulf & Western. Eisner decided to inform Davis during their meeting that he would be going to Disney. It seemed the honorable thing to do. After all, the Disney board was convening at eleven. Eisner felt he would appear a bit underhanded if he saw Davis, said nothing of Disney, and then an hour later Disney announced that it was hiring him as chief executive.

If Martin Davis was surprised or upset by Eisner's announcement, he didn't show it. He was sorry, he said, to see Eisner leave, but life would go on.

Eisner returned to his office to await word from Disney. Eleven o'clock came and went. So did twelve o'clock and one o'clock. Eisner began to become a little concerned. Finally, well past lunchtime, he received a call from Frank Wells. Disney's board, Wells informed him, had put off a decision and had instead formed a search committee. Eisner had the awful feeling he had made a most serious miscalculation.

Drained from the Disney board meeting, Stanley Gold returned to Shamrock, where, at three o'clock, Michael Eisner appeared and described the phone call from Frank Wells. He added that he had not even heard from Ray Watson.

"You mean Ray hasn't called you?" Gold asked.

"No."

"He doesn't have the guts to call you," Gold said. "No decision at all was made on you."

"What do you mean?" Eisner asked. "Ray told me I was in last night. He said I was going to be CEO."

"I don't know what Ray told you, but it's not done. The fat lady hasn't sung the last aria."

Eisner was furious. "What kind of an organization is this? Don't you have any management? Stanley, I thought you were running the company."

"I've barely got my oar in the water, kid," Gold said.

Eisner left in disgust, and Gold told himself all his work was in shambles. Absolute shambles.

"Disney's Chief Is Forced Out" proclaimed the headline of the lead business story in the *New York Times* on Saturday, September 8. "Premium Paid to Steinberg Was Criticized," said the subhead. Hal Vogel, entertainment analyst for Merrill Lynch, was quoted in the body of the piece: "This is not totally surprising," he said. "But there is an element of scapegoatism here, too. All of this activity in the last six months is not purely attributable to Ron Miller. The directors had a voice in all of this." The article also quoted Disney's head of public relations, Erwin Okun (whom the *Times* called Edwin) as saying the company was looking for a "recognized leader" to succeed Miller, someone with "a proven corporate background, an established name."

Writing in the wake of the resignation, James Flanigan, financial columnist for the *Los Angeles Times,* called Miller "a victim of the new math in corporate America," who had lost his job "not because the studio made money-losing pictures under his tenure . . . but because he bought off, rather than fought off, a raid on the corporation." That was the consensus on Wall Street, where Disney's stock closed up 62.5 cents on the day of the announcement.

16

AT TEN THIRTY in the morning on Monday, September 10, Ray Watson and Phil Hawley met with Dennis Stanfill at Hawley's office in downtown Los Angeles. The son of a Tennessee civil servant, Stanfill had graduated from Annapolis, studied economics as a Rhodes scholar at Oxford, and then served as the briefing officer on international affairs for the secretary of the navy. He had worked as an investment banker for Lehman Brothers, and as chief financial officer of the Times Mirror Company, which owned the *Los Angeles Times*. When Twentieth Century-Fox almost collapsed as a result of the $40 million disaster *Cleopatra*, Lehman Brothers, which had long been involved in Fox's affairs, arranged for Stanfill to join the studio. He had straightened out Fox's finances and had been appointed the studio's chief executive in 1971.

During Stanfill's reign, Fox had produced *Star Wars*, which had grossed more money—$267 million—than any film in history. He had used the cash to diversify into Coca-Cola bottling plants and resort real estate. Then, in 1979, Alan Ladd, Jr., who had chosen *Star Wars*, quit as president of the Fox film division in what was seen as yet another contest between the business and creative sides of a studio. Stanfill had replaced Ladd with Alan Hirschfield, the former chief executive of Columbia Pictures Industries, who had been fired from his job after disagreeing with his board over the correct response to the embezzlement of company funds by David Begelman, the president of Columbia's studio. Hirschfield and Stanfill, however, had soon begun feuding, and when Marvin Davis bought Fox in 1981, Stanfill had resigned to return to investment banking. Hirschfield had become chairman and chief executive officer. At the time Disney began searching for a new chief executive, Stanfill was the head of a venture capital fund called Carlyle Capital Corporation.

Dennis Stanfill was the virtual opposite of Michael Eisner in experience and temperament. At Fox, he had kept his distance from the creative side of the studio. "I think of myself as a business executive," he had once said, and to Phil Hawley the key word was *executive.* Stanfill had already run an important company; unlike Eisner, he had a track record. He could make decisions and articulate the reasoning behind them. He had the respect of investment bankers and corporate attorneys. He could conduct an annual meeting and fence with reporters. He could summon up just the precise measure of authority required to put an upstart dissident director like Stanley Gold in his place. In sum, Stanfill had exactly the establishment credentials and corporate manner Phil Hawley thought Disney needed.

But Stanfill was a rather aloof man, formal to the point of stiffness (Stanley Gold called him a martinet). After his meeting with Watson and Hawley, Watson wondered what impact Stanfill's remote, impersonal manner would have on the Disney culture.

That afternoon, Watson spoke to the roughly one thousand Disney employees at the studio. The company had been awash with rumors ever since the announcement of Ron Miller's resignation; official pronouncements had consisted entirely of Erwin Okun's statements that Disney was searching for a "recognized leader" and that Ray Watson was not a candidate. Filled with apprehension, the staff wondered who was going to be made chief executive—Eisner, Wells, Stanfill, and Hirschfield were all rumored candidates—and whom among management the new leader would fire. Some held that the company was going to be sold and that widespread layoffs would follow.

Watson tried to bolster morale. Disney was only as good as its staff, he said. They deserved the best leader and Watson had dedicated himself to finding the very best. "This is for you," he said of the executive search. "It will be over soon. Hang in there."

Michael Eisner had had a difficult few days. Friday afternoon, after learning from Frank Wells and then Stanley Gold that the board had delayed a decision, and was in fact looking for someone with somewhat different experience from his own, he had tried to backtrack with

Martin Davis. He was not sure about his desire to go to Disney, he told the G&W chairman, who reacted with characteristic reserve. That evening, Eisner had attended a party for the G&W board at Barry Diller's house—an awkward event, because Eisner not only had to conceal his anxiety over the turn of events at Disney, he also had to pretend that his conversation with Davis had never occurred.

On Saturday, there was another startling development: Diller called Eisner and told him that *he* was departing Paramount, to become chairman of Twentieth Century-Fox. Eisner had had no idea Diller had been negotiating with another studio.* Although he had not told Diller of his prospects at Disney—primarily because Diller was being so secretive himself—Eisner felt Diller should have warned him in advance that he might leave, since his departure would so profoundly affect Eisner's own position. Had Eisner known that the top job at Paramount was about to become available, he might well have handled the negotiations with Disney differently, and he almost certainly would not have tipped his hand to Martin Davis; whatever Davis's opinion of Eisner before that fateful Friday meeting, it was unlikely that, knowing what he now did of Eisner's dealings with Disney, he would offer him Diller's job.

During his conversation with Diller on Saturday, Eisner asked him to refrain from informing Davis for a few days so that he, Eisner, could consider his options and try to salvage something from what looked now to be a ruinous set of maneuvers. Diller agreed. But on Monday, Marvin Davis at Fox called Diller to say it would be necessary to make an announcement that day because he had already asked Alan Hirschfield, who had started his career as an investment banker for Allen & Company in New York, to resign as Fox's chairman and set up an investment banking operation for Davis. So Diller immediately called Martin Davis, who had gone back to New York, and resigned—a talk that took place while Michael Eisner happened to be at the dentist's.

When Eisner returned home, a series of phone messages from the Gulf & Western chairman awaited him. He was ordered to appear at

---

*The lawyer who negotiated Diller's deal with Marvin Davis was Bruce Ramer, Stanley Gold's law partner at Gang, Tyre & Brown.

the company headquarters at once. Eisner, however, had a policy of avoiding at all costs the overnight "red eye" flight from Los Angeles to New York because it invariably left him somewhat groggy the following day. Also, Eisner had a meeting at eight o'clock Tuesday morning with Ray Watson and Phil Hawley, which he had no intention of canceling. He told Davis he would come to New York Tuesday.

At his meeting with the two Disney directors, Eisner retraced for Hawley's benefit much of the ground Watson had covered with him in his private interviews. Then he and Paramount's head of production, Jeffrey Katzenberg, caught a plane to New York. It was conceivable that Martin Davis would ask Eisner to replace Diller as chairman of Paramount after all—conceivable, but not likely, given the circumstances. Besides, there had been a rumor around the studio that Davis favored Frank Mancuso, Paramount's marketing strategist and third-ranking executive, for the job. During the flight, Eisner decided that Davis was not going to offer him the chairmanship of Paramount, and that his best alternative was to force Davis into a breach of Eisner's contract with Gulf & Western.

The contract, drafted when Bluhdorn was still alive, required the company to name Eisner chairman of Paramount if the position became available. If someone else was given the job, G&W was obligated to pay Eisner an enormous sum and forgive him any outstanding loans, such as the $1.25 million Eisner had borrowed from the company to buy his house in Bel Air. Eisner figured Davis probably hadn't read his contract and might well breach it without realizing he was doing so.

The two men met late into the night at the Gulf & Western headquarters overlooking Central Park. Davis said he was still undecided on a replacement for Diller, and Eisner went back to his hotel room afraid that Davis had perhaps read his contract and might devise a way to circumvent it by giving Eisner the title of chairman but not the attendant power. Then, at 4 A.M., Jeff Katzenberg called Eisner and read to him an article from an early edition of the *Wall Street Journal* which stated that Mancuso was to be named chairman of Paramount; the sources cited for this information were anonymous Gulf & Western officials, but the article did quote Davis to the effect that, under Diller and Eisner, Paramount had neither produced a sufficient number of movies nor sold enough prime-time television shows to the networks. Someone at Gulf & Western—Davis later denied he was the source—appeared to be using the *Journal* to convey to Eisner the corporation's contempt for him.

Eisner told Katzenberg that the article constituted a job offer to Mancuso, and thus a breach of his, Eisner's, contract. At a meeting with Davis that afternoon, he resigned. "The untimely death of Charles Bluhdorn and this week's resignation of Barry Diller marked a period in my life to move," he said in a hastily drafted statement. "I will always be indebted to both men."

Eisner did receive a windfall settlement from Gulf & Western. And almost immediately, Diller called Eisner and suggested he come to Fox. Other studios inquired as well. ABC asked him to come back to the network and create a film division. By the end of the week, he had four job offers. But Eisner was tired of working for someone else. He wanted to be a chief executive himself.

His prospects at Disney, however, were looking rather dubious. So were those of Frank Wells, who had also met with Ray Watson and Phil Hawley on Tuesday morning, after their session with Eisner. When the meetings were over, Hawley again raised with Watson the issue of "corporate experience"—and both Eisner's and Wells's lack thereof.

Early on Thursday afternoon, Stanley Gold tried to reach Frank Wells. Wells's secretary at Warner Brothers said he was out of the office. When Gold tried his friend's home, he was told that Wells had been called downtown for a very special meeting with Ray Watson. But Ray Watson had no downtown office. Phil Hawley, however, did, and Gold suddenly became convinced that Watson and Hawley were going to offer the job of chief executive to Wells as a compromise between Eisner and Stanfill. After struggling for months—*years*—Walt Disney Productions was finally going to install a management team endorsed by Stanley Gold and his client Roy Disney. We're in, Gold thought. *We're in.*

As the afternoon wore on, however, Wells failed to telephone. Gold called Warner Brothers again. He called Gang, Tyre & Brown. He called the Wells household. He knew all Frank Wells's private numbers and he called them all, but he was unable to reach the man.

Still, Gold was not worried. At six o'clock he was sitting on his patio with Ilene and Mark Siegel, waiting confidently for the news.

"We've got it, we've got it, Siegel," Gold said. "I've beaten them."

A few minutes later the telephone rang.

"Frank?" Gold said.

"Schmucks," Wells said.

Gold was stunned. Wells said he was standing at a pay phone in downtown L.A. He was furious. Ray Watson had just delivered an incredible insult. "Can you believe it?" Wells asked. "Watson called me down here to ask me if I would consider what amounts to head of business affairs of the film division."

Watson, who a week earlier had told Eisner the job was his, had now, Gold decided, joined with Phil Hawley in supporting Stanfill; the job offer to Wells was a bone tossed in Roy Disney's direction.

At seven o'clock, Wells arrived at Gold's house. Mark Siegel was still there. Gold called Roy Disney over. Howard Bernstein, a friend of Gold's, also dropped by. They all sat with drinks on the patio.

"It's over," Wells said. "It's over."

"Frank," Gold said, "it's just started. But you've got to do me one favor. You've got to come out of the closet."

Up to that point, Eisner, Wells, and Stanfill had all behaved with extreme caution, maintaining publicly not only that they had not been approached for the job at Disney, but that they were not interested ("I don't even know where Disney is," Eisner had said).

"There are two creeds I live by," Gold said. "One is show me a good loser and I'll show you a loser. The other is lead, follow, or get out of the way."

Wells and Siegel had heard this before.

"We ain't going down losers," Gold told them. "We're going to fight. Wells, do me a favor. The only thing I'm asking from you now is to stop this I'm-not-interested crap. Just tell the world you fucking want the job."

Ray Watson had intended no offense in making the offer to Wells.* He was merely trying, with some desperation, to find an executive

*As a matter of fact, according to Watson, the position he had discussed with Wells was not head of business affairs of the film division but head of the entire film division: Richard Berger's

configuration acceptable to the board, to Disney's restive and dangerous shareholders Irwin Jacobs and Sid Bass, to the competing factions
of the Disney family, and to the candidates themselves. It was no easy
task. It required compromise from all parties. And Watson had had
no reason to think Frank Wells would find the position beneath him;
just three months before, during the negotiations for Roy Disney's
return to the board, Stanley Gold had tried to have Wells named to
a management position of that sort. In the intervening weeks, however, the stakes had been raised. Now no one, it seemed, would settle
for anything less than a top corporate role.

It was Phil Hawley, with his constant refrain about "corporate experience," who formed the primary obstacle on the board to both Michael
Eisner and Frank Wells, and in the aftermath of the "insulting" offer
to Wells, the dispute over Ron Miller's successor assumed for Stanley
Gold the dimensions of a personal struggle. It became a contest of
wills. It became Stanley Gold versus Phil Hawley.

On Friday afternoon, the screening committee met at Carter Hawley Hale, and Phil Hawley made a strong plea for Stanfill. Stanfill
knew his market; *Star Wars* was precisely the sort of family entertainment Disney ought to be making. Stanfill was smart; he could master
the most complex financial reports. He commanded respect on Wall
Street. He was well connected. And he was available. "That's the kind
of talent we need here," Hawley said. "We can always buy creative
talent."

"You're wrong, Phil," Stanley Gold retorted. "You think creative
talent can be bought as a commodity. You see guys like Eisner as a
little crazy or a little off the wall. I don't mean to be difficult with you,"
he went on, "but every great studio in this business has been run by
crazies. What do you think Walt Disney was? The guy was off the
goddamned wall. His brother Roy kept him in check."

Once Gold hit his stride, he was almost unstoppable. "This is a
creative institution," he said. "What's been wrong with this institution
over the past twenty years is that it hasn't been run by the crazies. It

---

job. And Watson says he had not offered Wells the job but had asked him if he would take it
if it were offered.

needs to be run by crazies again. Clean out your image of crazies. We're talking about creative crazies. That's what we ought to have. We can always buy M.B.A. talent."

Not surprisingly, Hawley disagreed. "I think you're wrong," he said. "I just can't bring myself to accept that. Eisner and Wells are very, very impressive, but they're divisional. They've never run anything but a division."

"I guess that's right," said Gold, "if you call Paramount Pictures a *division* of Gulf & Western. That's a billion-dollar division. If you call Warner Brothers a *division* of Warner Communications. That's a billion-dollar division."

Hawley suggested a compromise: to offer Eisner head of production and Wells head of business affairs. He knew as well as Gold, however, that Eisner had already said he would come to Disney only as chief executive and that Wells had turned down a less-than-senior corporate role. And he was unyielding in his refusal to recognize the two men as first-rate corporate material.

It seemed to Gold that the mere mention of the creative side of the movie business conjured up in Hawley's mind images of cocaine and limousines and starlets and Jacuzzis and est seminars. It was the same view as the one held by Martin Davis at Gulf & Western: that creative types were ultimately irresponsible and untrustworthy. It was a view bitterly resented by Eisner ("I don't wear a tutu," he once said. "I don't snort cocaine and go to wild parties. I can understand a P & L").

The meeting at Carter Hawley Hale lasted two hours. In the end, no one's mind was changed. The committee could not even decide on the qualifications Disney's chief executive should have, much less agree on a candidate. Nonetheless, Stanley Gold was not displeased. In articulating the philosophical issues surrounding the leadership question at Disney, he had, he thought, made perhaps the best argument of his career.

However, Roy Disney's supporters on the board were not dealing from a position of strength; indeed, a majority of the board appeared to side with Hawley, and even Ray Watson had dropped his support for Eisner. So the Brain Trust sought a compromise. Cliff Miller proposed that Eisner, Stanfill, and Wells share the office of president, forming a triumvirate. He arranged for Phil Hawley and Roy Disney to meet on Sunday morning to discuss the idea.

It was not a realistic proposal, Hawley told Roy at the meeting. Both Eisner and Stanfill would certainly reject it, though Wells might not.

Then Roy Disney tried a personal appeal. "Phil," he said, "I've got an idea of how the studio should be run. I've had it for ten years. Everyone else in the family has had a shot at running it his way, and it hasn't worked. So why not let me have my choice of management?"

Hawley was unmoved. He had, he said, a great deal of respect for Roy's ideas, but after what the company had been through, Dennis Stanfill was, in his opinion, the right man for the job. The fact that Hawley had no personal stake in Stanfill but was simply acting on his convictions, as a director was retained to do, did little to assuage Roy Disney's disappointment at the rejection. He was still not being taken seriously at Walt Disney Productions.

On Sunday afternoon, Dennis Stanfill visited Ray Watson in Newport Beach. Though it was the weekend, he wore a suit and a tie: That was his style, and this, after all, *was* a job interview.

"I've dealt with the corporate world," he told Watson. "I've had corporate experience at Fox." His corporate experience, he went on to say, would enable him to deal effectively with Wall Street, and with all the investors in Walt Disney Productions, be they institutional asset managers or arbitrageurs or raiders. "You've got to stand up to the corporate raiders," Stanfill said. "You've got to stand firm. You've got to be tough."

This talk of toughness struck Watson as irrelevant and meaningless; it was also disparaging to Ron Miller and to Watson himself. What did it mean to be "tough"? Nonetheless, Stanfill was impressive. Without a doubt he could run Walt Disney Productions. And he enjoyed the support of most of the directors.

While Ray Watson met with Dennis Stanfill, the Brain Trust convened at Stanley Gold's house in Beverly Hills. Gold did not see that he and his client had many options at this point. They had proposed Wells. They had proposed Eisner. They had proposed a triumvirate of Wells, Eisner, and Stanfill. None of the proposals had been accepted. There was one more possibility. The Brain Trust had discussed, on and off, an executive team composed of Wells and Eisner.

"With Frank's business background and Michael's creativity, we'd have an unbeatable duo," Gold said now, rather wistfully.

"Okay," Patty Disney said to Gold. "You're so smart, do something. Pull it off."

The board meeting to approve a new chief executive officer was scheduled for Saturday, September 22—six days later. When it came to a vote, most of the directors would side with Phil Hawley, whom they had known for years. Roy Disney and Stanley Gold, newcomers to the board, could count on no allies except for Peter Dailey. On top of that, there was a certain hostility to Disney and Gold, who some people believed were responsible for stirring up the trouble at the company in the first place.

"How are we going to get enough votes?" Mark Siegel asked.

"You're running scared," Gold said, summoning some pluck. "We're going to win it." He took out pen and paper and compiled a list of the directors, which, of course, no longer included Ron Miller. "We'll lose Hawley, we'll lose Lozano, and we'll lose Baldwin. Ahmanson's out of the country, so she won't be voting. We'll win all the rest. We'll win by nine to three."

"What are we going to do?" Siegel asked.

"We're going to run it my way," Gold said. "We're going to run it right down the middle of the street, where they're uncomfortable and where I'm comfortable. We're going to put on a fucking political campaign right out where everybody can see us. I'm tired of being told to be quiet because somebody's feelings are going to be hurt."

There was one small problem. Gold did not know if he had Michael Eisner. Eisner was understandably angry: Walt Disney Productions had left him standing at the altar. He was also the hottest property in town. The networks and the other studios all wanted to hire him. The Brain Trust could not expect him to come running when it called. But if a campaign was to succeed, Eisner had to join it.

Wells called Eisner, but it was Sunday, as it had been the first time he had invited Eisner to a meeting, and once again, Eisner was unable to come for a while. His kids had a baseball game. It was after dinner by the time he arrived with his lawyer Irwin Russell. Stanley Gold brought out the grappa and began to lobby.

The conversation lasted two hours. Among other things, there was considerable discussion of titles and job descriptions. Wells thought he and Eisner should each be co-chief executive; Eisner would handle the creative side, Wells the business side, but they would have equal status and equal compensation; Watson might even remain as chairman. Eisner, however, was adamant that he be chairman and sole chief executive officer. Things got a little touchy before Wells volunteered to be president, conceding the positions of chairman and chief executive officer to Eisner provided the two men would be equals in the sense that each of them would report directly to the board.

Gold thought Eisner was hooked by then, but Irwin Russell kept raising questions. He said Eisner had thought he had the job a week ago, that he had offers from elsewhere, and that if he campaigned for the Disney post he might jeopardize those other offers. He also wanted to discuss compensation. Finally, Gold cut him off. "I just want to know," he said to Eisner, "will you commit? Do you want to be chairman and CEO of Walt Disney Productions? It's the best job in the world. Give me a break. *Give me a break.*"

"I'll give you one week," Eisner said finally. "I'll do it." And so the campaign began.

The next day Stanley Gold compiled a master chart listing the names of every director and the director's friends, clients, customers, and business associates. He tried to determine the position of each director on the matter at hand, and to identify his vulnerable points. He called in every marker he had, phoning friends and industry leaders to persuade them to plead for Eisner and Wells with the directors. He had his law partners at Gang, Tyre & Brown phone the senior partners at Hufstedler, Miller, Carson & Beardsley, the firm of director Sam Williams. He also tried to line up support for "his boys" from Disney's shareholders. At the same time, Eisner and Wells put on coats and ties and visited each director personally to explain why they should run Walt Disney Productions.

Reaction from the other side was swift. On Tuesday Gold received a call from Joe Flom. The Skadden, Arps attorney was furious. Gold's efforts, he said, were unprofessional.

"Unprofessional?" Gold asked. "What have I done? I'm trying to persuade people that Eisner and Wells are the two better guys."

"You're *campaigning*," Flom said. "I've never seen anybody run something like this. If you don't stop, I'm going to tell Phil Hawley to pour on the coals."

As the crucial board meeting drew nearer, the pressure on Ray Watson began to mount again, growing more intense than it had been even during the decision to cancel Gibson. Everyone, it seemed, was calling Watson, urging him to support one candidate or another. Richard Nunis, the head of Disney's theme parks, wrote Watson a letter proposing himself as president. Caroline Ahmanson let Watson know she favored Dennis Stanfill. Stanley Gold called every three minutes (it seemed to Watson) to lobby for the Eisner-Wells team. Steven Spielberg called to promote Michael Eisner. Richard Rainwater phoned in from Fort Worth to say the candidate the Basses thought Watson should support was Frank Wells.

Although he mentioned it to no one, Watson was still inclined toward Eisner. He believed the company should have a creative head, a position consistent with the fact that, as a real estate developer, his background was in architecture, where the creative side usually ruled. But Watson also believed that his own inclinations were almost irrelevant. The most important task, Watson's *only* real task, was to produce a consensus among the directors and the shareholders for the chief executive—whoever it was—and thus finally to put an end to all the internecine wrangling that had made Disney so vulnerable. If Watson could build a consensus around Eisner, fine. But if the consensus formed instead around Stanfill, that was fine too.

Watson asked Gold to come to his office at three o'clock on Tuesday afternoon.

"I know you're out campaigning and pushing hard," Watson said, "and I admire that." The directors, however, were going to vote for Dennis Stanfill. The vote would be ten to three.* Watson was not even sure that Peter Dailey would go along with Gold, but he gave him Dailey's vote for the sake of argument.

---

*Unlike Gold, Watson was including Caroline Ahmanson in his count. In the end, Ahmanson, who was in China at the time, did not vote.

"Ray," Stanley Gold said, "in the words of one of the great poets: Go fuck yourself."

Watson broke into a huge smile. "I didn't think it was going to work," he said.

"You think I'm going to quit?" Gold asked. "You think I'm going to *quit?* Show me a good loser and I'll show you a loser. Nine months I've been working on this and you want me to capitulate for the sake of unanimity so that everyone will be happy? You're crazy. Who put you up to this?"

"Sit still, will you? Don't holler at me." Watson was still grinning. "Goddammit, Stan, just sit down."

When Gold was seated, Watson said, "It was my very own idea to call you in and tell you this. We have got to have a consensus on the candidate, whoever it is. The Basses are going in one direction, you and Roy are going in another, Phil Hawley in still another. It's not even clear who the Walt side of the family supports. Let me tell you something, Stan. Even Peter Dailey, your client's own brother-in-law, is calling me up and suggesting candidates. So I don't even know where *you* guys are. Saturday is the day of decision. Whoever can put together a coalition by Saturday will have the job. But if something doesn't change between now and Saturday, Dennis Stanfill will head this company."

"Ray," Gold said, "I'm going to win it and I'm going to get your goddamned vote. You're going to lead the vote for me."

"I only count three votes so far," Watson said. "And mine's not among them."

Stanley Gold came away from that meeting with the distinct impression that Watson had dropped his earlier support for Eisner and thrown in his lot with Hawley and Stanfill. It made the odds against his candidates even more formidable. Nonetheless, Gold reasoned, the support of the shareholders who had formed the alliance against Gibson could change those odds. At the board meeting on Saturday he wanted to be able to say that Irwin Jacobs, Ivan Boesky, the Basses, and all the rest of Disney's noisy and troublesome shareholders endorsed Eisner and Wells, and that if the board rejected this slate they risked provoking another proxy fight. Jacobs, who respected both

Eisner and Wells, and who could never turn down the opportunity to thwart an establishment figure like Phil Hawley, had readily agreed to cast his lot with Gold. So had Ivan Boesky.

The Basses, however, had proved more recalcitrant. Sid Bass and Richard Rainwater had never met Michael Eisner, and they had some of the same reservations about him that Phil Hawley did. They had been told that Eisner was a mere "movie man," someone who happened to have a knack for picking popular pictures, and little more. Eisner was said to lack depth. They thought Frank Wells, the businessman, should head the company. But Gold argued that under the management structure he envisioned, Wells and Eisner would be equal in the sense that both would report directly to the board. That, Gold said, was the way the company had originally been run, with Walt Disney, the "creative crazy," serving as chief executive, and Roy O. Disney, "the businessman," in the role of president.

At midweek, when Wells himself told Sid Bass that he endorsed this idea, the investor conceded. "I have enough confidence in you that I want you to be CEO," he told Wells. "And when you say 'Make Mike number one,' I have enough faith in you to take your word on it." Sid Bass then called to tell Gold he could inform the board that the Basses favored Eisner and Wells.

"Do me a favor," Gold said. "Call Cobb and make sure he's got things straight."

Sid Bass explained that Chuck Cobb was his own man. He would listen to advice but he would not take instructions. And Cobb had doubts. He too was a hard-asset man, an M.B.A., wary of Hollywood, where, as they liked to say, the assets left the lot at five.

Gold called Richard Rainwater.

"Richard, Cobb's wavering," Gold told him.

"Stanley, Stanley," Rainwater said, "have I taken care of my end of this deal?"

"Yes."

"He's on the program. Don't worry about what he's saying to people. Just count the vote."

"Okay, Richard."

Shortly after that, Gold called Ray Watson. He had an urge to taunt the chairman. "How am I doing, Ray?" Gold asked. "Is it still

ten to three? Do I have any more votes, yet? Do I have Cobb? Ten
to three—who are you kidding?"

Ray Watson laughed, but Gold's antics perturbed Frank Wells.

"Why are you calling him and tweaking him?" Wells asked Gold.
"You're making it personal. You're just asking for Flom and Hawley
to come after you with all they've got."

"Come on, Frank," Gold said. "Relax. We're going to win it."

That, however, was still far from certain; as Joe Flom had said he
might, Phil Hawley, together with Dennis Stanfill, had begun to campaign vigorously too. The two men called Stanley Gold's partners at
Gang, Tyre & Brown to persuade them to change Gold's mind.
Stanfill also visited Gold and Roy Disney to plead his case; they
listened politely, but that was more to satisfy the legal requirement
that as directors they act with "due diligence" than because they were
interested.

Stanfill then called Fort Worth to present his case to Sid Bass and
Richard Rainwater. In an attempt to appeal to their more conservative instincts, he described the range of his corporate experience. "The
company really needs someone with my qualifications," Stanfill said.

Stanley Gold, however, had been there first. "It's a hard decision
for us, but we've given Stanley our word that we'll support his candidates," Bass said.

Stanfill was clearly displeased. "Phil Hawley has the support of the
board," he said. "What will happen if I win the vote on Saturday?"

"If you win on Saturday, we'll start a proxy fight on Monday," Sid
Bass said. "We'll replace the board and appoint new officers."

Sid Bass had made up his mind to endorse Eisner and Wells, and
once Sid Bass arrived at a decision like that, he threw himself into the
fray.

As the week wore on, Bass was surprised to learn that Ray Watson
had shifted his support (as it appeared) from Eisner to Stanfill. Watson
seemed to him to flip back and forth on everything. He was against
greenmail, then he paid greenmail. He supported Gibson, then he
canceled it. He proposed Eisner to the board, then he dropped Eisner.
The guy changed his mind three times in five minutes. He was a
project-oriented architect rather than a manager. So Sid Bass called

Ray Watson to convey to him the same message he had given Stanfill.

"We've talked to all the large shareholders, Ray," Bass said, "and so far they all say that they want Eisner and Wells. That's 40 percent of the outstanding stock. So why are you going through this exercise of considering Stanfill? Don't do that, Ray. It's rather a cumbersome process. We've got the votes to elect brand-new directors. The new directors will fire the guy you've just hired and hire the guys we want to hire. Why go through all this pain?"

"A majority of the board is opposed to Eisner," Watson said.

"Listen to 40 percent of your shareholders," Bass said. "Why are you ignoring all of these people? We've talked and talked and talked and you can't convince us. You ought to give up trying to convince us and go and do it."

Shortly thereafter, Sid Bass called Stanley Gold. "What can I do to help you?" he asked.

"You're doing everything you can," Gold said. "Just keep up the support."

"I should tell you something. It's going to print in the next thirty seconds anyway."

"What's that?"

"You can go to the board and tell them your supporters control much more of Walt Disney Productions than they thought. We've just bought another million shares of Disney at about $60 a share."

Sid Bass had decided to send a message directly to the board. Since the Basses already owned more than 5 percent of Disney's stock, they had to file another 13D each time they increased their holdings by an additional percentage point, and they had bought close to 1 percent since closing on Arvida. Now Sid Bass told the Disney stock specialist on the floor of the New York Stock Exchange that he would take all the Disney stock that became available. At the end of the week Bass Brothers Enterprises publicly notified the SEC—and Disney—that they had raised their stake in the company from 5.5 percent to 8.6 percent of its outstanding shares.

Ray Watson, meanwhile, had been talking to the representatives of the Walt side of the Disney family. Ron Gother, the attorney for Lillian Disney and Sharon Disney Lund, said his clients opposed Stanfill (not creative enough) and Wells (a victory for Roy Disney). They were uncertain about Eisner. John Baity, the lawyer for Ron and Diane Miller, said his clients could not support anyone since they believed Ron himself should have the job. That was on Thursday. The board meeting was less than two days away and Watson felt he was as far from a consensus as he had ever been.

That same day Chuck Cobb arranged to meet Watson to discuss, Watson assumed, the strengths and weaknesses of Stanfill and the Eisner-Wells team. Instead, Cobb announced that *he* wanted to be the chief executive of Walt Disney Productions. One of the reasons he had agreed to the merger of Arvida and Disney, he said, was the possibility of one day running the combined company. He conceded that he had not been with Disney long enough for the directors to recognize his qualifications, and that this raised an obstacle to his quest. But, he went on, "Where I come out, Ray, is that none of these other people should become chief executive. *You* should become CEO, but say you'll only do it for a short time, eighteen months or so, until you find the right person. By then I'll have emerged as the natural candidate."

Watson could scarcely believe what he was hearing. "There's just no way, Chuck," he said. "It's just never going to fly. I am not a candidate for this job. I'm the wrong person for it. And I don't like the idea of an interim leader. We're trying to solve a problem, not drag it out." Nevertheless, Watson went on, he would do what the consensus wanted. If a consensus believed the company could be saved by what Cobb was proposing, he would go along.

"I'm going to go talk to the Basses," Cobb said.

"Well, you're welcome to do whatever you want to do."

Cobb flew down to Fort Worth that afternoon, and presented his idea. But Al Checchi, Richard Rainwater, and Sid Bass all said they couldn't support Cobb's proposal.

That evening, Watson telephoned Sid Bass at home. Bass had guests for dinner, but he excused himself to take the call. Watson, who wanted to approach the subject delicately, started off by asking about titles for Eisner and Wells.

"Which one should be chief executive?" he asked.

"Just ask them," Sid Bass said.

"You don't care?"

"Look, they're going to run the company. If they can't make a decision like that, then we're dead."

"Can they run it as equals?"

"I'll tell you what, Ray. I'm very opposed to the concept of a joint CEO. That is madness. There's got to be something wrong with someone who agrees to share the job."

"Do you think we should delay?" Watson asked, trying to hint at Chuck Cobb's proposition without raising it explicitly.

Sid Bass said again that he supported Eisner and Wells. The two men talked several times that evening and Sid Bass finally became impatient with the circular conversation. As a result, perhaps, Watson was left with the impression that Cobb had at the very least persuaded his acquaintances in Fort Worth to entertain his proposition if he could round up additional support for it—that Sid Bass, despite his protestations of support for Eisner and Wells, would agree to a postponement if others felt it was necessary. Things weren't coming together, they were flying apart.

The Brain Trust's effort had all the frenzy of a political campaign. Stanley Gold was working twenty hours a day, rising at four in the morning and going to bed at midnight. He and his team gathered every morning to put together a status report. By Thursday, they had commitments from four of the thirteen directors. They needed three more for a majority.

"The key is Card Walker," Gold told the Brain Trust. Walker himself had only one vote, of course, but Donn Tatum, the company's former chief executive, and Dick Nunis, the other Disney executive on the board, could be counted on to vote with him. If those three votes were added to the votes of Roy Disney, Stanley Gold, Peter Dailey, and Chuck Cobb (whose support Gold assumed he had), the total came to seven. But Walker had so far remained noncommittal. Frank Wells, Gold said, would have to persuade him. "I've pushed him off the executive committee and I have to give him something back," he went on. "I mean, he needs a little concession from me. I'll give up my seat on the board if it'll make peace." Wells was to tell Walker that Gold would resign in favor of Diane or Ron Miller, if they wanted to come back on the board, or, if they didn't, Sharon Lund.

But Card Walker had gone on a fishing trip to Arizona. On Friday, with less than twenty-four hours before the board was scheduled to meet, Wells flew there in the Shamrock jet to talk to the retired Disney chairman. That same afternoon, Michael Eisner, who had made a powerful presentation to director Sam Williams the day before, drove down to Newport Beach to try to persuade board member Ignacio Lozano to vote with Roy Disney and Stanley Gold.

On Friday night the Brain Trust gathered on Stanley Gold's patio to await word from Wells. The phone rang around seven o'clock. Wells was calling from the Shamrock jet.

"Bingo!" he said. "Card's committed to us. He wants to move the nomination and he wants to give the speech tomorrow. He says he'll work on it all night."

"A winner!" Gold shouted to his assembled friends. He turned and kicked a huge trash can off the patio. It sailed into the yard.

Five minutes after they heard from Wells, Eisner called in from the telephone in his car. He was driving back from Newport Beach, where he had been unable to change Lozano's mind.

"It doesn't matter," Gold said. "We've won!"

"I can't believe it," Eisner said. "I can't believe it."

"Do me a favor," Gold went on. "Be here tomorrow morning at six and we'll see if we can cut a deal. I need contracts to take to the board."

With that, Gold drank a big glass of Williams pear brandy, took two Valiums, and went to bed.

Ray Watson spent Friday night at the company apartment in Burbank. Around eight o'clock, Card Walker called him from Arizona and described Wells's visit. While he had been leaning toward Dennis Stanfill, he liked both Frank Wells and Michael Eisner. He knew they could run the company capably. But he was also intensely loyal to the Walt side of the Disney family. And Ron Miller's resignation meant that not a single member of the Walt side of the family had a seat on the board. That imbalance would be redressed if Stanley Gold resigned in favor of Diane Miller or Sharon Lund to promote unity. Also, Walker knew that the election of Dennis Stanfill would prolong the divisions among the major shareholders and possibly lead to another proxy fight. Stanley Gold had said he would not give up. Irwin Jacobs, Ivan Boesky, and the Basses had begun to see the issue as another Gibson. The company had to go with Eisner and Wells. "It all makes sense," Walker said. "I've written a statement that I want to read at tomorrow's meeting."

Watson then called each of the directors individually. He explained that he intended to recommend Eisner and Wells. A majority of the directors were in favor of the team, he said. And so were the major stockholders. Though he was slightly exaggerating the amount of formal support he actually had for Eisner and Wells, as he worked his way through the list of directors, enough of them let him know how they intended to vote to verify the outcome. He waited to call Phil Hawley last.

"How do you think it's going to come out?" Hawley asked.

"I think it's going to be unanimous," Watson said.

Stanley Gold arose at five thirty. Mark Siegel and Eisner and Wells arrived at six and quickly reconfirmed the deal Watson had worked out with Eisner when he had recommended Eisner to the board earlier in the month. Under its terms, which the board later approved, Disney's top two executives became among the highest paid in the industry. Ron Miller had earned about $500,000 a year after his so-called golden parachute raise went into effect. Eisner was to receive a salary of $750,000 a year and a performance bonus that could reach more than $1 million a year. He was also given a $750,000 signing bonus and options on 510,000 shares of Disney stock at $57 a share. Wells was given a salary of $400,000 and a similar, if slightly less grand, package of options and bonuses.

The board met at ten o'clock on the lot. Watson opened the meeting by raising the issue of the company's vulnerability. Only if its management enjoyed the support of both the Walt side and the Roy side of the Disney family, as well as the Basses, he said, could Disney remain independent.

The Walt side had been informed of Stanley Gold's willingness to resign in favor of one of their members if Wells and Eisner took over, and Ron Gother and John Baity were invited into the boardroom to declare their clients' support for the Eisner-Wells team. Roy Disney and Stanley Gold also spoke on the team's behalf. But Chuck Cobb urged the board to postpone a decision. "I think it's premature," he said. The board knew next to nothing about the candidates' strategy and goals for the company. It ought to take the time to find out.

Watson disagreed. For the company to go through further weeks of turmoil while the board discussed hypothetical goals would add nothing. Now was the time to decide. And like those who had spoken before him, he favored Eisner and Wells. "This is as close to a consensus as we are going to get," he said. "It's important that we show unity."

Then the inside directors left the room to allow the outsiders the opportunity to discuss the matter. The election of Eisner and Wells was a foregone conclusion, however, and the outside directors did little but confirm it. When the inside directors returned, Card Walker gave his speech formally nominating the two men. Watson moved that the board make it unanimous. And it did.

"Any other business?" Watson asked.

There was none. In his last official act as chairman of the board of Walt Disney Productions, Ray Watson adjourned the meeting. He then asked Stanley Gold to call Wells and Eisner, who were waiting at Eisner's house.

In an adjoining office, Gold gave the news to Disney's new management. Then Phil Hawley got on the phone. "I think it's terrific," he said. "Obviously there was some conflict here and some difficulty, but I want you both to know you have my full support."

Although he was to be replaced as chairman of Walt Disney Productions, Ray Watson harbored no bitterness. His ego did not require the position. When he had taken the job, he had not expected it to be more than a temporary, ceremonial post. He had agreed to help see the company through a period of transition. That transition had proved to be far more dramatic, wrenching, and profound than he had anticipated. But in the end, Watson felt that he had accomplished what he had been brought in to do.

After the board meeting, Stanley Gold and some of the other directors repaired to the Lakeside Golf Club to host a celebratory luncheon for

Eisner and Wells. When the meal was over, Gold drove alone to the shore, where he sat on the rocks and stared at the surf for several hours. It was Ilene's birthday, and Gold had promised to take her and a friend out for dinner. But when he arrived home early in the evening, he begged off, pleading exhaustion. He went to bed and slept for fourteen hours. On Sunday morning, he and Frank Wells went running. It was the last time they would run together for a long while. The following day, Wells would start his new job as president of Walt Disney Productions and he simply would not have the time.

17

A FEW DAYS AFTER the board meeting, Michael Eisner and Frank Wells flew to Fort Worth to see the Basses. They also sent a plane to Minneapolis to bring Irwin Jacobs down. The chief executive and the president of Walt Disney Productions wanted to thank the major stockholders personally for their support.

The previous week, at the height of the campaign, Jacobs had said in another filing with the SEC that he was raising his stake in Disney and might seek control of the company. He had repeated his intentions to Sid Bass in a phone conversation and had asked what the Basses' plans were. "We're keeping our options open," Bass had told him.

In a gathering in the offices of Bass Brothers Enterprises, where the walls were hung with paintings by such artists as Jasper Johns and Frank Stella, Disney's two top executives outlined their plans for the company. After half an hour, Richard Rainwater excused himself to take a phone call and Sid Bass went out with him. "I'm impressed," Bass told his associate. Rainwater said he was too. The company, they decided, was worth a substantial long-term investment. "Let's go back and tell them we're going to stay in for the next five years," Sid Bass said.

Before returning to the room, he asked Irwin Jacobs to step outside.

"So, what do you think?" Jacobs asked.

"It's a marvelous opportunity," Bass said. "The management is tremendous. I'm not selling."

Jacobs was flabbergasted. "Sid, did I just have a cerebral hemorrhage?" he asked. He had been under the impression that the Basses were short-term asset players who would want to sell their stock, which he thought he might want to buy.

"Irwin, I really like these guys," Sid Bass said. "I think they're smart. I'm with them for the next five years."

"Fine, you're entitled to your opinion," Jacobs said.

"I think I'm going to make a lot of money," Sid Bass went on. "That's why I'm doing it. I think you ought to do it, too. Let's both buy a lot of Disney stock."

The idea appealed to Jacobs. He said he would go back and talk to his confederates. "Maybe we'll stick in a hundred million," he added. "Maybe two hundred million. I don't know what we're going to do."

Upon returning to Minneapolis, Jacobs flirted with the idea of proceeding with an offer for Disney. Raising the money, however, might pose a problem. Jacobs put off a decision. "I've spoken to our people," he told Sid Bass two days later. "We're not ready to commit, but we're thinking favorably about going in for three hundred to five hundred million in additional stock."

While Jacobs equivocated, the Basses, convinced that under Wells and Eisner Disney would prove to be an enormously profitable investment, and believing, moreover, that to be associated in a positive way with this quintessentially American corporation might put some distance between themselves and the irritating greenmail charges, began to buy Disney stock aggressively. In early October they were approached by a broker who said Ivan Boesky was interested in selling his stake in the company; they bought him out: 1.52 million shares at $60 a share. Added to what they already owned, the block of stock gave them control of almost 16 percent of Walt Disney Productions.

Informed of the purchase by Sid Bass, Eisner and Wells issued a statement saying, "Management is enormously pleased with this development and sees it as a strong vote of confidence by the Bass family."

Irwin Jacobs, however, had just the opposite reaction. Fifteen minutes after the ticker carried the announcement that a large block of Disney had changed hands, he called Sid Bass.

"Did you buy Boesky's shares?" he asked.

Bass said he had. Jacobs asked about splitting the purchase; when he'd met with Sid Bass in Fort Worth, he had gotten the idea that Bass was suggesting they work in tandem, buy stock together. "I thought you weren't going to do anything until we made a decision," Jacobs said. "But if you did, we're entitled to half the stock, right?"

Sid Bass disagreed. His understanding was that he had simply told Jacobs that Disney was a good investment and that therefore they both would profit from acquiring its stock. Moreover, Jacobs had been unable to make up his mind what he wanted to do, and Sid Bass was not one to wait around while somebody else figured out a plan. If an opportunity came along, he seized it. That was how the game was played. "We're not giving you half the stock," he told Jacobs.

Jacobs felt he had been stiffed, and for a while he almost wanted to take on the Basses; he could, after all, buy enough shares to even himself with them quickly enough. But to do so would be to let himself be carried away by the passion for battle. And that could be dangerous. "What are we trying to accomplish here?" he asked his associates. "This is business, not a macho game."

Jacobs decided to offer to buy the Basses out. He called Sid Bass back. "Look, there isn't room for us both," he said. "You've got your star, I've got mine. We're prepared to offer you sixty-five dollars a share for all your stock, in cash."

"It's not for sale at any price," Sid Bass said. Jacobs's offer struck him as a subtle way of indicating that Jacobs's own stock might be available at that price. And indeed, Jacobs then said, "One of us is going to go. If you aren't selling, that means I should."

"We'll buy you out."

"I'll call you tomorrow morning before the market opens," Jacobs said. He went on: "You think seriously, Sid, about what you want to pay me. You're going to do a deal, but I want you to remember that I made this deal possible for everybody, including yourself." Jacobs thought he deserved a little gratitude. If it had not been for his fight against Gibson—a fight the Basses had been unwilling to join—Disney would have acquired the greeting card company and Bill Simon would have become Disney's largest shareholder. Simon would be running Disney's board. And Dennis Stanfill would be running the studio instead of Eisner and Wells.

The next morning, Jacobs called Sid Bass again.

"I'll pay you sixty dollars a share," Bass said. It was the same price he had just paid for Boesky's stock.

Jacobs reacted as if he found Bass a source of continual amazement. "Sid," he said, "I offered you *sixty-five* a share for your stock. Now, just tell me you can't afford that, or tell me it isn't worth it. Sid, I want to hear you say the stock isn't worth sixty-five, so maybe you'll sell me yours for that price."

"No, that isn't the case," said Bass. But Sid Bass knew he had Irwin Jacobs overpowered and outmaneuvered. "I'll tell you what," he said. "I'll give you sixty-one."

"Fine," Jacobs said. "The trade will go up right now." Irwin Jacobs hung up knowing he had probably made one of the worst deals of his life—even though he and his associates would come out of it with a profit of almost $29 million (some days you win, some days you lose). But money wasn't the issue, Jacobs told himself. His business style was. He had lost control of the situation and he had to move on.

With the addition of Jacobs's stock, the holdings of Bass Brothers Enterprises in Walt Disney Productions rose to more than 24 percent, making the Basses by far the largest shareholders. And despite persistent rumors that they intended some sort of asset play, such as forcing Disney to sell its Florida real estate, they were content to remain passive shareholders. They had no interest in participating in Disney's day-to-day management, they said in a statement. The Basses, Michael Eisner announced happily, "are exactly the kind of investors that this company needs."

EPILOGUE

In a matter of months, Eisner and Wells had transformed Walt Disney Productions almost beyond recognition. A week after he joined the company, Eisner brought Jeff Katzenberg over from Paramount to become president of the movie and television operations. As a result, Richard Berger resigned as head of production (he later became president of United Artists), and within days, Katzenberg announced that he had signed a contract for the company's first R-rated movie. It was to star Nick Nolte, Richard Dreyfuss, and Bette Midler and to be directed by Paul Mazursky, best known for his romantic—and distinctly adult—comedies, *An Unmarried Woman* and *Bob and Carol and Ted and Alice.* The new movie, titled *Down and Out in Beverly Hills,* was released in December 1985 under Ron Miller's Touchstone label, the Disney name appearing nowhere in the ads. It was well reviewed and in short order overtook *Splash* to become the studio's most successful film.

An outpouring of similarly "un-Disneylike" projects followed the signing of Mazursky and his cast. Katzenberg brought in the writers who had collaborated on *Beverly Hills Cop,* the producers who had made *Risky Business,* and actors Dennis Hopper, Kirk Douglas, Burt Lancaster, and Sidney Poitier. He also pursued the rock singer Madonna, whose campy crucifix-and-corset costumes would have been anathema to Walt Disney, in hopes of persuading her to appear in a "black comedy."

The company's new approach to film-making was shown to be even more daring in the summer of 1986, when Bette Midler, who had signed a three-picture contract with the studio, appeared in *Ruthless People,* a gag-filled farce about the kidnapped wife of a businessman

that was based on a story by O. Henry. The movie was by and large
applauded by the critics, who praised it as "screamingly funny," but
also called it "raucous," "raunchy," "rude," "vulgar," and "offensive." And though, as with *Down and Out in Beverly Hills, Ruthless
People* was released under the Touchstone label, the press certainly
connected it with Disney: *Newsday*'s reviewer decided it was "the
randiest movie ever made by the studio." No such misgivings, however, appeared to greet Touchstone's third R-rated release, *The Color
of Money*, which hit theaters in October 1986. Directed by Martin
Scorsese and starring Paul Newman and Tom Cruise in a continuation
of the story in *The Hustler,* the film garnered almost universally
rapturous reviews as well as solid box-office receipts.

Inevitably, some people—Richard Berger was one—complained
that Disney was losing its uniqueness, that the projects the new team
had put in development looked and sounded no different from the
movies and television shows produced by Hollywood's other studios.
It was certainly true that, under Eisner and Wells, Disney was not
what it had been under Ron Miller and Card Walker, and still less
what it had been under Walt and Roy Disney. And *Down and Out in
Beverly Hills, Ruthless People,* and *The Color of Money* did resemble
many of the films Eisner and Katzenberg had made at Paramount.
Supporters of the new regime, however, insisted that, in adapting to
the times, the studio was remaining faithful on the most fundamental
level—the level that valued and nourished creativity—to the legacy of
Walt Disney. In the summer of 1986, Richard Nunis, the head of the
theme parks, who had remained at the company despite his long
friendship with the departed Ron Miller and who had known the
founder for years, said that "If Walt Disney were alive today, he
would agree with what we are doing."

The new "Team Disney," as Eisner and his cohorts soon were
known, also devoted a great deal of energy to recapturing the company's once prominent position in television. By the fall of 1985, one
year after his tenure began, Katzenberg had sold the television networks two Saturday morning cartoon shows and a prime-time comedy
series called *Golden Girls,* which proved a phenomenal success for
NBC. Even more important for the company's image, he arranged for
ABC to schedule "The Disney Sunday Movie," the package of family-

oriented made-for-television movies that had been under discussion but had never gotten off the ground during Ron Miller's reign.

While much of the new emphasis was on adults, the company remained staunchly committed to children, though often with a distinctly contemporary twist. Capitalizing on the vogue for high technology, for example, Disney signed a licensing agreement with a San Francisco corporation that made electronic toys. The company also revived Walt Disney comic books and, when Katzenberg's attempts to sign a contract with Madonna failed, unveiled a new, "updated" Minnie Mouse who had her own rock record, "Totally Minnie," and who made appearances in punk-rock outfits.

Management's innovations extended to the theme parks. George Lucas agreed to produce, Francis Ford Coppola agreed to direct, and Michael Jackson agreed to star in, a twelve-minute 3-D short called *Captain Eo* that was to be a permanent attraction at Disneyland and Epcot. The company also launched an aggressive campaign, featuring photographs of Eisner wearing Mickey Mouse ears, to promote Walt Disney World as a center for business meetings and conventions, and relaxed somewhat its notoriously puritanical code of behavior. For the first time, beer and wine were allowed at Disneyland—though only after dark, and only at private corporate parties attended by at least five hundred people—and single-sex dancing, once forbidden at the theme parks, began to be discreetly overlooked.

It was perhaps a fitting coincidence then, that, along with all this modernizing and updating, Disney characters suddenly assumed a certain chic in the fashion world. Men and women—*adults*—appeared on the streets of New York and Hollywood and Paris wearing jackets and sweaters emblazoned with the faces of Minnie and Mickey Mouse. The fad, according to the company's 1985 annual report, was the result of "a European and American trend of blending pop culture with haute couture into witty, whimsical, and wearable clothes."

By the time Eisner and Wells had been in place a year, it seemed as if nothing at the company remained untouched. Park benches had been pulled up along Mickey Avenue. The studio barbershop was closed. The executive offices in the animation building were redesigned to look sleek and modern, with plush carpeting, track lighting, and walls covered in beige fabric. In a sort of culmination to the "Disney revolution," as Hollywood had taken to calling it, the company, at its 1986 annual meeting, officially changed its name from Walt Disney Productions to The Walt Disney Company. A study had found that the name Walt Disney Productions connoted involvement in motion pictures and television, slighting the company's other enterprises. The new name, according to a statement from Erwin Okun's office, "enables the company to publicly clarify ambiguities that have existed between the parent corporation and its operating units."

The revolution wrought by Eisner and Wells, however, went well beyond product innovation and fresh marketing. One of the reasons for Disney's takeover troubles in 1984 was that the management in charge at the time had failed to appreciate the new and harsher investment environment in which all public companies were forced to operate in the 1980s. The institutional investors—whose instant access to a vast array of complex market information gave them a profound edge over the individual who based his investment decisions primarily on what he read in the morning paper, and who might buy a few shares in a company and hold them for years—continuously rotated in and out of stocks. Given such restlessness, it was not surprising that takeovers proliferated, particularly in the early 1980s, when economic recession and a slump in the stock market meant that many companies were undervalued; indeed, it was the rising prices of the stocks of companies being acquired that helped drive the long market rally which began in 1982. And takeovers continued even after the economic recovery was well under way. In 1984 alone, according to *Mergers & Acquisitions* magazine, there were 3,126 mergers and acquisitions, up from 1,529 five years before; many of the takeover targets were companies whose executives were believed by Wall Street (correctly or not, depending on one's point of view) to be performing poorly. According to the Street, Disney under Ron Miller was simply one more of dozens of firms that had failed to show enough hustle.

And Wall Street was uniformly remorseless toward a company that failed to provide an acceptable return on investment—a return that was measured not even annually but quarterly. Had institutional investors been willing to wait for Ron Miller to complete his second year as head of the company, they probably would have seen Disney's stock rise as *Splash* generated substantial revenues, and as Touchstone and the real estate development projects contemplated by Ray Watson gathered momentum. But Wall Street was not willing to wait. Or, more accurately, it was not capable of waiting. For had those institutional investors holding Disney's stock endured its slump, the clients whose accounts they managed would have begun to complain, and would probably have shifted their accounts to other, more aggressive money managers who produced a better return on investment.

Thus the pressure on corporate executives like those at Disney reflected to a large extent the pressure on institutional investors, who by the mid-eighties controlled a good 30 percent of many Fortune 500 companies. If earnings fell, such investors quickly became eager to dump their shares, which caused the company's stock to fall, and which in turn made it vulnerable to a takeover, usually by someone prepared to sell off its assets piecemeal to obtain a sum considerably greater than the value of the company as a whole on the stock market. Since at the prospect of a takeover, the arbitrage community could be counted on to accumulate at least 10 percent of the company's stock, some 40 percent of the company's "owners" were willing, not to say eager, to sell their shares for a quick profit. A raider, then, could acquire a mere 10 percent of an undervalued company (as Saul Steinberg did), then offer to buy the 40 percent controlled jointly by the institutional investors and the arbitrageurs (as Steinberg did) by issuing junk bonds and promising to liquidate the company once the takeover was complete (as Steinberg did). And once a company was "in play," management's alternatives, as Disney's executives learned, were few and all unpleasant.

Greatly compounding the difficulties of a target company like Disney, moreover, was its having to contend with the fine-spun web of relationships that bound together arbitrageurs, raiders, investment bankers, and lawyers, and gave this uniquely mercenary group distinct advantages in combat. When, for example, Roy Disney decided against attempting a takeover of Walt Disney Productions, it was an easy matter for Mike Milken to carry Drexel's financing package over to Saul Steinberg virtually intact. Indeed, the world of takeover professionals is so small, so circumscribed, so interwoven that, like some remote Appalachian village, everyone in one way or another is related to everyone else. For observers, one of the most delicious ironies of the Disney affair occurred when Kekst and Company—the very firm that represented Saul Steinberg—went to work for Disney side by side with Hill and Knowlton. And it is interesting to note that Fried, Frank, in addition to working for Stanley Gold and Roy Disney, had Ivan Boesky as its long-time client, and represented him when he emerged at the center of the Wall Street insider trading scandal in 1986.

All the uproar surrounding that scandal, in which a Drexel Burnham managing director, Dennis Levine, admitted to profiting from advance knowledge of impending corporate takeovers and to selling that information to Boesky, has also drawn attention to the far more pervasive, and perfectly legal, exchange of non-confidential but not widely known information, and the exploitation of personal contacts. Stanley Gold's friendship with the broker Boyd Jefferies brought about his meeting with Irwin Jacobs and helped forge the alliance between the two dissident shareholders. And Irwin Jacobs's knowledge that the Disney board was split over Gibson certainly informed his decisions regarding his investment in the company. Arbitrageurs are particularly hungry for that type of information, since they often depend on the "mosaic method," or the collection of vast quantities of details, to decide whether they should invest in a takeover stock. As Boesky did throughout the Disney affair, they telephone investment bankers, raiders, and corporate executives, often relying on hints or tones of voice rather than outright disclosures of fact. For their part, the raiders and their investment bankers are interested in seeing as much of a target company's stock as possible pass into the hands of the arbs. Investment banks also cultivate arbs to find out what companies are takeover targets, then approach those companies and offer to represent them. With no violation of insider trading laws, much can be intimated during telephone conversations between professionals from the types of questions asked, the guarded replies given, and even the refusal to answer a particular question.

It is true that the privileged relationships which exist on Wall Street, and the opportunities they yield, do not always work against a target company's management. In fact, one measure of the abilities of a target's lawyers and investment bankers lies in the strength of precisely those sorts of contacts. Joe Flom *was* able to arrange a meeting between Ray Watson and Saul Steinberg, even if Steinberg later cancelled. And Don Drapkin's acquaintance with Larry Tisch provided the opening for the greenmail negotiations.

Despite the SEC investigation into possible insider trading at the time of the greenmail, no one has been accused of doing anything illegal regarding Disney. And no evidence exists to suggest that anything illegal was done. But the battle for Disney unfolded in the manner it did, and assumed the outcome it finally did, because the arbs, brokers, bankers, and lawyers all knew one another. If they didn't all share the same values, they did speak the same language and employ the same frame of reference. They were all *insiders.* And in large part because he was not an insider in this sense, Ron Miller was at a hopeless disadvantage.

Critics of the raiders, such as John Kenneth Galbraith, say that they have forced corporations to expend vast amounts of time and money defending themselves in useless takeover battles, draining valuable resources that ought to be invested in increasing productivity at a time when many American industries—from textiles to oil to steel—are in the throes of crisis, when in fact the health of the American economy overall is at stake. Further, the focus of the institutional investors on quarterly returns, which has made raiding possible, has forced executives to sacrifice long-term strategies like capital investment and research and development that almost inevitably lead to reduced earnings in the short term, in favor of temporary tactics that prop up their company's stock price.

The raiders, however, have their defenders as well—including *In Search of Excellence* co-author Tom Peters—who have cited Steinberg's takeover attempt on Disney as an outstanding example of the useful role raiders play in identifying underperforming companies and forcing changes which improve that performance. If Steinberg's bid for Disney produced the chaos that forced out Ron Miller and brought in Eisner and Wells, hostile takeovers, to the extent that generalizations are possible, would seem to benefit corporate America. Yet it was management's resistance to Steinberg as much as Steinberg's tender offer that ended with the arrival of Eisner and Wells. For, had Steinberg succeeded with his takeover, what is now The Walt Disney Company would not exist. Kirk Kerkorian would own the studio, Steinberg would have the theme parks, the Fisher brothers would control much of the real estate. There would have been nothing there for Michael Eisner and Frank Wells to reinvigorate.

Whether Steinberg destroyed or saved Disney—arguments about the "morality" of raiding will divide economists for years—the investment environment in which he and the other raiders operated required all chief executives to be as concerned, if not more concerned, with their company's stock price as with any other indicator of its performance. And it was not enough simply to keep an eye on the Quotron; the institutional shareholders needed constant and artful massaging. Unlike his predecessor, Ron Miller, Michael Eisner assiduously cultivated Wall Street, for, unlike Miller, he recognized that it was no longer enough for Disney's chief executive just to make sure the company was providing entertainment for families with small children or even producing films that reflected current sensibilities. Indeed, one of the chief executive's main responsibilities was to promote the company's image in the investment community—which was why among the first moves Eisner and Frank Wells made after assuming control was to travel to Fort Worth to meet with their two largest stockholders, Sid Bass and Irwin Jacobs. And almost immediately thereafter, the two men flew to New York to talk up the company's stock with investment analysts. They displayed polish, sophistication, and confidence as they described their plans for the studio, for developing the Florida real estate, and for stimulating attendance at the theme parks. To all concerned, in short, they showed hustle.

They were also lucky. In the summer of 1986, Disney produced an animated feature called *The Great Mouse Detective.* It proved an astonishing success, grossing more than $25 million in three months. So did the videocassette of *Pinocchio,* which sold 500,000 copies within a year of its release to become one of the best-selling cassettes ever put on the market. The general explanation for this phenomenon was that it heralded a revival of family entertainment; the postwar generation that had thrived on Disney in the fifties and rejected it in the seventies was now having children of its own. And these parents, remembering their own childhood, were taking their offspring to see Disney films and buying them videocassettes of Disney cartoons.

Within two years of his ouster the sort of benign family-oriented project associated with the regime of Ron Miller and his mentor Card Walker was suddenly more popular and profitable than ever.

When the shape and extent of the Eisner-Wells revolution at Disney became clear, analysts began recommending Disney stock to their clients. The result was a run-up that was nothing less than astonishing, even in the midst of the boom Wall Street was then enjoying. From a price of $55 a share when the Basses bought out Irwin Jacobs in September 1984, Disney rose to $61 by the end of the year. By the following June it had reached $90, and it continued to climb. By September 1985, before any of the movies produced by the new team had even reached the theaters, it was closing on its all-time high, and by the following January, the month after *Down and Out in Beverly Hills* opened, it had reached $120 a share. Some financial journalists equated Eisner with the prince who awakened Sleeping Beauty. And at *Business Week,* where the writers have a particular weakness for puns involving Disney characters, it was reported that Disney shares had risen to "Goofy heights." On January 13, 1986, the company announced plans for a four-for-one stock split. By March, when the new shares were distributed, the stock had climbed to $145, the highest price it had ever fetched. The announcement of the split set off such a scramble for Disney shares that Stanley Gold was inundated with calls from brokers begging him to sell off some of Shamrock's holdings.

Disney's stock was a favorite on Wall Street all through the great market run-up of 1987. But that was understandable, given the fact that in many ways the year was one of the best in the company's history. The studio, fulfilling Roy Disney's dream that it become a power center in Hollywood, produced fourteen movies in 1987, including such hits as *Tin Men,* starring Richard Dreyfuss, *Stakeout,* which also featured Dreyfuss, and *Outrageous Fortune,* Bette Midler's third film for Disney (the three movies Midler did for the company proved so successful that she agreed to another three-picture deal).

The year was also the fiftieth anniversary of *Snow White and the Seven Dwarfs* and Disney naturally exploited this occasion for its maximum public-relations value. Snow White and the dwarfs made a number of appearances, even at one point parading onto the floor of the New York Stock Exchange. Disney also tracked down ninety-three of the women who had played Snow White at the theme parks at various times and gathered them all together for two well-publicized reunions. The movie itself was re-released as well. It was eventually shown in forty-two countries—playing for the first time ever in Moscow and the first time since the revolution in China—and at the end of the run Disney claimed that "More people have seen *Snow White and the Seven Dwarfs* than any other film ever released." Such exhaustive marketing efforts helped revenues for Disney's filmed entertainment division climb to $875 million in 1987, thereby making it the third largest studio in Hollywood. The following year looked even more promising as *Three Men and a Baby,* a comedy released late in 1987, became the first movie in Disney's history to gross more than $100 million in its initial release.

At the same time, revenues were soaring at the theme parks. Early on, Eisner and Wells had made what with hindsight would seem to be the rather simple discovery that admission prices at the parks had failed to keep pace with inflation. When Card Walker and Ron Miller had run the company, executives had been afraid that price increases would discourage customers; Eisner and Wells reasoned that if a visit to the theme parks meant so much that families were willing to travel across the country to get there, they would hardly be deterred by higher admission. During Eisner and Wells's first two years on the job, they raised prices at the parks by 45 percent. Far from being discouraged, ever greater numbers of people flocked to Disneyland, Walt Disney World, and Tokyo Disneyland; in 1987, the parks were visited by more than 50 million people.

But even with such record-breaking attendance figures, Eisner and Wells believed the theme parks to be underdeveloped. Early in 1987, Disney announced that it was selling Arvida to a Chicago real estate company for "$400 million in cash, notes, and assumed debts." It used much of this money to undertake an ambitious expansion program at its Orlando properties. New rides, such as Typhoon Lagoon, and new pavilions, such as the Wonders of Life, were constructed, as was an actual production and animation studio that was to be open for tours. The noted post-modern architect Michael Graves was retained to design a convention hotel for the resort, and while not actually using Disney characters, Graves did produce a whimsical building that features statues of a cavorting dolphin and swan.

Eisner and Wells embarked on all sorts of other ventures as well. They opened the first of a planned series of Disney retail stores, and they realized one of Walt Disney's old ambitions when they acquired the Wrather Corporation, and with it the Disneyland Hotel. The range of accomplishments brought about by its new management enabled Disney's stock to weather with relatively little damage the market's crash in October 1987. While the stock did drop, it recovered much of its value and closed out the year at around $60 a share. That was due to the fact that not only were Disney's businesses considered to be "recession resistant," but the management of Eisner and Wells had made the company, in the words of one Wall Street analyst, "a haven of quality" in an uncertain time for investors.

In fact, Disney's management had been celebrated throughout the year; Eisner appeared on the cover of *Business Week* ("Disney's Magic: It's Back!"), of *Parade* ("What's New at Disney"), of *Marketing and Media Decisions* ("The Mouse Roars"), and of *Business Month,* which named Disney one of the five best-managed companies of 1987. An even more telling illustration of Eisner's success could be found in his finances. In the three years since he had joined the company, Eisner had, under the terms of the contract Ray Watson had negotiated with him, received options to buy more than 2 million Disney shares at a price, accounting for the stock's split, of roughly $14 a share. With Disney's stock trading at $60, those options meant Eisner was worth more than $90 million. Similarly, Frank Wells had options that made him worth more than $80 million. By the end of 1987, however, Eisner and Wells had exercised few of those option. They were keeping their money in their company.

In the aftermath of the Eisner-Wells victory, Gold had ordered vanity license plates saying "10-3" for his Mercedes convertible. He had also left the board—as did Peter Dailey and eventually Philip Hawley— and Sharon Disney Lund had joined it. And when Disney's stock rose, Gold did indeed sell a substantial portion of Shamrock's holdings. With the proceeds Shamrock made a tender offer for, and subsequently acquired, Central Soya, the country's biggest soybean processor. Friends found the move difficult to comprehend, but Gold, who was soon spending much of his time in Fort Wayne, Indiana, trying to straighten out the ailing agribusiness company, explained that he was a "real contrarian" and that he and Roy Disney believed in "basic American industry."

By 1987, Gold had sold off most of Central Soya for a tidy profit. In September of that year a seat on the Disney board became vacant when Chuck Cobb, who had little to do at Disney after Arvida was sold, resigned as a director to become an Assistant Secretary of Commerce in the Reagan Administration. Gold took Cobb's place, permanently joining his client Roy Disney and his friends Eisner and Wells on the board, and bringing to final conclusion Roy's decision, made three and a half years earlier, to go "all the way in."

Ray Watson, who remained a director, was named chairman of the executive committee (the one from which he had had to ask Card Walker and Donn Tatum to resign). Foregoing for the time being a return to real estate development, he taught a class at the University of California's Irvine business school on the running of a modern corporation. He was also sought out at times for advice by executives at companies threatened with hostile takeovers.

Ron Miller, showing no interest in an independent production contract at Disney, spent a lot of time traveling with Diane and tending to his vineyard, Silverado. A year after his resignation, the animated movie *Black Cauldron,* listing Miller as executive producer, was released to good reviews, though, as with the first runs of many of Disney's animated classics, it proved a disappointment at the box office in a year in which theater attendance was down generally. Meanwhile, Roy Disney, who never could draw, was named head of the animation department, acquiring the influential studio job he had yearned for ever since he had left the company; it was he who supervised the final cut of *Black Cauldron,* the movie his cousin-by-marriage had hoped would restore the studio's tradition of glorious animation.

As for the Bass brothers, their Disney investment turned out to be the single most lucrative deal they ever put together, and it is undoubtedly one of the most successful financial maneuvers in mod-

ern times. By the fall of 1986 the Disney stock Bass Brothers received in exchange for its $14 million investment in Arvida, together
with its subsequent purchases of the company's shares, was worth
more than $950 million, which amounted to a capital gain of $850
million. But by then, Bass Brothers Enterprises no longer existed. In
1985 the company was liquidated and the assets divided up among
the four brothers. The following year, Al Checchi left Fort Worth to
pursue a political career and Richard Rainwater went into business
on his own. The interests of Sid Bass himself seemed to shift somewhat from finance to culture and society, and he began spending
more time in New York.

The Walt Disney Company continued to be embroiled in the various
legal cases brought on by the decision to pay Saul Steinberg greenmail.
Most of the suits revolved around the fact that when Disney bought
back Steinberg's stock for $70 a share (excluding expenses), it failed
to treat all shareholders equally by offering to buy their stock for the
same price. Had those unhappy shareholders been willing to hold on
to their shares for another eighteen months, they could have sold them
for more than double what Steinberg was paid—and what they were
insisting in their suits they were entitled to be paid. Steinberg himself
clearly realized this, for, in the final irony of the greenmail saga,
Reliance—which by a court order had been barred from spending the
money it received in the buyback—sued Disney demanding the return
of the shares it had sold to the company. Reliance claimed it had been
"forced" to part with the stock by Disney's threat of a self-tender and
it wanted those shares back. Disney issued a statement labeling the
suit "without merit."

INDEX

Merrill Lynch, 174, 213
Metropolitan Museum of Art (New York), 52
MGM/United Artists, 47, 112
Mickey and Minnie Mouse characters, 7
Mickey Mouse Club, 10
Midler, Bette, 240, 248
Milken, Michael (Mike), 69 and *n.,* 70–1, 89–90, 96, 106–14 *passim,* 136, 175, 244
Miller, Clifford, 6, 67, 107, 134, 143, 144, 148, 152, 189, 194, 196, 221
Miller, Diane Disney, 6, 12, 18–21, 45, 95, 125, 126, 147, 195, 205, 230, 231, 232, 251
Miller, Ronald (Ron), 6, 12, 13, 14–15, 18, 23, 24, 27–8, 39, 46, 49, 53, 64, 68, 95, 111, 141–2, 163–4, 173–5, 185 and *n.,* 202, 230, 231, 241–2, 248, 249, 251; accomplishments of, 211; and Bass Bros. and Arvida acquisition deal, 82, 84–8; career of, 19–21, 23, 29, 35–8; criticisms of his management, 175, 176, 179, 192, 195–9, 208, 213, 243, 246–7; Disney's CEO, 29, 35–8; Disney's president, 29, 36, 38; and Gibson deal, 93–4, 97, 106, 157–8, 161–2, 166, 189, 191; marital separation, 21, 125, 179, 205; and 1984 annual stockholders' meeting, 21, 30–1, 42–3; ouster of, 200, 203–4, 205, 208–13, 215, 232, 246; overtures to Gold/Roy Disney, 96, 98–100, 143–4, 146–9, 152; salary and contract, 76–7, 233; and Steinberg's tender offer, 115, 117–19, 120–4, 125–7, 130–1, 134–5; and takeover threat, 40–1, 56–8, 60, 74, 78–9, 111; and (Frank) Wells, 45, 125, 144, 145–7, 186
Minnie Mouse, 7, 242
Minstar Company, 73, 108
MM Acquisition Corporation, 112–13
Montgomery Securities, 24
Moonpilot (Disney show), 20
Morgan Stanley & Company, 37, 41, 55, 56, 59–61, 72, 73, 74, 78–9, 81–2 and *n.,* 84–5, 88, 92, 101, 103, 115–16, 119, 128, 130–1, 143, 151, 158, 161–2, 165, 173–4, 180, 187, 191, 194–5, 197

Morrow, Richard, 95, 96, 184
Murdoch, Rupert, 55, 58
Myers, Alan, 124
My Science Project (film), 65

Nash, Clarence, 120
National Broadcasting Company (NBC), 27, 206, 241
National Coalition on Television Violence, 25
NBC (National Broadcasting Company), 27, 206, 241
Neiman-Marcus, 187 and *n.*
Never Cry Wolf (film), 24, 31 *n.,* 142, 175
Newman, Paul, 241
Newport Beach Development, 33, 38
Newsday, 241
Newsweek, 163, 201
New York *Daily News,* 146
New York magazine, 201
New York *Post,* 55
New York State anti-takeover bill (vetoed), 137
New York Stock Exchange, 115, 130, 132 and *n.,* 133–4, 170 *n.,* 249
New York Times, The, 53, 55, 56, 74, 136, 137, 167, 213
Nichols, Mike, 202
Night Crossing (film), 24
Nine Old Men (animators), 22
Nixon, Richard, 13 *n.,* 102
Nolte, Nick, 240
nudity in films, 30–1 and *n.,* 48
Nunis, Richard, 25, 131, 144, 147, 225, 231, 241

Officer and a Gentleman, An (film), 200
Okun, Erwin, 74–5, 209–11, 213, 215, 243
Old Yeller (film), 19
On Golden Pond (film), 27
Ordinary People (film), 200
Outrageous Fortune (film), 248

Pabst Brewing Company, 109
Paine Webber, 137, 174
Parade, 250
Paramount Pictures Corporation, 28, 45, 47, 200–2, 207, 208, 216–18, 221, 240